THE MAN WHO SOLVED THE MARKET

Advance praise for *THE MAN WHO SOLVED THE MARKET*

'Zuckerman vividly tells the story of how Jim Simons and his team of scientists developed the most successful quantitative trading operation in history . . . Immensely enjoyable'
Edward O. Thorp, author of *A Man for All Markets*

'An extremely well-written and engaging book . . . a must read, and a fun one at that'
Mohamed A. El-Erian, author of *The Only Game in Town*

'Leave it to the *Wall Street Journal*'s Greg Zuckerman to lay open the golden mysteries of quantitative investing. With this fine, humane, and eye-opening book, he's well and truly broken the code'
James Grant, Grant's Interest Rate Observer

Praise for *THE GREATEST TRADE EVER*

'Simply terrific. Easily the best of the post-crash financial books'
Malcolm Gladwell

'The definitive account of a strange and wonderful subplot of the financial crisis'
Michael Lewis

Praise for *THE FRACKERS*

'Fast-paced, densely interesting' *New Republic*

'Reads like a blockbuster thriller' *Publishers Weekly*

ABOUT THE AUTHOR

GREGORY ZUCKERMAN is the author of *The Greatest Trade Ever* and *The Frackers* and is a special writer at the *Wall Street Journal*. At the *Journal*, Zuckerman writes about financial firms, personalities, and trades, as well as hedge funds and other investing and business topics. He's a three-time winner of the Gerald Loeb Award, the highest honour in business journalism.

Zuckerman appears regularly on CNBC, Fox Business, and other networks and radio stations, and gives speeches around the globe.

THE MAN WHO SOLVED THE MARKET

How Jim Simons Launched the Quant Revolution

Gregory Zuckerman

BUSINESS

PENGUIN BUSINESS

UK | USA | Canada | Ireland | Australia
India | New Zealand | South Africa

Penguin Business is part of the Penguin Random House group of companies
whose addresses can be found at global.penguinrandomhouse.com.

First published in the United States of America by Portfolio / Penguin,
an imprint of Penguin Random House LLC 2019
First published in Great Britain by Penguin Business 2019
002

Grateful acknowledgment is made for permission to reprint the following photographs:
Insert page 2 (top) Courtesy of Lee Neuwirth © Lee Neuwirth
Insert page 3 (top) Courtesy of Seth Rumshinsky
Insert page 3 (bottom) Photo by Rick Mott, taken at the NJ Open Go Tournament,
provided with permission, courtesy of Stefi Baum
Insert page 4 (top, bottom) Courtesy of Brian Keating
Insert page 5 (top) Courtesy of David Eisenbud
Insert page 5 (bottom) Courtesy of *Wall Street Journal* and Jenny Strasburg
Insert page 6 Patrick McMullan/Getty Images

Printed at Thomson Press India Ltd, New Delhi

A CIP catalogue record for this book is available from the British Library

HARDBACK ISBN: 978–0–241–42215–1
TRADE PAPERBACK ISBN: 978–0–241–30972–8

Follow us on LinkedIn: linkedin.com/company/penguinbusiness

www.greenpenguin.co.uk

CONTENTS

To Gabriel and Elijah
My signals in the noise

CAST OF CHARACTERS

James Simons	Mathematician, code breaker, and founder of Renaissance Technologies
Lenny Baum	Simons's first investing partner and author of algorithms that impacted the lives of millions
James Ax	Ran the Medallion fund and developed its first trading models
Sandor Straus	Data guru who played key early role at Renaissance
Elwyn Berlekamp	Game theorist who managed the Medallion fund at a key turning point
Henry Laufer	Mathematician who moved Simons's fund toward short-term trades
Peter Brown	Computer scientist who helped engineer Renaissance's key breakthroughs
Robert Mercer	Renaissance's co-CEO, helped put Donald Trump in the White House
Rebekah Mercer	Teamed up with Steve Bannon to upend American politics
David Magerman	Computer specialist who tried to stop the Mercers' political activities

A TIMELINE OF KEY EVENTS

1938 Jim Simons born

1958 Simons graduates MIT

1964 Simons becomes code breaker at the IDA

1968 Simons leads math department at Stony Brook University

1974 Simons and Chern publish groundbreaking paper

1978 Simons leaves academia to start Monemetrics, a currency trading firm, and a hedge fund called Limroy

1979 Lenny Baum and James Ax join

1982 Firm's name changes to Renaissance Technologies Corporation

1984 Baum quits

1985 Ax and Straus move the company to California

1988 Simons shuts down Limroy, launches the Medallion fund

1989 Ax leaves, Elwyn Berlekamp leads Medallion

1990 Berlekamp departs, Simons assumes control of the firm and fund

1992 Henry Laufer becomes full-time employee

1993 Peter Brown and Robert Mercer join

1995 Brown, Mercer achieve key breakthrough

2000 Medallion soars 98.5 percent

2005 Renaissance Institutional Equities Fund launches

2007 Renaissance and other quant firms suffer sudden losses

2010 Brown and Mercer take over firm

2017 Mercer steps down as co-CEO

INTRODUCTION

"You do know—no one will speak with you, right?"

I was picking at a salad at a fish restaurant in Cambridge, Massachusetts, in early September 2017, trying my best to get a British mathematician named Nick Patterson to open up about his former company, Renaissance Technologies. I wasn't having much luck.

I told Patterson that I wanted to write a book about how James Simons, Renaissance's founder, had created the greatest moneymaking machine in financial history. Renaissance generated so much wealth that Simons and his colleagues had begun to wield enormous influence in the worlds of politics, science, education, and philanthropy. Anticipating dramatic societal shifts, Simons harnessed algorithms, computer models, and big data before Mark Zuckerberg and his peers had a chance to finish nursery school.

Patterson wasn't very encouraging. By then, Simons and his representatives had told me they weren't going to provide much help, either. Renaissance executives and others close to Simons—even those I once considered friends—wouldn't return my calls or emails. Even archrivals begged out of meetings at Simons's request, as if he was a Mafia boss they dared not offend.

Over and over, I was reminded of the iron-clad, thirty-page nondisclosure agreements the firm forced employees to sign, preventing even retirees from divulging much. I got it, guys. But come on. I'd been at the *Wall Street Journal* for a couple of decades; I knew how the game was played. Subjects, even recalcitrant ones, usually come around. After all, who doesn't want a book written about them? Jim Simons and Renaissance Technologies, apparently.

I wasn't entirely shocked. Simons and his team are among the most secretive traders Wall Street has encountered, loath to drop even a hint of how they'd conquered financial markets, lest a competitor seize on any clue. Employees avoid media appearances and steer clear of industry conferences and most public gatherings. Simons once quoted Benjamin, the donkey in *Animal Farm*, to explain his attitude: "'God gave me a tail to keep off the flies. But I'd rather have had no tail and no flies.' That's kind of the way I feel about publicity."[1]

I looked up from my meal and forced a smile.

This is going to be a battle.

I kept at it, probing defenses, looking for openings. Writing about Simons and learning his secrets became my fixation. The obstacles he put up only added allure to the chase.

There were compelling reasons I was determined to tell Simons's story. A former math professor, Simons is arguably the most successful trader in the history of modern finance. Since 1988, Renaissance's flagship Medallion hedge fund has generated average annual returns of 66 percent, racking up trading profits of more than $100 billion (see Appendix 1 for how I arrive at these numbers). No one in the investment world comes close. Warren Buffett, George Soros, Peter Lynch, Steve Cohen, and Ray Dalio all fall short (see Appendix 2).

In recent years, Renaissance has been scoring over $7 billion annually in trading gains. That's more than the annual revenues of brand-name corporations including Under Armour, Levi Strauss, Hasbro, and Hyatt Hotels.

Here's the absurd thing—while those other companies have tens of thousands of employees, there are just three hundred or so at Renaissance.

I've determined that Simons is worth about $23 billion, making him wealthier than Elon Musk of Tesla Motors, Rupert Murdoch of News Corp, and Laurene Powell Jobs, Steve Jobs's widow. Others at the firm are also billionaires. The average Renaissance employee has nearly $50 million just in the firm's own hedge funds. Simons and his team truly create wealth in the manner of fairy tales full of kings, straw, and lots and lots of gold.

More than the trading successes intrigued me. Early on, Simons made a decision to dig through mountains of data, employ advanced mathematics, and develop cutting-edge computer models, while others were still relying on intuition, instinct, and old-fashioned research for their own predictions. Simons inspired a revolution that has since swept the investing world. By early 2019, hedge funds and other quantitative, or *quant*, investors had emerged as the market's largest players, controlling about 30 percent of stock trading, topping the activity of both individual investors and traditional investing firms.[2] MBAs once scoffed at the thought of relying on a scientific and systematic approach to investing, confident they could hire coders if they were ever needed. Today, coders say the same about MBAs, if they think about them at all.

Simons's pioneering methods have been embraced in almost every industry, and reach nearly every corner of everyday life. He and his team were crunching statistics, turning tasks over to machines, and relying on algorithms more than three decades ago—long before these tactics were embraced in Silicon Valley, the halls of government, sports stadiums, doctors' offices, military command centers, and pretty much everywhere else forecasting is required.

Simons developed strategies to corral and manage talent, turning raw brainpower and mathematical aptitude into astonishing wealth. He made money from math, and a lot of money, at that. A few decades ago, it wasn't remotely possible.

Lately, Simons has emerged as a modern-day Medici, subsidizing the salaries of thousands of public-school math and science teachers, developing autism treatments, and expanding our understanding of the origins of life. His efforts, while valuable, raise the question of whether one individual should enjoy so much influence. So, too, does the clout of his senior executive,* Robert Mercer, who is perhaps the individual most responsible for Donald Trump's presidential victory in 2016. Mercer, Trump's biggest financial supporter, plucked Steve Bannon and Kellyanne Conway from obscurity and inserted them into the Trump campaign, stabilizing it during a difficult period. Companies formerly owned by Mercer and now in the hands of his daughter Rebekah played key roles in the successful campaign to encourage the United Kingdom to leave the European Union. Simons, Mercer, and others at Renaissance will continue to have broad impact for years to come.

The successes of Simons and his team prompt a number of challenging questions. What does it say about financial markets that mathematicians and scientists are better at predicting their direction than veteran investors at the largest traditional firms? Do Simons and his colleagues enjoy a fundamental understanding of investing that eludes the rest of us? Do Simons's achievements prove human judgment and intuition are inherently flawed, and that only models and automated systems can handle the deluge of data that seems to overwhelm us? Do the triumph and popularity of Simons's quantitative methods create new, overlooked risks?

I was most fascinated by a striking paradox: Simons and his team *shouldn't have been the ones* to master the market. Simons never took a single finance class, didn't care very much for business, and, until he turned forty, only dabbled in trading. A decade later, he still hadn't made much headway.

---

*Mercer is no longer Renaissance's co-CEO but he remains a senior employee of the firm.

Heck, Simons didn't even do applied mathematics, he did *theoretical* math, the most impractical kind. His firm, located in a sleepy town on the North Shore of Long Island, hires mathematicians and scientists who *don't know anything* about investing or the ways of Wall Street. Some are even outright suspicious of capitalism. Yet, Simons and his colleagues are the ones who changed the way investors approach financial markets, leaving an industry of traders, investors, and other pros in the dust. It's as if a group of tourists, on their first trip to South America, with a few odd-looking tools and meager provisions, discovered El Dorado and proceeded to plunder the golden city, as hardened explorers looked on in frustration.

Finally, I hit my own pay dirt. I learned about Simons's early life, his tenure as a groundbreaking mathematician and Cold War code-breaker, and the volatile early period of his firm. Contacts shared details about Renaissance's most important breakthroughs as well as recent events featuring more drama and intrigue than I had imagined. Eventually, I conducted more than four hundred interviews with more than thirty current and former Renaissance employees. I spoke with an even larger number of Simons's friends, family members, and others who participated in, or were familiar with, the events I describe. I owe deep gratitude to each individual who spent time sharing memories, observations, and insights. Some accepted substantial personal risk to help me tell this story. I hope I rewarded their faith.

Even Simons spoke with me, eventually. He asked me not to write this book and never truly warmed to the project. But Simons was gracious enough to spend more than ten hours discussing certain periods of his life, while refusing to discuss Renaissance's trading and most other activities. His thoughts were valuable and appreciated.

This book is a work of nonfiction. It is based on first-person accounts and recollections of those who witnessed or were aware of the events I depict. I understand that memories fade, so I've done my best to check and confirm every fact, incident, and quote.

I've tried to tell Simons's story in a way that will appeal to the general reader as well as to professionals in quantitative finance and mathematics. I will refer to hidden Markov models, kernel methods of machine learning, and stochastic differential equations, but there also will be broken marriages, corporate intrigue, and panicked traders.

For all his insights and prescience, Simons was blindsided by much that took place in his life. That may be the most enduring lesson of his remarkable story.

THE MAN WHO SOLVED THE MARKET

PROLOGUE

Jim Simons wouldn't stop calling.

It was the fall of 1990 and Simons was in his office on the thirty-third floor of a midtown Manhattan high-rise, his eyes glued to a computer screen flashing the latest moves in global financial markets. Friends didn't understand why Simons was still at it. Fifty-two years old, Simons had already lived a full life, enjoying enough adventure, accomplishment, and prosperity to satisfy the ambitions of his peers. Yet, there he was, overseeing an investment fund, sweating the market's daily eruptions.

Simons stood nearly five foot ten, though a slight stoop and a head of graying, thinning hair suggested someone a bit shorter and older. Creases enveloped his brown eyes, the likely result of a smoking habit he couldn't kick—or just didn't want to. Simons's rugged, craggy features, and the glint of mischief in his eyes, reminded friends of the late actor Humphrey Bogart.

On Simons's uncluttered desk sat an oversize ashtray awaiting the next flick of his burning cigarette. On his wall was a rather gruesome painting of a lynx feasting on a rabbit. Nearby, on a coffee table next to a couch and two comfortable leather chairs, sat a complicated mathematics research paper, a reminder of the thriving academic career Simons had discarded to the bewilderment of his fellow mathematicians.

By then, Simons had spent twelve full years searching for a successful investing formula. Early on, he traded like others, relying on intuition and instinct, but the ups and downs left Simons sick to his stomach. At one point, Simons became so discouraged an employee worried he was contemplating suicide. Simons recruited two renowned and headstrong mathematicians to trade with him, but those partnerships crumbled amid losses and acrimony. A year earlier, Simons's results had been so awful he had been forced to halt his investing. Some expected him to pull the plug on his entire operation.

Now on his second marriage and third business partner, Simons decided to embrace a radical investing style. Working with Elwyn Berlekamp, a game theorist, Simons built a computer model capable of digesting torrents of data and selecting ideal trades, a scientific and systematic approach partly aimed at removing emotion from the investment process.

"If we have enough data, I *know* we can make predictions," Simons told a colleague.

Those closest to Simons understood what really was driving him. Simons had earned a PhD at the age of twenty-three and then became an acclaimed government code-breaker, a renowned mathematician, and a groundbreaking university administrator. He needed a new challenge and a bigger canvas. Simons told a friend that solving the market's age-old riddle and conquering the world of investing "would be remarkable." He wanted to be the one to use math to beat the market. If he could pull it off, Simons knew he could make millions of dollars, maybe even more, perhaps enough to influence the world beyond Wall Street, which some suspected was his true goal.

In trading, as in mathematics, it's rare to achieve breakthroughs in midlife. Yet, Simons was convinced he was on the verge of something special, maybe even historic. A Merit cigarette lodged between two fingers, Simons reached for the phone to call Berlekamp one more time.

"Have you seen gold?" Simons asked, the accent of his gravelly voice hinting at his Boston upbringing.

Yes, I've seen gold prices, Berlekamp responded. And, no, we don't need to adjust our trading system. Simons didn't push, hanging up politely, as usual. Berlekamp was becoming exasperated by Simons's pestering, however. Serious and slim with blue eyes behind thick glasses, Berlekamp worked on the other side of the country in an office that was a short walk from the campus of University of California, Berkeley, where he continued to teach. When Berlekamp discussed his trading with graduates of the university's business school, they sometimes mocked the methods he and Simons had embraced, calling them "quackery."

"Oh, come on. Computers can't compete with human judgment," one had told Berlekamp.

"We're gonna do things *better* than humans can," Berlekamp responded.

Privately, Berlekamp understood why their approach screamed of modern-day alchemy. Even he couldn't fully explain why their model was recommending certain trades.

It wasn't just on campus where Simons's ideas seemed out of touch. A golden age for traditional investing had dawned as George Soros, Peter Lynch, Bill Gross, and others divined the direction of investments, financial markets, and global economies, producing enormous profits with intelligence, intuition, and old-fashioned economic and corporate research. Unlike his rivals, Simons didn't have a clue how to estimate cash flows, identify new products, or forecast interest rates. He was digging through reams of price information. There wasn't even a proper name for this kind of trading, which involved *data cleansing*, *signals*, and *backtesting*, terms most Wall Street pros were wholly unfamiliar with. Few used email in 1990, the internet browser hadn't been invented, and algorithms were best known, if at all, as the step-by-step procedures that had enabled Alan Turing's machine to break coded Nazi messages during World War II. The idea that these formulas might guide, or even help govern, the day-to-day lives of hundreds of millions of individuals, or that a couple of former math professors might employ computers to trounce seasoned and celebrated investors, seemed far-fetched if not outright ludicrous.

Simons was upbeat and confident by nature, though. He detected early signs of success for his computer system, sparking hope. Besides, Simons didn't have a lot of options. His once-thriving venture investments weren't going anywhere, and he sure didn't want to return to teaching.

"Let's work on the system," Simons told Berlekamp in one more urgent phone call. "Next year, I know, we can be up 80 percent."

Eighty percent in a year? Now he's really gone too far, Berlekamp thought.

Such enormous returns weren't likely, he told Simons. And you really don't need to call so much, Jim. Simons couldn't stop, though. Eventually, it all became too much—Berlekamp quit, a fresh blow for Simons.

"The hell with it, I'm just going to run it myself," Simons told a friend.

Around the same time, in a different part of New York State fifty miles away, a tall, handsome, middle-aged scientist stared at a whiteboard, grappling with his own challenges. Robert Mercer was working in a sprawling IBM research center in a Westchester suburb searching for ways to get computers to do a better job transcribing speech into text and even translate languages, among other tasks. Rather than follow conventional methods, Mercer was tackling his problems with an early form of large-scale machine learning. He and his colleagues were feeding their computers with enough data to enable them to perform tasks on their own. Mercer was nearing his second decade at the computer giant, however, and it still wasn't clear how much he and the team could accomplish.

Colleagues couldn't figure Mercer out, not even those who had spent years working closely with him. Mercer was unusually gifted. He was also odd and socially awkward. Every day for lunch, Mercer ate either a tuna or peanut-butter-and-jelly sandwich packed in a used brown paper bag. Around the office, Mercer constantly hummed or whistled, usually classical tunes, wearing a look of detached amusement.

Much of what came out of Mercer's mouth was brilliant, even profound, though it could also be utterly jarring. Once, Mercer told colleagues he believed he would live forever. The staffers *thought* he was serious, though historic precedent didn't seem on his side. Later, colleagues would learn of Mercer's deep-seated hostility toward government and of radical political views that would come to dominate his life and affect the lives of many others.

At IBM, Mercer spent long hours huddled with a younger colleague named Peter Brown, a charming, creative, and outgoing mathematician whose dark glasses, thick mane of unruly brown hair, and kinetic energy brought to mind a mad professor. The two men didn't spend much time discussing money or markets. Personal turmoil would lead Mercer and Brown to join forces with Simons, however. His unlikely quest to crack the market's code and lead an investing revolution would become theirs.

=

Simons wasn't aware of the imposing obstacles in his way. Nor did he know that tragedy stalked him, or that political upheaval would upend his firm.

Looking out from his office onto the East River that day in the fall of 1990, Simons just knew he had a difficult problem to solve.

"There are patterns in the market," Simons told a colleague. "I know we can find them."

PART ONE

Money Isn't Everything

CHAPTER ONE

Jimmy Simons grabbed a broom and headed upstairs.

It was the winter of 1952 and the fourteen-year-old was trying to earn some spending money at Breck's garden supply near his home in Newton, Massachusetts, the leafy Boston suburb. It wasn't going well. Working in a stockroom downstairs, the young man found himself so lost in thought that he had misplaced the sheep manure, planting seeds, and most everything else.

Frustrated, the owners asked Jimmy to walk the store's narrow aisles and sweep its hardwood floors, a mindless and repetitive task. To Jimmy, the demotion felt like a stroke of luck. Finally, he was left alone to ponder what mattered most in his life. Math. Girls. The future.

They're paying me to think!

Weeks later, his Christmas-time job complete, the couple who owned the store asked Jimmy about his long-term plans.

"I want to study mathematics at MIT."

They burst out laughing. A young man so absentminded that he couldn't keep track of basic gardening supplies hoped to be a math major—at the Massachusetts Institute of Technology, no less?

"They thought it was the funniest thing they had ever heard," Simons recalls.

The skepticism didn't bother Jimmy, not even the giggles. The teenager was filled with preternatural confidence and an unusual determination to accomplish something special, the result of supportive parents who had experienced both high hopes and deep regrets in their own lives.

Marcia and Matthew Simons welcomed James Harris to the family in the spring of 1938. She and Matty poured time and energy into their son, who remained their only child after Marcia suffered a series of subsequent miscarriages. A sharp intellect with an outgoing personality and subtle wit, Marcia volunteered in Jimmy's school but never had the opportunity to work outside the home. She funneled her dreams and passions into Jimmy, pushing him academically and assuring him that success was ahead.

"She was ambitious for me," Simons recalls. "She saw me as her project."

Matty Simons had a different perspective on both life and parenting. From the age of six, Matty, one of ten children, hustled to make money for the family, selling newspapers in the streets and hauling bags for travelers at a nearby train station. When he reached high school age, Matty began working full time. He tried going to night school but quit, too tired to concentrate.

As a father, Matty was kind, soft-spoken, and easygoing. He enjoyed coming home and spinning tall tales for Marcia, telling her about Cuba's imminent plans to build a bridge to Florida, for example, as Jimmy did his best to mask a grin. Marcia might have been the family's intellect, but she also was remarkably gullible. Matty would concoct increasingly outrageous stories until Marcia finally picked up on the fibs, a family game guaranteed to crack Jimmy up.

"She didn't usually get it," Simons says, "but I did."

Matty worked as a sales manager for 20th Century Fox, driving to theaters around New England to pitch the studio's latest films. Shirley

Temple, the era's biggest star, was under contract to Fox, so Matty cobbled her films with four or five others and convinced theaters to pay for the package. Matty enjoyed his job and was promoted to sales manager, sparking hopes that he might rise in the corporate ranks. Matty's plans changed when his father-in-law, Peter Kantor, asked him to work at his shoe factory. Peter promised an ownership stake, and Matty felt obligated to join the family business.

Peter's factory, which produced upscale women's shoes, was a success, but money flew out almost as fast as it came in. A heavyset, flamboyant man who favored expensive clothing, drove a succession of late-model Cadillacs, and wore elevator shoes to compensate for his five-foot-four stature, Peter blew much of his wealth on horse races and a series of paramours. On paydays, Peter let Jimmy and his cousin Richard Lourie hold piles of cash "as high as our heads," Richard recalls. "We both loved it."[1]

Peter projected a certain insouciance and a love of life, attitudes Jimmy later would adopt. A native of Russia, Peter shared naughty stories about the old country—most of which featured wolves, women, caviar, and a lot of vodka—and he taught his grandsons a few key Russian phrases—"Give me a cigarette" and "Kiss my ass"—sending the boys into fits of laughter. Peter placed the bulk of his cash in a safe-deposit box, likely to shield it from taxes, but he made sure to have $1,500 in his breast pocket at all times. He was found with that exact amount the day he died, surrounded by Christmas cards from dozens of appreciative female friends.

Matty Simons spent years as the general manager of the shoe factory, but he never received the ownership share Peter had promised. Later in life, Matty told his son he wished he hadn't forgone a promising and exciting career to do what was expected of him.

"The lesson was: Do what you like in life, not what you feel you 'should' do," Simons says. "It's something I never forgot."

What Jimmy liked to do more than anything else was think, often about mathematics. He was preoccupied with numbers, shapes, and slopes. At the age of three, Jimmy doubled numbers and divided them in half, figuring out all the powers of 2 up to 1,024 before becoming bored. One day, while taking the family to the beach, Matty stopped for gasoline, perplexing the young boy. The way Jimmy reasoned, the family's automobile could never have run out of gas. After it used half its tank, there would be another half remaining, then they could use half of that, and so on, without ever reaching empty.

The four-year-old had stumbled onto a classic mathematical problem involving a high degree of logic. If one must always travel half the remaining distance before reaching one's destination, and any distance, no matter how small, can be halved, how can one ever reach one's destination? The Greek philosopher Zeno of Elea was the first to address the dilemma, the most famous of a group of paradoxes that challenged mathematicians for centuries.

Like many children without siblings, Jimmy sat with his thoughts for long stretches of time and even talked to himself. In nursery school, he would climb a nearby tree, sit on a branch, and ponder. Sometimes Marcia had to come and force him to climb down and play with the other children.

Unlike his parents, Jimmy was determined to focus on his own passions. When he was eight, Dr. Kaplan, the Simons family's doctor, suggested a career in medicine, saying it was the ideal profession "for a bright Jewish boy."

Jimmy bristled.

"I want to be a mathematician or a scientist," he replied.

The doctor tried to reason with the boy. "Listen, you can't make any money in mathematics."

Jimmy said he wanted to try. He didn't quite understand what mathematicians did, but it likely involved numbers, which seemed good enough. Anyway, he knew perfectly well he didn't want to be a doctor.

In school, Jimmy was smart and mischievous, displaying his mother's self-assurance and his father's impish humor. He loved books, frequently visiting a local library to take out four a week, many well above his grade level. Mathematical concepts captivated him most, however. At the Lawrence School in Brookline, which counts television newscasters Mike Wallace and Barbara Walters as alumni, Jimmy was elected class president and finished close to the top of his grade, losing out in the latter case to a young woman who didn't find herself lost in thought nearly as often as he did.

During that time, Jimmy had a friend who was quite wealthy, and he was struck by the comfortable lifestyle his family enjoyed.

"It's nice to be very rich. I observed that," Simons later said. "I had no interest in business, which is not to say I had no interest in money."[2]

Adventures occupied much of Jimmy's time. Sometimes he and a friend, Jim Harpel, rode trolleys to Bailey's Ice Cream in Boston to enjoy a pint. When they were older, the pair sneaked into burlesque shows at the Old Howard Theatre. One Saturday morning, as the boys headed out the door, Harpel's father noticed binoculars around their necks.

"You boys going to the Old Howard?" he asked.

Busted.

"How'd you know, Mr. Harpel?" Jimmy asked.

"Not much bird watching around here," Mr. Harpel replied.

After ninth grade, the Simons family moved from Brookline to Newton, where Jimmy attended Newton High School, an elite public school well equipped to nurture his emerging passions. As a sophomore, Jimmy enjoyed debating theoretical concepts, including the notion that two-dimensional surfaces could extend forever.

After graduating high school in three years, Simons, thin and solidly built, set off on a cross-country drive with Harpel. Everywhere they went, the seventeen-year-olds—middle-class and, until then, largely sheltered from hardship—conversed with locals. Crossing into Mississippi, they saw African Americans working as sharecroppers and living in chicken coops.

"Reconstruction had left them as tenant farmers, but it was the same as slavery," Harpel recalls. "It was a bit of a shock to us."

Camping in a state park, the boys visited a swimming pool but saw no African Americans, which surprised them. Simons asked a heavyset, middle-aged park employee why no one of color was around.

"We don't allow no n——s," he said.

Visiting other cities, Simons and Harpel saw families living in abject poverty, experiences that left a mark on the boys, making them more sensitive to the plight of society's disadvantaged.

Simons enrolled at MIT, as he had hoped, and even skipped the first year of mathematics thanks to advanced-placement courses he took in high school. College brought immediate challenges, however. Early on, Simons dealt with stress and intense stomach pain, losing twenty pounds and spending two weeks in the hospital. Doctors eventually diagnosed colitis and prescribed steroids to stabilize his health.

Overconfident during the second semester of his freshman year, Simons registered for a graduate course in abstract algebra. It was an outright disaster. Simons was unable to keep up with his classmates and couldn't understand the point of the assignments and course topics.

Simons bought a book on the subject and took it home for the summer, reading and thinking for hours at a time. Finally, it clicked. Simons aced subsequent algebra classes. Though he received a D in an upper-level calculus course in his sophomore year, the professor allowed him to enroll in the next level's class, which discussed Stokes' theorem, a generalization of Isaac Newton's fundamental theorem of calculus that relates line integrals to surface integrals in three dimensions. The young man was fascinated—a theorem involving calculus, algebra, and geometry seemed to produce simple, unexpected harmony. Simons did so well in the class that students came to him seeking help.

"I just blossomed," Simons says. "It was a glorious feeling."

The way that powerful theorems and formulas could unlock truths and unify distinct areas in math and geometry captured Simons.

"It was the elegance of it all, the concepts were beautiful," he says.

When Simons studied with students like Barry Mazur—who graduated in two years and later would win top mathematics awards and teach at Harvard University—Simons concluded he wasn't quite at their level. He was close, though. And Simons realized he had a unique approach, mulling problems until he arrived at original solutions. Friends sometimes noticed him lying down, eyes closed, for hours at a time. He was a ponderer with imagination and "good taste," or the instinct to attack the kinds of problems that might lead to true breakthroughs.

"I realized I might not be spectacular or the best, but I could do something good. I just had that confidence," he says.

One day, Simons saw two of his professors, renowned mathematicians Warren Ambrose and Isadore Singer, in deep discussion after midnight at a local café. Simons decided he wanted that kind of life—cigarettes, coffee, and math at all hours.

"It was like an epiphany . . . a flash of light," he says.

Away from mathematics, Simons did everything he could to avoid courses demanding too much of him. MIT students were required to enroll in a physical-fitness course, but Simons didn't want to waste time showering and changing, so he signed up for archery. He and another student, Jimmy Mayer, who had come to MIT from Colombia, decided to make the class a bit more interesting, betting a nickel on every shot. They became fast friends, wooing girls and playing poker with classmates into the night.

"If you lost five dollars, you practically shot yourself," Mayer recalls.

Simons was funny, friendly, spoke his mind, and often got into trouble. As a freshman, he enjoyed filling water pistols with lighter fluid and then using a cigarette lighter to create a homemade flame thrower. Once, after Simons created a bathroom bonfire in Baker House, a dormitory on Charles

River, he flushed a pint of lighter fluid down a toilet and closed the door behind him. Glancing back, Simons saw an orange glow around the door frame—the inside of the bathroom was aflame.

"Don't go in there!" he screamed to approaching classmates.

Inside the toilet, the fluid had heated up and ignited into a fireball. Luckily, the dorm was built with dark red rustic bricks and the fire failed to spread. Simons confessed to his crime and paid the school fifty dollars total in ten-week installments for the necessary repairs.

By 1958, after three years at MIT, Simons had enough credits to graduate at the age of twenty, earning a bachelor of science in mathematics. Before entering graduate school, though, he yearned for a new adventure. Simons told a friend, Joe Rosenshein, that he wanted to do something that would "go down in the records" and would be "historic."

Simons thought a long-distance roller-skating trip might attract attention but it seemed too tiring. Inviting a news crew to follow him and his friends on a water-skiing trip to South America was another possibility, but the logistics proved daunting. Hanging out in Harvard Square with Rosenshein one afternoon, Simons saw a Vespa motor scooter race by.

"I wonder if we could use one of those?" Simons asked.

He developed a plan to undertake a "newsworthy" trip, convincing two local dealerships to give him and his friends discounts on Lambretta scooters, the top brand at the time, in exchange for the right to film their trip. Simons, Rosenshein, and Mayer set out for South America, a trip they nicknamed "Buenos Aires or Bust." The young men drove west through Illinois before heading south to Mexico. They traveled on country roads and slept on porches, in abandoned police stations, and in forests, where they set up jungle hammocks with mosquito netting. A family in Mexico City warned the boys about bandits and insisted they buy a gun for protection, teaching the young men to say a crucial phrase in Spanish: "If you move, we'll kill you."

Driving with a noisy, broken muffler through a small southern Mexican town around dinnertime, wearing leather jackets and looking like the motorcycle gang in Marlon Brando's classic film *The Wild One,* the boys stopped to find a place to eat. When the locals saw visitors disturbing their traditional evening stroll, they turned furious.

"Gringo, what are you doing here?" someone called out.

Within minutes, fifty hostile young men, some holding machetes, surrounded Simons and his friends, pushing their backs up against a wall. Rosenshein reached for the gun but remembered it only had six bullets, not nearly enough to handle the swelling crowd. Suddenly, police officers emerged, pushing through the throng to arrest the MIT students for disturbing the peace.

The boys were thrown in jail. Soon, it was surrounded by a mob, which screamed and whistled at them, causing such commotion that the mayor sent someone to investigate. When the mayor heard that three college kids from Boston were causing trouble, he had them brought directly to his office. It turned out that the mayor had graduated from Harvard University and was eager to hear the latest news from Cambridge. Moments after fending off an angry mob, the boys sat down with local officials for a sumptuous, late-night dinner. Simons and his friends made sure to get out of town before dawn, though, to avoid additional trouble.

Rosenshein had enough of the drama and headed home, but Simons and Mayer pushed on, making it to Bogotá in seven weeks, through Mexico, Guatemala, and Costa Rica, overcoming mudslides and raging rivers along the way. They arrived with almost no food or money, thrilled to stay in the luxurious home of another classmate, Edmundo Esquenazi, a native of the city. Friends and family lined up to meet the visitors, and they spent the rest of the summer playing croquet and relaxing with their hosts.

When Simons returned to MIT to begin his graduate studies, his advisor suggested he finish his PhD at the University of California, Berkeley, so he could work with a professor named Shiing-Shen Chern, a former math prodigy from China and a leading differential geometer and topologist. Simons had some unfinished business to take care of, though. He had begun dating a pretty, petite, dark-haired eighteen-year-old named Barbara Bluestein, who was in her first year at nearby Wellesley College. After four consecutive nights of intense conversation, they were enamored and engaged.

"We talked and talked and talked," Barbara recalls. "He was going to Berkeley, and I wanted to join him."

Barbara's parents were furious about the quicksilver relationship. Barbara was too young to wed, her mother insisted. She also worried about a potential power imbalance between Barbara and her self-assured fiancé.

"Years later, he's going to wipe the floor with you," she warned Barbara.

Determined to marry Simons despite her parents' objections, Barbara negotiated a compromise—she'd go with him to Berkeley, but they'd wait until her sophomore year to wed.

Simons received a fellowship to study in Berkeley. Arriving on campus in the late summer of 1959, he got an early and unhappy surprise—Chern was nowhere to be found. The professor had just left for a year-long sabbatical. Simons began working with other mathematicians, including Bertram Kostant, but he met frustrations. One night, in early October, Simons visited Barbara's boardinghouse and told her his research wasn't going well. She thought he looked depressed.

"Let's get married," she recalls telling him.

Simons was on board. They decided to go to Reno, Nevada, where they wouldn't have to wait days for a blood test, as was required in California. The young couple had almost no money, so Simons's roommate lent him enough to purchase two bus tickets for the two-hundred-mile trip. In Reno, Barbara persuaded the manager of a local bank to let her cash an out-of-state check so they could buy a marriage license. After a brief ceremony, Simons used the remaining money to play poker, winning enough to buy his new bride a black bathing suit.

Back in Berkeley, the couple hoped to keep their wedding a secret, at least until they figured out how to break the news to their families. When Barbara's father wrote a letter saying he was planning a visit, they realized they'd have to own up. Simons and his new bride wrote to their respective parents, filling several pages with mundane news about school and classes, before adding identical postscripts:

"By the way, we got married."

After Barbara's parents cooled down, her father arranged for a local rabbi to marry the couple in a more traditional ceremony. The newlyweds rented an apartment on Parker Street, near a campus buzzing with political activity, and Simons made progress on a PhD dissertation focused on differential geometry—the study of curved, multidimensional spaces using methods from calculus, topology, and linear algebra. Simons also spent time on a new passion: trading. The couple had received $5,000 as a wedding gift, and Simons was eager to multiply the cash. He did a bit of research and drove to a Merrill Lynch brokerage office in nearby San Francisco, where he bought shares of United Fruit Company, which sold tropical fruit, and Celanese Corporation, a chemical company.

The shares barely budged in price, frustrating Simons.

"This is kind of boring," he told the broker. "Do you have anything more exciting?"

"You should look at soybeans," he said.

Simons knew nothing about commodities or how to trade futures (financial contracts promising the delivery of commodities or other investments at a fixed price at a future date), but he became an eager student. At the time, soybeans sold for $2.50 per bushel. When the broker said Merrill Lynch's analysts expected prices to go to three dollars or even higher, Simons's eyes widened. He bought two futures contracts, watched soybeans soar, and scored several thousand dollars of profits in a matter of days.

Simons was hooked.

"I was fascinated by the action and the possibility I could make money short-term," he says.

An older friend urged Simons to sell his holdings and pocket his profits, warning that commodity prices are volatile. Simons disregarded the advice. Sure enough, soybean prices tumbled, and Simons barely broke even. The roller-coaster ride might have discouraged some novice investors, but it only whet Simons's appetite. He began getting up early to drive to San Francisco so he could be at Merrill Lynch's offices by 7:30 a.m., in time for the opening of trading in Chicago. For hours, he would stand and watch prices flash by on a big board, making trades while trying to keep up with the action. Even after heading home to resume his studies, Simons kept an eye on the markets.

"It was kind of a rush," Simons recalls.

It became too much, though. Schlepping into San Francisco at the crack of dawn while trying to complete a challenging thesis proved taxing. When Barbara became pregnant, there were too many balls for Simons to juggle. Reluctantly, he put a stop to his trading, but a seed had been planted.

For his doctoral thesis, Simons wanted to develop a proof for a difficult, outstanding problem in the field, but Kostant doubted he could pull it off. World-class mathematicians had tried and failed, Kostant told him. Don't waste your time. The skepticism seemed only to spur Simons. His resulting thesis, "On the Transitivity of Holonomy Systems," completed in 1962 after just two years of work, dealt with the geometry of multidimensional curved spaces. (When Simons speaks to novices, he likes to define *holonomy* as "parallel transport of tangent vectors around closed curves in multiple-dimensional curved spaces." Really.) A respected journal accepted the thesis for publication, helping Simons win a prestigious three-year teaching position at MIT.

Even as he made plans with Barbara to return to Cambridge with their baby, Elizabeth, Simons began to question his future. The next few decades seemed laid out for him all too neatly: research, teaching, more research, and still more teaching. Simons loved mathematics, but he also needed new adventure. He seemed to thrive on overcoming odds and defying skepticism, and he didn't see obstacles on the horizon. At just twenty-three, Simons was experiencing an existential crisis.

"Is this it? Am I going to do this my whole life?" he asked Barbara one day at home. "There has to be more."

After a year at MIT, Simons's restlessness got the better of him. He returned to Bogotá to see if he could start a business with his Colombian schoolmates, Esquenazi and Mayer. Recalling the pristine asphalt tile in his MIT dormitory, Esquenazi complained about the poor quality of floor material in Bogotá. Simons said he knew someone who made flooring, so they decided to start a local factory to produce vinyl floor tile and PVC piping. The financing mostly came from Esquenazi's father-in-law, Victor Shaio, but Simons and his father also took small stakes.

The business seemed in good hands, and Simons didn't feel he had much to contribute, so he returned to academia, accepting a research position at Harvard University in 1963. There, he taught two classes, including an advanced graduate course on partial differential equations, an area within geometry he anticipated would become important. Simons didn't know much about partial differential equations (PDEs), but he figured teaching the course was a good way to learn. Simons told his students he was learning the topic just a week or so before they were, a confession they found amusing.

Simons was a popular professor with an informal, enthusiastic style. He cracked jokes and rarely wore a jacket or tie, the outfit of choice among many faculty members. His jovial exterior masked mounting pressures, however. Simons's research was going slowly, and he didn't enjoy the Harvard community. He had borrowed money to invest in the floor-tile factory Esquenazi and the others were building, and he had persuaded his parents to mortgage their home for their own share of the deal. To pad his income, Simons began teaching two additional courses at nearby Cambridge Junior College, work that added to his stress, though he kept it secret from his friends and family.

Simons was hustling for money, but it wasn't simply to pay off his debts. He hungered for true wealth. Simons liked to buy nice things, but he wasn't extravagant. Nor did he feel pressure from Barbara, who still sometimes wore items of clothing from her high school days. Other motivations seemed to be driving Simons. Friends and others suspected he wanted to have some kind of impact on the world. Simons saw how wealth can grant independence and influence.

"Jim understood at an early age that money is power," Barbara says. "He didn't want people to have power over him."

As he sat in a Harvard library, his earlier career doubts resurfaced. Simons wondered if another kind of job might bring more fulfillment and excitement—and perhaps some wealth, at least enough to pay off his debts.

The mounting pressures finally got to Simons. He decided to make a break.

CHAPTER TWO

Q: What's the difference between a PhD in mathematics and a large pizza?

A: A large pizza can feed a family of four.

In 1964, Simons quit Harvard University to join an intelligence group helping to fight the ongoing Cold War with the Soviet Union. The group told Simons he could continue his mathematics research as he worked on government assignments. Just as important, he doubled his previous salary and began paying off his debts.

Simons's offer came from the Princeton, New Jersey, division of the Institute for Defense Analyses, an elite research organization that hired mathematicians from top universities to assist the National Security Agency—the United States' largest and most secretive intelligence agency—in detecting and attacking Russian codes and ciphers.

Simons joined during a tumultuous period for the IDA. High-level Soviet codes hadn't been cracked on a regular basis in more than a decade. Simons and his colleagues at the IDA's Communications Research Division were tasked with securing US communications and making sense of stubbornly impenetrable Soviet code. The IDA taught Simons how to develop mathematical models to discern and interpret patterns in seemingly meaningless data. He began using statistical analysis and probability theory, mathematical tools that would influence his work.

To break codes, Simons would first determine a plan of attack. Then, he'd create an algorithm—a series of steps for his computer to follow—to test and implement his strategy. Simons was awful at designing computer programs, forcing him to rely on the division's in-house programmers for the actual coding, but he honed other skills that would prove valuable later in his career.

"I learned I liked to make algorithms and testing things out on a computer," Simons later said.[1]

Early on, Simons helped develop an ultrafast code-breaking algorithm, solving a long-standing problem in the group. Soon thereafter, intelligence experts in Washington discovered an isolated instance in which the Soviets sent a coded message with an incorrect setting. Simons and two colleagues seized on the glitch, which provided rare insight into the internal construction of the enemy's system, and helped devise ways to exploit it. The advances made Simons a sleuthing star and earned the team a trip to Washington, DC, to accept personal thanks from Defense Department officials.

The only problem with his new job: Simons couldn't share his accomplishments with anyone outside the organization. Members of the group were sworn to secrecy. The word the government used to describe how it classified the IDA's work was, itself, classified.

"What did you do today?" Barbara would ask when Simons came home from work.

"Oh, the usual," he'd reply.

Before long, Barbara gave up asking.

Simons was struck by the unique way talented researchers were recruited and managed in his unit. Staff members, most of whom had doctorates, were hired for their brainpower, creativity, and ambition, rather than for any specific expertise or background. The assumption was that researchers would find problems to work on and be clever enough to solve them. Lenny Baum, among the most accomplished code-breakers, developed a saying that became the group's credo: "Bad ideas is good, good ideas is terrific, no ideas is terrible."

"It was an idea factory," says Lee Neuwirth, the division's deputy director, whose daughter, Bebe, later became a Broadway and television star.

Researchers couldn't discuss their work with those outside the organization. Internally, however, the division was structured to breed an unusual degree of openness and collegiality. Most of the twenty-five or so employees—all mathematicians and engineers—were given the same title: *technical staff member*. The team routinely shared credit and met for champagne toasts after discovering solutions to particularly thorny problems. Most days, researchers wandered into one another's offices to offer assistance or lend an ear. When staffers met each day for afternoon tea, they discussed the news, played chess, worked on puzzles, or competed at Go, the complicated Chinese board game.

Simons and his wife threw regular dinner parties at which IDA staffers became inebriated on Barbara's rum-heavy Fish House Punch. The group played high-stakes poker matches that lasted until the next morning, with Simons often walking away with fistfuls of his colleagues' cash.

One evening, the gang came over but Simons was nowhere to be found.

"Jim was arrested," Barbara told the crew.

Simons had racked up so many parking tickets in his beat-up Cadillac, and had ignored so many of the resulting summonses, that the police threw him in jail. The mathematicians piled into a few cars, drove to the police station, and chipped in to bail Simons out.

The IDA was filled with unconventional thinkers and outsize personalities. One large room hosted a dozen or so personal computers for the staff.

One morning, a guard discovered a cryptologist in the room wearing a bathrobe and nothing more; he had been thrown out of his home and had been living in the computer room. Another time, late at night, someone noticed a staffer typing away on a keyboard. What was shocking was that the employee was typing with his bare, smelly toes, rather than his fingers.

"His fingers were bad enough," Neuwirth says. "It was really disgusting. People were furious."

Even as Simons and his colleagues were uncovering Soviet secrets, Simons was nurturing one of his own. Computing power was becoming more advanced but securities firms were slow to embrace the new technology, continuing to rely on card-sorting methods for accounting and other areas. Simons decided to start a company to electronically trade and research stocks, a concept with the potential to revolutionize the industry. The twenty-eight-year-old Simons shared the idea with his boss, Dick Leibler, as well as the IDA's best programmer. They both agreed to join his company, to be named iStar.

Accustomed to top-secret schemes, the group worked surreptitiously on the company. One day, though, Neuwirth got wind of the plot. Upset that the pending departures would gut the group, Neuwirth stormed into Leibler's office.

"Why are you guys leaving?"

"How did you find out?" Leibler responded. "Who else knows?"

"Everyone—you guys left the last sheet of your business plan on the Xerox machine."

Their strategy was more Maxwell Smart than James Bond, it turned out.

In the end, Simons failed to raise enough money to get the business off the ground, eventually dropping the idea. It didn't feel like much of a setback, because Simons was finally making progress in his research on *minimal varieties,* the subfield of differential geometry that had long captivated him.

Differential equations—which are used in physics, biology, finance, sociology, and many other fields—describe the derivatives of mathematical quantities, or their relative rates of change. Isaac Newton's famous physics equation—the net force on an object is equal to its mass times its acceleration—is a differential equation because acceleration is a second derivative with respect to time. Equations involving derivatives with respect to time *and* space are examples of partial differential equations and can be used to describe elasticity, heat, and sound, among other things.

An important application of PDEs to geometry is in the theory of minimal varieties, which had been the focus of Simons's research since his first semester as an MIT instructor. A classic illustration in the field concerns the surface formed by a soap film stretching across a wire frame that has been dipped in soap solution and lifted out. Such a surface has minimal area compared with any other surface with the same wire frame as its boundary. Experimenting with soap films in the nineteenth century, Belgian physicist Joseph Plateau asked whether such surfaces with "minimal" areas always exist, and whether they are so smooth that every point looks alike, no matter how complicated or twisted the wire frame. The answer to what became known as Plateau's problem was yes, at least for ordinary, two-dimensional surfaces, as proved by a New York mathematician in 1930. Simons wanted to know if the same would be true for minimal surfaces in higher dimensions, something geometers call minimal varieties.

Mathematicians who focus on theoretical questions often immerse themselves in their work—walking, sleeping, even dreaming about problems for years on end. Those with no exposure to this kind of mathematics, which can be described as *abstract* or *pure*, are liable to dismiss it as pointless. Simons wasn't merely solving equations like a high school student, however. He was hoping to discover and codify universal principles, rules, and truths, with the goal of furthering the understanding of these mathematical objects. Albert Einstein argued that there is a natural order in the world; mathematicians like Simons can be seen as searching for evidence of that structure. There is true beauty to their work, especially when it succeeds in revealing something about the universe's natural order. Often, such theories find practical applications, even many years later, while advancing our knowledge of the universe.

Eventually, a series of conversations with Frederick Almgren Jr., a professor at nearby Princeton University who had solved the problem in three dimensions, helped Simons achieve a breakthrough. Simons created a partial differential equation of his own, which became known as the Simons equation, and used it to develop a uniform solution through six dimensions. He also proposed a counterexample in dimension seven. Later, three Italians, including Fields Medal winner Enrico Bombieri, showed the counterexample to be correct.

In 1968, Simons published "Minimal Varieties in Riemannian Manifolds," which became a foundational paper for geometers, proved crucial in related fields, and continues to garner citations, underscoring its enduring significance. These achievements helped establish Simons as one of the world's preeminent geometers.

=

Even as Simons realized success in code-breaking and mathematics, he kept searching for new ways to make money. The IDA granted its researchers a remarkable amount of flexibility in their work, so Simons spent time examining the stock market. Working with Baum and two other colleagues, Simons developed a newfangled stock-trading system. The quartet published an internal, classified paper for the IDA called "Probabilistic Models for and Prediction of Stock Market Behavior" that proposed a method of trading that the researchers claimed could generate annual gains of at least 50 percent.

Simons and his colleagues ignored the basic information most investors focus on, such as earnings, dividends, and corporate news, what the code breakers termed the "fundamental economic statistics of the market." Instead, they proposed searching for a small number of "macroscopic variables" capable of predicting the market's short-term behavior. They posited that the market had as many as eight underlying "states"—such as "high variance," when stocks experienced larger-than-average moves, and "good," when shares generally rose.

Here's what was really unique: The paper didn't try to identify or predict these states using economic theory or other conventional methods, nor did the researchers seek to address *why* the market entered certain states. Simons and his colleagues used mathematics to determine the set of states best fitting the observed pricing data; their model then made its bets accordingly. The *whys* didn't matter, Simons and his colleagues seemed to suggest, just the strategies to take advantage of the inferred states.

For the majority of investors, this was an unheard-of approach, but gamblers would have understood it well. Poker players surmise the mood of their opponents by judging their behavior and adjusting their strategies accordingly. Facing off against someone in a miserable mood calls for certain tactics; others are optimal if a competitor seems overjoyed and overconfident. Players don't need to know *why* their opponent is glum or exuberant to profit from those moods; they just have to identify the moods themselves. Simons and the code-breakers proposed a similar approach to predicting stock prices, relying on a sophisticated mathematical tool called a hidden Markov model. Just as a gambler might guess an opponent's mood based on his or her decisions, an investor might deduce a market's state from its price movements.

Simons's paper was crude, even for the late 1960s. He and his colleagues made some naive assumptions, such as that trades could be made "under ideal conditions," which included no trading costs, even though the model required heavy, daily trading. Still, the paper can be seen as something of a trailblazer. Until then, investors generally sought an underlying economic rationale to explain and predict stock moves, or they used simple *technical analysis*, which involved employing graphs or other representations of past price movements to discover repeatable patterns. Simons and his colleagues were proposing a third approach, one that had similarities with technical trading but was much more sophisticated and reliant on tools of math and science. They were suggesting that one could deduce a range of "signals" capable of conveying useful information about expected market moves.

Simons and his colleagues weren't alone in suggesting that stock prices are set by a complex process with many inputs, including some that are hard or even impossible to pin down and not necessarily related to traditional, fundamental factors. Around that time, Harry Markowitz, the University of Chicago Nobel laureate and father of modern portfolio theory, was searching for anomalies in securities prices, as was mathematician Edward Thorp. Thorp would attempt an early form of computerized trading, gaining a head start on Simons. (Stay tuned for more, dear reader.)

Simons was part of this vanguard. He and his colleagues were arguing that it wasn't important to understand all the underlying levers of the market's machine, but to find a mathematical system that matched them well enough to generate consistent profits, a view that would inform Simons's approach to trading years later. Their model foreshadowed revolutions in finance—including *factor investing*, the use of models based on unobservable states, and other forms of quantitative investing—that would sweep the investing world decades later.

=

By 1967, Simons was thriving at the IDA. He was matching wits with Russians, making progress in his math research, learning how to manage big brains, and gaining a better understanding of the power of computation. His ability to identify the most promising ideas of his colleagues was especially distinctive.

"He was a terrific listener," Neuwirth says. "It's one thing to have good ideas, it's another to recognize when others do. . . . If there was a pony in your pile of horse manure, he would find it."

By then, Leibler had begun discussing retirement, and Simons was in line to become the division's deputy director. A bump in salary and increased prestige seemed within reach.

The Vietnam War changed everything. That fall, protests cropped up around the country, including on the campus of Princeton University. Few Princeton students realized a division supporting the NSA was in their neighborhood until an article appeared in the school newspaper, the *Daily Princetonian*, alerting the community to the fact. Simons and his colleagues weren't doing work related to the war, and many of them were vehemently against the effort. That summer, when Jim and Barbara's daughter Liz went to sleepaway camp, her friends received packages of candy from their parents; Liz got peace necklaces.

The code breakers' unhappiness with the war didn't stop Princeton students from launching a series of protests, including a sit-in blocking the IDA's entrance. At one point, the building was trashed, Neuwirth's car was pelted with eggs, and he was called a "baby killer."[2]

As debate about the war heated up across the country, the *New York Times* published an opinion piece by General Maxwell D. Taylor as the cover story of its Sunday magazine. In the piece, General Taylor—the decorated war veteran who had served as chairman of the Joint Chiefs of Staff and had convinced President John F. Kennedy to send combat troops to the region—made a forceful argument that the United States was winning the war and that the nation should rally around the effort.

It was too much for Simons, who didn't want readers to be left with an impression that all IDA employees backed the war. He wrote a six-paragraph letter to the paper arguing that there were better uses of the nation's resources than conducting war in Vietnam.

"It would make us a stronger country to rebuild Watts than it would to bomb Hanoi," Simons wrote. "It would make us stronger to construct decent transportation on our East Coast than it would to destroy all the bridges in Vietnam."

After the newspaper published the letter, Simons was rather pleased with himself. He didn't get much reaction from colleagues and figured Taylor was fine with a little difference of opinion. A bit later, a stringer for *Newsweek* working on an article about Defense Department employees opposed to the war contacted Simons, asking how they handled their qualms. Simons said he and his colleagues generally worked on personal projects half the time, while spending the rest of their time on government projects. Since he opposed the war, Simons said, he had decided to devote all his time to his own mathematics research until the fighting ended, and then he'd only do Defense Department work, to even things out.

In truth, Simons hadn't formally established any kind of clean break from defense work. It was a personal goal, one he probably shouldn't have shared with the public.

"I was twenty-nine," Simons explains. "No one had ever asked to interview me. . . . And I was a wise guy."

Simons told Leibler about the interview, and Leibler gave Taylor a heads-up about the forthcoming *Newsweek* article. A short while later, Leibler returned with some disturbing news.

"You're fired," he said.

"What? You can't fire me," Simons responded. "I'm a *permanent* member."

"Jim, the only difference between a permanent member and temporary member is a temporary member has a contract," Leibler said. "You don't."

Simons came home in the middle of the day, shell-shocked. Three days later, President Lyndon Johnson announced the halting of US bombing missions, a sign the war effort was coming to an end. Simons figured the news meant he could reclaim his job. Leibler told him not to bother coming in.

By then, Simons had three young children. He had little idea what he was going to do next, but getting fired so abruptly convinced him that he needed to gain some control over his future. He wasn't quite sure how, though.

Simons's minimal-varieties paper was gaining attention, and he fielded offers from some schools, as well as companies including IBM. He told Leonard Charlap, a friend and fellow mathematician, that teaching mathematics seemed too dull. Simons said he might join an investment bank to sell convertible bonds. When Charlap said he didn't know what convertible bonds were, Simons launched into a long description. Charlap was disappointed in his friend. Simons was one of the world's premier young mathematicians, not someone meant to hawk Wall Street's latest product.

"That's ridiculous," Charlap said. "What's your ideal job?"

Simons confessed that he'd prefer to chair a large math department, but he was too young and didn't know the right people. Charlap said he had an idea. A bit later, a letter arrived for Simons from John Toll, president of SUNY Stony Brook, a public university on Long Island about sixty miles from New York City. The school had spent five years searching for someone to lead its math department. To the extent that the school had a reputation, it was for having a problem with drug use on campus.[3]

"The only thing we had heard was that there were some drug raids there," Barbara says.

Toll was determined to change things. A physicist who had been recruited by New York Governor Nelson Rockefeller, Toll was leading a $100 million, government-funded drive to turn the school into the "Berkeley of the East." He already had recruited Nobel Prize–winning physicist Chen Ning Yang and was now focusing on revitalizing his math department. Toll offered Simons the position of chairman, dangling the chance to be his own boss and build the department as he wished.

"I want it," Simons told Toll.

=

In 1968, at the age of thirty, Simons moved his family to Long Island, where he began charming recruits and building a department. Early on, Simons targeted a Cornell University mathematician named James Ax, who, a year earlier, had won the prestigious Cole Prize in number theory. Ax seemed unlikely to bolt the Ivy League powerhouse for an unheralded school like Stony Brook. He had a wife, a young son, and a bright future at Cornell. But Simons and Ax had been friendly as graduate students at Berkeley and they had stayed in touch, giving Simons some hope as he and Barbara drove five hours northwest to Ithaca, New York, to meet with the younger mathematician.

Simons wooed Ax, promising him a major salary increase. Later, he and Barbara hosted Ax and his family in Stony Brook, where Simons drove his guests to West Meadow Beach in nearby Brookhaven, on Long Island Sound, hoping the picturesque views might sway them. Back in Ithaca, Ax and his wife, also named Barbara, received care packages from Simons packed with pebbles and other reminders of Stony Brook's more temperate climate.

Ax took his time deliberating, frustrating Simons. One day, Simons walked into his Stony Brook office in a tennis outfit, flung his racket to the ground, and told a colleague, "If this job requires any more ass-licking I'm out of here!" The entreaties paid off, though. Ax became the first brand-name academic to join Stony Brook.

"He really wore us down with his little tricks," Barbara Ax says.

Ax's decision sent a message that Simons meant business. As he raided other schools, Simons refined his pitch, focusing on what it might take to lure specific mathematicians. Those who valued money got raises; those focused on personal research got lighter class loads, extra leave, generous research support, and help evading irritating administrative requirements.

"Jim, I don't want to be on a committee," one potential hire told him.

"How about the library committee?" Simons said. "It's a committee of one."

Courting accomplished candidates, Simons developed a unique perspective on talent. He told one Stony Brook professor, Hershel Farkas, that he valued "killers," those with a single-minded focus who wouldn't quit on a math problem until arriving at a solution. Simons told another colleague that some academics were "super smart" yet weren't original thinkers worthy of a position at the university.

"There are guys and there are *real* guys," he said.

Simons worked to create a collegial, stimulating environment, just as he had enjoyed at the IDA. To keep his academics happy, Simons kept teaching loads at reasonable levels and invited colleagues to join him and Barbara on their newly purchased twenty-three-foot boat docked on Long Island Sound. Unlike some top-flight academics, Simons relished interacting with colleagues. He'd wander into a professor's office, asking what projects he was working on and how he could be helpful, much like he had at the IDA.

"It's unusual for someone to think of the well-being of colleagues," Farkas says.

Simons put mathematicians and students at ease, dressing more informally than others at the school. He rarely wore socks, even in the frigid New York winters, a practice he would continue into his eighties.

"I just decided it takes too much of my time to put them on," Simons says.

Simons and Barbara hosted weekly parties at which academics, artists, and left-leaning intellectuals removed their shoes and mingled on the Simons's white shag carpet, enjoying drinks and chatting about politics and other topics of the day.

Simons made mistakes—including letting future Fields Medal winner Shing-Tung Yau get away after the young geometer demanded tenure—but he assembled one of the world's top centers of geometry, hiring twenty mathematicians while learning to identify the nation's best minds and how to recruit and manage them.

=

As Simons's department expanded, his personal life came unglued.

Simons's charisma attracted a range of students to his office, at all hours. He was receiving acclaim from his minimal-varieties work and enjoying the power of his chairmanship amid a period in which sexual norms—and restraints—were rapidly loosening. A best-selling book of the time, *Open Marriage,* encouraged spouses to "strip marriage of its antiquated ideals" and explore sexual relationships outside of wedlock. At the same time, the women's liberation movement encouraged women to discard the perceived shackles of society, including conservative dress and even monogamy.

"There seemed to be a contest among the secretaries as to who could wear the shortest skirt," recalls Charlap, the Stony Brook professor.

Simons was thirty-three years old and feeling restless once again. Rumors emerged of an extramarital dalliance with the department's attractive secretary. At least once, Simons made a crude joke about a female academic, surprising his colleagues.

At the time, Barbara felt overshadowed by her husband's accomplishments and was frustrated that early marriage and motherhood had stunted her own academic career. Barbara was smart and ambitious, but she had married at eighteen and had a daughter at nineteen.

"I felt a little trapped," she says.

One day, Simons heard Barbara was conducting a relationship with a younger colleague whom Simons had recruited and mentored. Simons was shaken. At a dinner party, when someone asked why Simons was so upset, noting that Jim's relationship with Barbara hadn't been ideal and he didn't seem especially committed to her, a drunken Simons slammed his hand against a wall, a colleague recalls.

Simons decided to take a sabbatical year at the University of California, Los Angeles, so he could undergo primal therapy, which was emerging as something of a cultural phenomenon. The approach involved screaming or otherwise articulating repressed pain "primally," as a newborn emerging from the womb. Simons, who sometimes woke up screaming at night, was intrigued by the approach.

After a few weeks of therapy, Simons had second thoughts. When his instructor suggested he might make more progress if he used marijuana, Simons decided to bolt.

This seems like a hoax, he thought.

Simons moved back to the East Coast, spending the year at the Institute for Advanced Study in Princeton. His marriage with Barbara couldn't be salvaged, and they eventually divorced. Barbara would head to UC Berkeley, where she completed a PhD in computer science in 1981. In her dissertation, Barbara solved an open problem in theoretical computer science. She would join IBM as a researcher and become president of ACM, the largest educational and scientific computing society. Later, Barbara emerged as a national expert on the security problems of computerized voting, demonstrating an interest in technology and addressing broader societal challenges that Simons would share.

"We just married too young," Barbara says. "My parents were right."

=

Back on Long Island, this time on his own, Simons searched for a live-in nanny to lend a hand when his three children were with him. One day, he interviewed Marilyn Hawrys, a pretty, twenty-two-year-old blond who later became a graduate student in economics at Stony Brook. Shortly after employing Marilyn, Simons asked her on a date. For a while, the relationship was off-and-on. Eventually Marilyn left to become a nanny for James Ax's children, helping out as Ax and his wife went through a painful divorce. Marilyn lived with Barbara Ax and her two sons, Kevin and Brian, playing late-night games of Scrabble with the family, cooking a mean mac and cheese, and providing a shoulder for the kids to cry on.

"Marilyn was a godsend to all of us," recalls Ax's son, Brian Keating.

Over time, Jim and Marilyn forged a romantic bond. Marilyn made progress on a PhD in economics, while Simons enjoyed a breakthrough with Shiing-Shen Chern, the professor he had followed to UC Berkeley, only to realize he was on leave.

On his own, Simons made a discovery related to quantifying shapes in curved, three-dimensional spaces. He showed his work to Chern, who realized the insight could be extended to all dimensions. In 1974, Chern and Simons published "Characteristic Forms and Geometric Invariants," a paper that introduced Chern-Simons *invariants*—an invariant is a property that remains unchanged, even while undergoing particular kinds of transformations—which proved useful in various areas of mathematics.

In 1976, at the age of thirty-seven, Simons was awarded the American Mathematical Society's Oswald Veblen Prize in Geometry, the highest honor in the field, for his work with Chern and his earlier research in minimal varieties. A decade later, theoretical physicist Edward Witten and others would discover that Chern-Simons theory had applications to a range of areas in physics, including condensed matter, string theory, and supergravity. It even became crucial to methods used by Microsoft and others in their attempts to develop quantum computers capable of solving problems vexing modern computers, such as drug development and artificial intelligence. By 2019, tens of thousands of citations in academic papers—approximately three a day—referenced Chern-Simons theory, cementing Simons's position in the upper echelon of mathematics and physics.

=

Simons had reached a pinnacle of his profession. Just as quickly, he drifted from mathematics, desperate for a new summit to ascend.

In 1974, the floor-tile company Simons had started with his friends Edmundo Esquenazi and Jimmy Mayer sold a 50 percent stake, delivering profits to Simons and the other owners. Simons recommended that Esquenazi,

Mayer, and Victor Shaio invest their money with Charlie Freifeld, who had taken a course with Simons at Harvard. An offshore trust Shaio had established for Simons also placed money with Freifeld.

Freifeld employed a different strategy from most. He built *econometric* models to forecast the prices of commodities, including sugar, using economic and other data as his inputs. If crop production fell, for example, Freifeld's models computed the price rise that likely would result, an early form of quantitative investing.

Freifeld's tactics paid off as sugar prices nearly doubled. The value of the group's partnership soared, tenfold, to $6 million. Some of the investors reacted in unexpected ways to the shocking windfall.

"I was depressed," says Mayer, Simons's friend from Colombia. "We'd made all this money, but there was no socially redeeming value in what we were doing."

Simons had a very different response. The rapid-fire gains got his speculative juices flowing once more, reminding him of the rush trading could bring. Freifeld's style even shared some similarities to the math-based trading system described by Simons and his colleagues in their paper at the IDA. He thought using models to trade was an idea that held promise.

"Jim got the bug," Mayer says.

Despite his recent acclaim, Simons needed a break from mathematics. He and Jeff Cheeger, a protégé who was emerging as a star in the field of geometry, had been trying to show that certain geometrically defined numbers, such as pi, are irrational in almost every case. They weren't getting anywhere and were growing frustrated, even hopeless.

"There was bigger game there, and we weren't able to get it," Simons says. "It was driving me crazy."[4]

Simons was also dealing with confusion in his personal life. He was growing closer to Marilyn but was still pained by the breakup of his marriage.

After four years of dating, Simons confided to a friend that he was contemplating proposing marriage but was unsure about getting back into a serious relationship.

"I've met this woman; she's really special," he told a friend. "I don't know what I'm going to do."

Jim and Marilyn married, but he continued pondering his life's direction. Simons reduced his obligations at Stony Brook to spend half his time trading currencies for a fund established by Shaio. By 1977, Simons was convinced currency markets were ripe for profit. World currencies had begun to *float*, moving freely without regard to the price of gold, and the British pound had tumbled. It seemed to Simons that a new, volatile era had begun. In 1978, Simons left academia to start his own investment firm focusing on currency trading.

Simons's father told him he was making a big mistake giving up a tenured position. Mathematicians were even more shocked. Until then, most had only a vague awareness that Simons had outside interests. The idea that he might leave to play the market full-time was confounding. Mathematicians generally have a complicated relationship with money; they appreciate the value of wealth, but many see the pursuit of lucre as a lowly distraction from their noble calling. Academics wouldn't say it to Simons directly, but some were convinced he was squandering rare talent.

"We looked down on him, like he had been corrupted and had sold his soul to the devil," says René Carmona, who taught at Cornell at the time.

Simons had never completely fit into the world of academia, though. He loved geometry and appreciated the beauty of mathematics, but his passion for money, curiosity about the business world, and need for new adventures set him apart.

"I've always felt like something of an outsider, no matter what I was doing," he later would say.[5] "I was immersed in mathematics, but I never felt quite like a member of the mathematics community. I always had a foot [outside that world]."

Simons had been a star cryptologist, had scaled the heights of mathematics, and had built a world-class math department, all by the age of forty. He was confident he could conquer the world of trading. Investors had spent centuries trying to master markets, rarely finding huge success. Once again, rather than deter Simons, the challenges seemed to spark enthusiasm.

"He really wanted to do unusual things, things others didn't think possible," his friend Joe Rosenshein says.

Simons would find it harder than he expected.

CHAPTER THREE

Getting fired can be a good thing.
You just don't want to make a habit of it.

Jim Simons

Weeks after leaving Stony Brook University's expansive, tree-lined cam-pus in the early summer of 1978, Simons found himself just a few miles down the road, yet a world away.

Simons sat in a storefront office in the back of a dreary strip mall. He was next to a women's clothing boutique, two doors down from a pizza joint, and across from the tiny, one-story Stony Brook train station. His space, built for a retail establishment, had beige wallpaper, a single computer terminal, and spotty phone service. From his window, Simons could barely see the aptly named Sheep Pasture Road, an indication of how quickly he had gone from broadly admired to entirely obscure.

The odds weren't in favor of a forty-year-old mathematician embarking on his fourth career, hoping to revolutionize the centuries-old world of investing. Indeed, Simons appeared closer to retirement than any sort of historic breakthrough. His graying hair was long and stringy, almost to his shoulders. A slight paunch made him look even more like an aging professor out of step with modern finance.

Until then, Simons had dabbled in investing but hadn't demonstrated any special talent. Sure, the stake Simons and his father had in Charlie Freifeld's investment partnership had grown to about a million dollars after Freifeld correctly anticipated a surge in sugar prices, but disaster had barely been averted. Just weeks after Freifeld dumped the group's holdings, sugar prices had plummeted. Neither Freifeld nor Simons had anticipated the fall. They had simply agreed to cash out if they ever scored a substantial profit.

"It was incredible," Simons says, "but it was completely lucky."[1]

Somehow, Simons was bursting with self-confidence. He had conquered mathematics, figured out code-breaking, and built a world-class university department. Now he was sure he could master financial speculation, partly because he had developed a special insight into how financial markets operated. Some investors and academics saw the markets' zigs and zags as random, arguing that all possible information was already baked into prices, so only news, which is impossible to predict, could push prices higher or lower. Others believed that price shifts reflected efforts by investors to react to and predict economic and corporate news, efforts that sometimes bore fruit.

Simons came from a different world and enjoyed a unique perspective. He was accustomed to scrutinizing large data sets and detecting order where others saw randomness. Scientists and mathematicians are trained to dig below the surface of the chaotic, natural world to search for unexpected simplicity, structure, and even beauty. The emerging patterns and regularities are what constitute the laws of science.[2]

Simons concluded that markets didn't always react in explainable or rational ways to news or other events, making it difficult to rely on traditional research, savvy, and insight. Yet, financial prices did seem to feature at least some defined patterns, no matter how chaotic markets appeared, much as the apparent randomness of weather patterns can mask identifiable trends.

It looks like there's some structure here, Simons thought.

He just had to find it.

Simons decided to treat financial markets like any other chaotic system. Just as physicists pore over vast quantities of data and build elegant models to identify laws in nature, Simons would build mathematical models to identify order in financial markets. His approach bore similarities to the strategy he had developed years earlier at the Institute for Defense Analyses, when he and his colleagues wrote the research paper that determined that markets existed in various hidden states that could be identified with mathematical models. Now Simons would test the approach in real life.

There must be some way to model this, he thought.

Simons named his new investment company Monemetrics, combining the words "money" and "econometrics" to indicate that he would use math to analyze financial data and score trading gains. At the IDA, Simons had built computer models to spot "signals" hidden in the noise of the communications of the United States' enemies. At Stony Brook, he had identified, courted, and managed talented mathematicians. Now Simons would hire a team of big brains to pore through the market's data to identify trends and develop mathematical formulas to profit from them.

Simons wasn't sure where to start. All he knew was that currency markets had become unshackled, presenting profit potential. He did have an ideal partner in mind for his fledgling firm: Leonard Baum, one of the coauthors of the IDA research paper and a mathematician who had spent time discerning hidden states and making short-term predictions in chaotic environments. Simons just had to convince Baum to risk his career on Simons's radical, unproven approach.

═

Lenny Baum was born in 1931, the son of immigrants who had fled Russia for Brooklyn to escape rampant poverty and anti-Semitism. At the age of thirteen, Lenny's father, Morris, began work on the floor of a hat factory, where he eventually became the manager and owner. As a teenager, Lenny was six feet tall with a barrel chest, his high school's top sprinter and a member of its tennis team, though his delicate hands suggested someone more comfortable turning the pages of a textbook than competing on a court.

One day, while visiting nearby Brighton Beach with friends, Lenny spotted a vivacious and attractive young woman chatting with friends. Julia Lieberman had come with her family to the United States at the age of five from a small village in Czechoslovakia, clutching her favorite doll as they escaped the Nazis on the last boat from Europe in 1941. Once in New York, Julia's father, Louis, spent months unsuccessfully searching for a job. Discouraged, he decided to show up at a local factory and try to blend in with its workers. Louis proved such a tireless laborer that he was added to the payroll. Later, Louis operated a laundromat in the family's small row house, but the Lieberman family would always struggle financially.

Lenny and Julia fell in love and eventually married and moved to Boston, where Lenny attended Harvard University, graduating in 1953 and then earning a PhD in mathematics. Julia finished fourth in her class at Boston University before obtaining a master of arts in education and history at Harvard. After joining the IDA in Princeton, Baum was even more successful breaking code than Simons, receiving credit for some of the unit's most important, and still classified, achievements.

"Lenny and some others were definitely higher than Jim in what we in management used to call 'lifeboat order,'" Lee Neuwirth says.

Balding and bearded, Baum pursued math research while juggling government assignments, just like Simons. Over the course of several summers in the late 1960s, Baum and Lloyd Welch, an information theorist working down the hall, developed an algorithm to analyze Markov chains, which are sequences of events in which the probability of what happens next depends only on the current state, not past events. In a Markov chain, it is impossible to predict future steps with certainty, yet one can observe the chain to make educated guesses about possible outcomes. Baseball can be seen as a Markov game. If a batter has three balls and two strikes, the order in which they came and the number of fouls in between don't matter. If the next pitch is a strike, the batter is out.

A *hidden* Markov process is one in which the chain of events is governed by unknown, underlying parameters or variables. One sees the results of the chain but not the "states" that help explain the progression of the chain. Those not acquainted with baseball might throw their hands up when receiving updates of the number of runs scored each inning—one run in this inning, six in another, with no obvious pattern or explanation. Some investors liken financial markets, speech recognition patterns, and other complex chains of events to hidden Markov models.

The Baum-Welch algorithm provided a way to estimate probabilities and parameters within these complex sequences with little more information than the output of the processes. For the baseball game, the Baum-Welch algorithm might enable even someone with no understanding of the sport to guess the game situations that produced the scores. If there was a sudden jump from two runs to five runs, for example, Baum-Welch might suggest the probability that a three-run home run had just been hit rather than a bases-loaded triple. The algorithm would allow someone to infer a sense of the sport's rules from the distribution of scores, even as the full rules remained hidden.

"The Baum-Welch algorithm gets you closer to the final answer by giving you better probabilities," Welch explains.

Baum usually minimized the importance of his accomplishment. Today, though, Baum's algorithm, which allows a computer to teach itself states and probabilities, is seen as one of the twentieth century's notable advances in machine learning, paving the way for breakthroughs affecting the lives of millions in fields from genomics to weather prediction. Baum-Welch enabled the first effective speech recognition system and even Google's search engine.

For all of the acclaim Baum-Welch brought Lenny Baum, most of the hundreds of other papers he wrote were classified, which grated on Julia. She came to believe her husband was getting neither the recognition nor the pay he deserved. The Baum children had little idea what their father was up to. The few times they asked, he told them his work was classified. Baum did tell them what he *wasn't* working on.

"We're not making bombs," he reassured his daughter Stefi one day, as controversy about the Vietnam War flared.

Unlike Simons, Baum was a homebody who spent little time socializing, playing poker, or interacting with others. Most evenings, he sat quietly on a faux-leopard-skin couch in his family's modest Princeton home, scribbling on a yellow pad with a pencil. When Baum ran into a particularly challenging problem, he'd stop, gaze far into the distance, and ponder. Baum fit the stereotype of an absentminded professor—once, he came to work with half a beard, explaining that he had become distracted thinking about mathematics while shaving.

During his tenure at the IDA, Baum had noticed his eyesight deteriorating. Doctors eventually determined he suffered from cone-rod dystrophy, a disorder affecting the cone cells on the retina. Baum found it difficult to engage in activities requiring visual clarity, such as tennis. Once, at the net, a ball hit Baum square in the head. The same thing happened in Ping-Pong; his clear blue eyes would see the ball for a moment and then lose it, forcing Baum to drop the sports.

He remained surprisingly upbeat, focusing on pleasures he still could enjoy, such as walking two miles a day near the Princeton campus. Grateful he could read and write, despite the decline of his fine, sharp, straight-ahead vision, Baum maintained an unbreakable optimism.

"Let the problem be," Baum liked to say, usually with a smile, when his kids came to him with concerns. "It will solve itself."

After Simons left the IDA to lead Stony Brook's mathematics department, however, the Baum family began to detect uncharacteristic frustration in their patriarch. When Baum broke a Russian code and identified a spy but the FBI proved too slow arresting the suspect, he expressed irritation. Baum became discouraged about his unit's future, writing an internal memo emphasizing the need for better recruitment.

"It is obvious that the loss of Simons is serious for us, both because we need him mathematically and because of the manner of his departure," Baum wrote, referring to Simons's firing. "During the period of seven months when Simons supposedly wasn't working on defense material, he, in fact, did more work on defense projects than some of our members have done in the last few years."[3]

One day in 1977, Simons reached out to Baum, asking if he would spend a day at Monemetrics' office on Long Island helping Simons set up a trading system to speculate on currencies. Baum chuckled at the invitation. He didn't know much about trading, despite his earlier theoretical paper with Simons, and cared so little about investing that he left the family's portfolio entirely in his wife's hands. Nonetheless, Baum agreed to spend some time assisting Simons, as a favor to his old friend.

At the office, Simons set charts depicting the daily closing values of various major currencies in front of Baum, as if he was presenting him with a mathematical problem. Scrutinizing the data, Baum quickly determined that, over stretches of time, some currencies, especially the Japanese yen, seemed to move in steady, straight lines. Perhaps Simons was right, Baum thought, there did seem to be some inherent structure in the markets. Baum hypothesized that the yen's steady climb might be due to the Japanese government, under pressure from foreign nations, intervening to buy the currency "in precise Japanese manner" to make Japanese exports a bit less competitive. Either way, Baum agreed with Simons that a mathematical model might be developed to map out and ride trends in various currencies.

Baum began working with Simons once a week. By 1979, Baum, then forty-eight years old, was immersed in trading, just as Simons had hoped. A top chess player in college, Baum felt he had discovered a new game to test his mental faculties. He received a one-year leave of absence from the IDA and moved his family to Long Island and a rented, three-bedroom Victorian house lined with tall bookcases. Because his eyesight had worsened, Julia drove her husband back and forth to Simons's office each day.

"Let's see if we can make a model," Simons told him, as they prepared to focus on markets.

It didn't take Baum long to develop an algorithm directing Monemetrics to buy currencies if they moved a certain level below their recent trend line and sell if they veered too far above it. It was a simple piece of work, but Baum seemed on the right path, instilling confidence in Simons.

"Once I got Lenny involved, I could see the possibilities of building models," Simons later said.[4]

Simons called some friends, including Jimmy Mayer and Edmundo Esquenazi, asking if they would invest in his new fund. Simons showed them the same charts he had presented Baum, wowing them with how much he and Baum would have made had they used their mathematics-focused trading strategy over the course of the previous several years.

"He came with this chart and impressed us with the possibilities," Mayer says.

Simons failed to raise the $4 million he was shooting for, but he came close enough to begin his fund, which also held his own money. He called his new investment fund Limroy, an amalgam of Lord Jim, the protagonist of the Joseph Conrad novel of the same name, and the Royal Bank of Bermuda, which handled the new company's money transfers so that it could glean the advantages, tax-related and otherwise, of being located offshore. The name blended high-finance with a character known for wrestling with ideals of honor and morality, a fitting choice for someone who long had one foot in the world of business and another in mathematics and academia.

Simons decided Limroy would be a *hedge fund*, a loosely defined term for private investment partnerships that manage money for wealthy individuals and institutions and pursue a variety of strategies, including trying to hedge, or protect, themselves from losses in the overall market.

Monemetrics would invest a bit of money for Simons, testing strategies in a variety of markets. If the tactics looked profitable, Simons would place the same trades in Limroy, which was much bigger and would invest for outsiders as well as for Simons. Baum would share in the 25 percent cut the firm claimed from all its trading profits.

Simons hoped he and Baum could make big money relying on a trading style that combined mathematical models, complicated charts, and a heavy dose of human intuition. Baum became so certain their approach would work, and so hooked on investing, that he quit the IDA to work full-time with Simons.

To make sure he and Baum were on the right track, Simons asked James Ax, his prized recruit at Stony Brook, to come by and check out their strategies. Like Baum a year or so earlier, Ax knew little about investing and cared even less. He immediately understood what his former colleagues were trying to accomplish, though, and became convinced they were onto something special. Not only could Baum's algorithm succeed in currencies, Ax argued, but similar predictive models could be developed to trade commodities, such as wheat, soybeans, and crude oil. Hearing that, Simons persuaded Ax to leave academia, setting him up with his own trading account. Now Simons was *really* excited. He had two of the most acclaimed mathematicians working with him to unlock the secrets of the markets and enough cash to support their efforts.

A year or two earlier, Baum couldn't stop thinking about math; now it was trading that occupied his mind. Lying on a beach with his family one morning during the summer of 1979, Baum mulled the extended weakness in the value of the British pound. At the time, the conventional wisdom was that the currency could only fall in value. One expert who advised Simons and Baum on their trading made so much selling pounds that he named his son Sterling.

Relaxing on the beach that morning, Baum sat straight up, overcome with excitement. He was convinced a buying opportunity was at hand. Baum raced to the office, telling Simons that Margaret Thatcher, Britain's new prime minister, was keeping the currency at unsustainably low levels.

"Thatcher is sitting on the pound," Baum said. "She can't hold it down much longer."

Baum said they needed to buy pounds, but Simons was amused, rather than swayed, by Baum's sudden conviction.

"Lenny, it's too bad you didn't come in earlier," Simons responded, smiling. "Thatcher stood up. . . . The pound just rose five cents."

That morning, it turned out, Thatcher had decided to let the pound rise in price. Baum was unfazed.

"That's nothing!" he insisted. "It's going to go up fifty cents—maybe more!"[5]

Baum was right. He and Simons kept buying British pounds, and the currency kept soaring. They followed that move with accurate predictions for the Japanese yen, West German deutsche mark, and Swiss franc, gains that had the South American investors calling Simons with congratulations and encouragement as the fund grew by tens of millions of dollars.

Fellow mathematicians still scratched their heads about why Simons had discarded a promising career to sit in a makeshift office trading currency contracts. They were just as stunned that Baum and Ax had joined him. Even Simons's father seemed disappointed. In 1979, at a bar mitzvah party for Simons's son Nathaniel, Matty Simons told a Stony Brook mathematician, "I liked to say, 'My son, the professor,' not 'My son, the businessman.'"

Simons spent little time looking back. After racking up early currency winnings, Simons amended Limroy's charter to allow it to trade US Treasury bond futures contracts as well as commodities. He and Baum—who now had their own, separate investment accounts—assembled a small team to build sophisticated models that might identify profitable trades in currency, commodity, and bond markets.

Simons was having a blast exploring his lifelong passion for financial speculation while trying to solve markets, perhaps the greatest challenge he had encountered. Besides, he joked, his wife Marilyn at last could "hang out with people and know what they were talking about."[6]

The fun wouldn't last.

═

Searching for someone to program his computers, Simons heard about a nineteen-year-old on the verge of getting kicked out of the California Institute of Technology. Greg Hullender was sharp and creative, but he had trouble focusing on his schoolwork and did poorly in many of his courses. Later in life, he would be diagnosed with attention-deficit disorder. At the time, Hullender was frustrated by his struggles, as were the school's administrators. The last straw came when he was caught running an unauthorized, high-stakes trading operation out of his dorm room. Friends pooled their cash and handed it to Hullender, who purchased stock options before a market rally in 1978, turning $200 into $2,000 in a matter of days. Soon, everyone in the dorm wanted in on the operation, throwing money at

Hullender, who began repackaging stock options purchased through a brokerage account at Merrill Lynch and reselling them to eager students.

"It was like my own stock exchange," Hullender says, with pride.

Merrill Lynch officials weren't amused by his ingenuity. Citing Hullender for violating the terms of his account, the brokerage pulled the plug on his venture and the school kicked him out. Sitting in his dorm room, waiting to be expelled, Hullender was startled by a seven a.m. phone call from Simons. Simons had heard about Hullender's unlicensed trading operation through a Caltech grad student and was impressed by Hullender's understanding of financial markets, as well as his moxie. Simons offered Hullender a salary of $9,000 a year, as well as a share of his firm's profits, to come to New York to program Limroy's trades.

With a round, cherubic face, shaggy brown hair, and a boyish smile, Hullender looked like a teenager heading off to summer camp, not someone cut out for a cross-country trip to join an unknown trading operation. Rail-thin with thick, oversize glasses, Hullender kept pens in his front pocket, along with a brown case for his spectacles, a look that made him appear especially guileless.

Hullender hadn't met Simons or Baum and was wary of the job offer.

"Jim's firm sounded like the shadiest thing in the world," he says.

The young man didn't hesitate to accept Simons's offer, however.

"I was in my dorm room waiting to get kicked out—it's not like I had a lot of options."

Hullender moved to Long Island, staying with Simons and his family for several weeks until he rented a room in a nearby Stony Brook dormitory. The young man didn't have a driver's license, so Simons lent him a bicycle to get to work. At the office, Simons, wearing his usual open-collared cotton shirt and loafers, gave Hullender a tutorial on how he approached trading. Currency markets are affected by the actions of governments and others,

Simons told him, and his firm hoped to develop detailed, step-by-step algorithms to identify "trends that result from hidden actors influencing the market," not unlike what Simons did at the IDA to break enemy code.

Hullender began by writing a program to track the new firm's results. Within six months, Hullender's figures showed disturbing losses—Simons's shift to bond trading had gone awry. Clients kept calling, but now they were asking why they were losing so much money, rather than extending congratulations.

Simons seemed to take the downturn hard, growing more anxious as the losses increased. On one especially rough day, Hullender found his boss lying supine on a couch in his office. Hullender sensed Simons wanted to open up to him, perhaps even make some kind of confession.

"Sometimes I look at this and feel I'm just some guy who doesn't really know what he's doing," Simons said.

Hullender was startled. Until that moment, Simons's self-confidence seemed boundless. Now he appeared to be second-guessing his decision to ditch mathematics to try to beat the market. Still on the couch, as if in a therapist's office, Simons told Hullender about Lord Jim, which centers on failure and redemption. Simons had been fascinated with Jim, a character who had a high opinion of himself and yearned for glory but failed miserably in a test of courage, condemning himself to a life filled with shame.

Simons sat up straight and turned to Hullender.

"He had a really good death, though," he said. "Jim died nobly."

Wait, is Simons contemplating suicide?

Hullender worried about his boss—and about his own future. Hullender realized he had no money, was alone on the East Coast, and had a boss on a couch talking about death. Hullender tried reassuring Simons, but the conversation turned awkward.

In the following days, Simons emerged from his funk, more determined than ever to build a high-tech trading system guided by algorithms, or step-by-step computer instructions, rather than human judgment. Until then, Simons and Baum had relied on crude trading models, as well as their own instincts, an approach that had left Simons in crisis. He sat down with Howard Morgan, a technology expert he'd hired to invest in stocks, and shared a new goal: building a sophisticated trading system fully dependent on preset algorithms that might even be automated.

"I don't want to have to worry about the market every minute. I want models that will make money while I sleep," Simons said. "A pure system without humans interfering."

The technology for a fully automated system wasn't there yet, Simons realized, but he wanted to try some more sophisticated methods. He suspected he'd need reams of historic data, so his computers could search for persistent and repeating price patterns across a large swath of time. Simons bought stacks of books from the World Bank and elsewhere, along with reels of magnetic tape from various commodity exchanges, each packed with commodity, bond, and currency prices going back decades, some to before World War II. This was ancient stuff that almost no one cared about, but Simons had a hunch it might prove valuable.

Hullender's five-foot-tall, blue-and-white PDP-11/60 computer couldn't read some of the older data Simons was amassing because its formatting was outdated, so Hullender surreptitiously carried the reels to the nearby headquarters of Grumman Aerospace, where his friend Stan worked. Around midnight, when things slowed down at the defense contractor, Stan let Hullender fire up a supercomputer and spend hours converting the reels so they could be read on Simons's computer. As the reels spun, the friends caught up over coffee.

To gather additional data, Simons had a staffer travel to lower Manhattan to visit the Federal Reserve office to painstakingly record interest-rate histories and other information not yet available electronically. For more recent pricing data, Simons tasked his former Stony Brook secretary and new office manager, Carole Alberghine, with recording the closing prices of major currencies. Each morning, Alberghine would go through the *Wall Street Journal* and then climb on sofas and chairs in the firm's library room to update various figures on graph paper hanging from the ceiling and taped to the walls. (The arrangement worked until Alberghine toppled from her perch, pinching a nerve and suffering permanent injury, after which Simons enlisted a younger woman to scale the couches and update the numbers.)

Simons recruited his sister-in-law and others to input the prices into the database Hullender created to track prices and test various trading strategies based on both mathematical insights and the intuitions of Simons, Baum, and others. Many of the tactics they tried focused on various momentum strategies, but they also looked for potential correlations between commodities. If a currency went down three days in a row, what were the odds of it going down a fourth day? Do gold prices lead silver prices? Might wheat prices predict gold and other commodity prices? Simons even explored whether natural phenomena affected prices. Hullender and the team often came up empty, unable to prove reliable correlations, but Simons pushed them to keep searching.

"There's a pattern here; there *has* to be a pattern," Simons insisted.

Eventually, the group developed a system that could dictate trades for various commodity, bond, and currency markets. The office's single computer wasn't powerful enough to incorporate all the data, but it could identify a few reliable correlations.

The trading system had live hogs as a component, so Simons named it his "Piggy Basket." The group built it to digest masses of data and make trading recommendations using the tools of linear algebra. The Piggy Basket produced a row of numbers. The sequence "0.5, 0.3, 0.2," for example, would signify that the currency portfolio should be 50 percent yen, 30 percent deutsche marks, and 20 percent Swiss francs. After the Piggy Basket churned out its recommendations for about forty different futures contracts, a staffer would get in touch with the firm's broker and deliver buy-and-sell instructions based on those proportions. The system produced automated trade recommendations, rather than automated trades, but it was the best Simons could do at the time.

For a few months, the Piggy Basket scored big profits, trading about $1 million of Monemetrics' money. The team generally held its positions for a day or so, then sold them. Encouraged by the early results, Simons transferred several million dollars of additional cash from the Limroy account into the model, scoring even larger gains.

Then, something unexpected happened. The computerized system developed an unusual appetite for potatoes, shifting two-thirds of its cash into futures contracts on the New York Mercantile Exchange that represented millions of pounds of Maine potatoes. One day, Simons got a call from unhappy regulators at the Commodity Futures Trading Commission: Monemetrics was close to cornering the global market for these potatoes, they said, with some alarm.

Simons had to stifle a giggle. Yes, the regulators were grilling him, but they had to realize Simons hadn't meant to accumulate so many potatoes; he couldn't even understand why his computer system was buying so many of them. Surely, the CFTC would understand that.

"They think we're trying to corner the market on spuds!" he told Hullender, with some amusement, after hanging up the phone.

The regulators somehow missed the humor in Simons's misadventure. They closed out his potato positions, costing Simons and his investors millions of dollars. Soon, he and Baum had lost confidence in their system. They could see the Piggy Basket's trades and were aware when it made and lost money, but Simons and Baum weren't sure *why* the model was making its trading decisions. Maybe a computerized trading model wasn't the way to go, after all, they decided.

In 1980, Hullender quit to go back to school. Leaving college prematurely weighed on him, and he was ashamed he couldn't help Simons make more progress on his computerized trading system. Hullender couldn't understand the math Simons and Baum were using, and he was lonely and miserable. Weeks earlier, he had revealed to colleagues that he was gay. They tried to make him comfortable, but the young man felt increasingly out of place.

"I just felt I had a better chance meeting someone compatible in California," says Hullender, who eventually earned his degree and became a machine-learning specialist for Amazon and Microsoft. "Some things are more important than money."

=

With Hullender gone and the Piggy Basket malfunctioning, Simons and Baum drifted from predictive mathematical models to a more traditional trading style. They began looking for undervalued investments while reacting to market-moving news, investing $30 million in various markets.

Simons thought it might help if they could get their hands on news from Europe before their rivals, so he hired a Parisian studying at Stony Brook to read an obscure French financial newsletter and translate it before others had a chance. Simons also consulted with an economist named Alan Greenspan, who later would become Federal Reserve chair. At one point, Simons set up a red phone in his office that rang whenever urgent financial news broke, so he and Baum could enter trades before others. Sometimes the phone rang and they were nowhere to be found, sending new office manager Penny Alberghine, Carole's sister-in-law, racing to find them, be it in a local restaurant or shop or even the men's room, where she'd pound on the door to get their attention.

"Come back in!" Alberghine screamed once. "Wheat's down thirty points!"

Simons's cheeky, irreverent sense of humor put his team at ease. He'd tease Alberghine about her thick New York accent, and she'd mock the remains of his Boston inflection. Once, Simons became elated when he received an especially high interest rate for money the firm held in a bank account.

"Investors are getting eleven and seven-*fucking*-eighths!" he exclaimed.

When a young employee gasped at his blue language, Simons flashed a grin.

"I know—that *is* an impressive rate!"

A few times a week, Marilyn came by to visit, usually with their baby, Nicholas. Other times, Barbara checked in on her ex-husband. Other employees' spouses and children also wandered around the office. Each afternoon, the team met for tea in the library, where Simons, Baum, and others discussed the latest news and debated the direction of the economy. Simons also hosted staffers on his yacht, *The Lord Jim*, docked in nearby Port Jefferson.

Most days, Simons sat in his office, wearing jeans and a golf shirt, staring at his computer screen, developing new trades—reading the news and predicting where markets were going, like most everyone else. When he was especially engrossed in thought, Simons would hold a cigarette in one hand and chew on his cheek. Baum, in a smaller, nearby office, trading his own account, favored raggedy sweaters, wrinkled trousers, and worn Hush Puppies shoes. To compensate for his worsening eyesight, he hunched close to his computer, trying to ignore the smoke wafting through the office from Simons's cigarettes.

Their traditional trading approach was going so well that, when the boutique next door closed, Simons rented the space and punched through the adjoining wall. The new space was filled with offices for new hires, including an economist and others who provided expert intelligence and made their own trades, helping to boost returns. At the same time, Simons was developing a new passion: backing promising technology companies, including an electronic dictionary company called Franklin Electronic Publishers, which developed the first hand-held computer.

In 1982, Simons changed Monemetrics' name to Renaissance Technologies Corporation, reflecting his developing interest in these upstart companies. Simons came to see himself as a venture capitalist as much as a trader. He spent much of the week working in an office in New York City, where he interacted with his hedge fund's investors while also dealing with his tech companies.

Simons also took time to care for his children, one of whom needed extra attention. Paul, Simons's second child with Barbara, had been born with a rare hereditary condition called ectodermal dysplasia. Paul's skin, hair, and sweat glands didn't develop properly, he was short for his age, and his teeth were few and misshapen. To cope with the resulting insecurities, Paul asked his parents to buy him stylish and popular clothing in the hopes of fitting in with his grade-school peers.

Paul's challenges weighed on Simons, who sometimes drove Paul to Trenton, New Jersey, where a pediatric dentist made cosmetic improvements to Paul's teeth. Later, a New York dentist fitted Paul with a complete set of implants, improving his self-esteem.

Baum was fine with Simons working from the New York office, dealing with his outside investments, and tending to family matters. Baum didn't need much help. He was making so much money trading various currencies using intuition and instinct that pursuing a systematic, "quantitative" style of trading seemed a waste of time. Building formulas was difficult and time-consuming, and the gains figured to be steady but never spectacular. By contrast, quickly digesting the office's news ticker, studying newspaper articles, and analyzing geopolitical events seemed exciting and far more profitable.

"Why do I need to develop those models?" Baum asked his daughter Stefi. "It's so much easier making millions in the market than finding mathematical proof."

Simons respected Baum too much to tell him how to trade. Besides, Baum was on a roll, and the firm's computer firepower was limited, making any kind of automated system likely impossible to implement.

Baum liked to pore over economic and other data, close the door to his office, and lie back on his green sofa, reflecting for long periods on his next market move.

"He'd lose track of time," Penny Alberghine says. "He was a bit spacey."

When Baum emerged, he usually placed buy orders. An optimist by nature, Baum liked to purchase investments and sit on them until they rose, no matter how long it took. Courage was needed to hold on to investment positions, Baum told friends, and he was proud he didn't buckle when others grew weak in the knees.

"If I don't have a reason for doing something, I leave things as they are and do nothing," he wrote to family members, explaining his trading tactics.

"Dad's theory was buy low and hold on forever," Stefi says.

The strategy enabled Baum to ride out market turbulence and rack up more than $43 million in profits between July 1979 and March 1982, nearly double his original stake from Simons. In the latter year, Baum grew so bullish about stocks that he insisted on missing the firm's annual outing on Simons's yacht, preferring to monitor the market and buy more stock futures. Around noon, when Baum grudgingly joined his colleagues, Simons asked why he looked so glum.

"I got half of what I wanted," Baum said. "Then I had to come to this lunch."

Baum probably should have stayed in the office. He had correctly identified that year's historic bottoming out of the US stock market. As stocks soared and his profits piled up, Lenny and Julia purchased a six-bedroom, turn-of-the-century home on Long Island Sound. Julia still drove an old Cadillac, but she no longer worried about money. The trading life had a less salutary impact on her husband, despite his mounting gains. Once relaxed and upbeat, Baum turned serious and intense, fielding calls from Simons and others well into the evening as they debated how to react to news of the day.

"He was like a different person," Stefi recalls.

═

Baum's penchant for holding on to investments eventually caused a rift with Simons. The tension started back in the fall of 1979, when they each purchased gold-futures contracts at around $250 an ounce. Late that year, the Iranian government took fifty-two American diplomats and citizens hostage and Russia invaded Afghanistan to support that country's communist regime. The resulting geopolitical jitters pushed gold and silver prices higher. Visitors to the Long Island office watched as Baum, normally quiet and introspective, stood, exuberantly cheering gold higher. Simons sat nearby, smiling.

By January 1980, gold and silver prices were soaring. When gold topped $700 in a frenzied two-week period, Simons dumped his position, locking in millions of dollars of profits. As usual, Baum couldn't bear to sell. One day, Simons was speaking with a friend who mentioned that his wife, a jeweler, was rifling through his closet, removing gold cuff links and tie clips to sell.

"Are you going broke or something?" Simons asked with concern.

"No—she can cut the line to sell," the friend responded.

"There's a *line* to sell gold?"

The friend explained that people around the country were queuing up to sell jewelry, taking advantage of surging prices. Simons turned scared; if the supply of gold was swelling, that could crush prices.

Back in the office, Simons gave Baum an order.

"Lenny, sell right now."

"No—the trend will continue."

"Sell the fucking gold, Lenny!"

Baum ignored Simons, driving him crazy. Baum was sitting on more than $10 million of profits, gold had skyrocketed past $800 an ounce, and he was sure more gains were ahead.

"Jim nagged me," Baum later told his family. "But I couldn't find any specific reason or news for action, so I did nothing."

Finally, on January 18, Simons dialed the firm's broker and pressed the phone to Baum's ear.

"Tell him you're selling, Lenny!"

"Alright, alright," Baum grumbled.

Within months, gold had raced past $865 an ounce, and Baum was bitterly complaining that Simons had cost him serious money. Then the bubble burst; just a few months later, gold was under $500 an ounce.

A bit later, Baum discovered a native of Colombia who worked at the brokerage firm E. F. Hutton and claimed to have insights into the coffee-futures market. When the Colombian predicted higher prices, Baum and Simons built some of the largest positions in the entire market. Almost immediately, coffee prices dropped 10 percent, costing them millions. Once again, Simons dumped his holdings but Baum couldn't bear selling. Eventually, Baum lost so much money he had to ask Simons to get rid of the coffee investment for him; he was unable to do it himself. Baum later described the episode as "the dumbest thing I ever did in this business."

Baum's eternal optimism was beginning to wear on Simons.

"He had the buy-low part, but he didn't always have the sell-high part," Simons later said.[7]

By 1983, Baum and his family had moved to Bermuda, where they enjoyed the island's idyllic weather and favorable tax laws. The island's beauty reinforced Baum's upbeat nature and bullish instincts. US inflation seemed under control, and Federal Reserve Chair Paul Volcker predicted a decline in interest rates, so Baum purchased tens of millions of dollars of US bonds, an ideal investment for that kind of environment.

But panic selling overcame the bond market in the late spring of 1984 amid surging bond issuance by the administration of President Ronald Reagan and rapid US economic growth. As his losses grew, Baum maintained his typical equanimity, but Simons feared the troubles could take the firm down.

"Lighten up, Lenny. Don't be stubborn," Simons said.

Baum's losses kept growing. A huge wager that the yen would continue to appreciate also backfired, placing Baum under even more pressure.

"This cannot continue!" Baum said one day, staring at his computer screen.

When the value of Baum's investment positions had plummeted 40 percent, it triggered an automatic clause in his agreement with Simons, forcing Simons to sell all of Baum's holdings and unwind their trading affiliation, a sad denouement to a decades-long relationship between the esteemed mathematicians.

Ultimately, Baum proved prescient. In subsequent years, both interest rates and inflation tumbled, rewarding bond investors. By then, Baum was trading for himself, and he and Julia had returned to Princeton. The years with Simons had been filled with such stress that Baum rarely enjoyed a full night's sleep. Now he was rested and had time to return to mathematics. As he grew older, Baum focused on prime numbers and an unsolved and well-known problem, the Riemann hypothesis. For fun, he traveled the country competing in Go tournaments, memorizing the board or standing over it to compensate for his ever-declining eyesight.

In his eighties, Baum enjoyed walking two miles from his home to Witherspoon Street, near Princeton University's campus, stopping to smell budding flowers along the way. Passing drivers sometimes slowed to offer assistance to the slow, well-dressed older gentleman, but he always declined the help. Baum would spend hours sitting in the sun at coffee shops, striking up conversations with strangers. Family members sometimes found him gently comforting homesick undergraduates. In the summer of 2017, weeks after finalizing his latest mathematics paper, Baum passed away at the age of eighty-six. His children published the paper posthumously.

=

Baum's losses in the 1984 trading debacle left deep scars on Simons. He halted his firm's trading and held disgruntled investors at bay. Once staffers eagerly greeted the frequent calls from Simons's friends, who asked, "How are we doing?" Now that the fund was losing millions of dollars daily, Simons instituted a new rule with clients—no performance results until the end of each month.

The losses had been so upsetting that Simons contemplated giving up trading to focus on his expanding technology businesses. Simons gave clients the opportunity to withdraw their money. Most showed faith, hoping Simons could figure out a way to improve the results, but Simons himself was racked with self-doubt.

The setback was "stomach-wrenching," he told a friend. "There's no rhyme or reason."

Simons had to find a different approach.

CHAPTER FOUR

Truth . . . is much too complicated to allow
for anything but approximations.

John von Neumann

Jim Simons was miserable.

He hadn't abandoned a flourishing academic career to deal with sudden losses and grumpy investors. Simons had to find a different method to speculate on financial markets; Lenny Baum's approach, reliant on intellect and instinct, just didn't seem to work. It also left Simons deeply unsettled.

"If you make money, you feel like a genius," he told a friend. "If you lose, you're a dope."

Simons called Charlie Freifeld, the investor who had made him a millionaire speculating on sugar contracts, to share his frustrations.

"It's just too hard to do it this way," Simons said, sounding exasperated. "I have to do it mathematically."

Simons wondered if the technology was yet available to trade using mathematical models and preset algorithms, to avoid the emotional ups and downs that come with betting on markets with only intelligence and intuition. Simons still had James Ax working for him, a mathematician who seemed perfectly suited to build a pioneering computer trading system. Simons resolved to back Ax with ample support and resources, hoping something special would emerge.

For a while, it seemed an investing revolution was at hand.

═

No one understood why James Ax was always so angry.

There was the time he drove his foot through a department wall, the fistfight he started with a fellow mathematician, and the invective he regularly directed at colleagues. Ax squabbled about credit due, seethed if someone let him down, and shouted if he didn't get his way.

The rage didn't make much sense. Ax was an acclaimed mathematician with chiseled good looks and a biting sense of humor. He enjoyed professional success and acclaim from his peers. Yet, most days, Ax was a disagreement away from a frightening eruption of pique and dudgeon.

His gifts emerged at a young age. Born in the Bronx, Ax attended Stuyvesant High School in lower Manhattan, New York City's most prestigious public school. Later, he graduated with high honors from the Polytechnic Institute of Brooklyn, a school claiming notable contributions to the development of microwave physics, radar, and the US space program.

Ax concealed deep suffering that wasn't immediately apparent amid his academic achievement. When he was seven, his father had abandoned the family, leaving the boy disconsolate. Growing up, Ax battled constant stomach pain and fatigue. It took doctors until his late teens to deliver a diagnosis of Crohn's disease, prompting a series of treatments that helped ameliorate his condition.

In 1961, Ax earned a PhD in mathematics from the University of California, Berkeley, where he became friends with Simons, a fellow graduate student. Ax was the first to greet Simons and his wife in the hospital after Barbara gave birth to their first child. As a mathematics professor at Cornell University, Ax helped develop a branch of pure mathematics called number theory. In the process, he forged a close bond with a senior, tenured academic named Simon Kochen, a mathematical logician. Together, the professors tried to prove a famous fifty-year-old conjecture made by the famed Austrian mathematician Emil Artin, meeting immediate and enduring frustration. To blow off steam, Ax and Kochen initiated a weekly poker game with colleagues and others in the Ithaca, New York, area. What started as friendly get-togethers, with winning pots that rarely topped fifteen dollars, grew in intensity until the men fought over stakes reaching hundreds of dollars.

Ax was a decent poker player, but he couldn't find a way to beat Kochen. Growing more infuriated with each loss, Ax became convinced Kochen was gaining a crucial advantage by reading his facial expressions. Ax had to hide his tell. One summer evening, as the poker players sat down to play in a brutal heat wave, Ax showed up wearing a heavy, woolen ski mask to conceal his face. Sweating profusely and barely able to see through the mask's narrow openings, Ax somehow lost to Kochen again. Ax stalked away from the game, fuming, never to uncover Kochen's secret.

"It wasn't his face," Kochen says. "Jim tended to straighten up in his chair when he had a good hand."

Ax spent the 1970s searching for new rivals and ways to best them. In addition to poker, he took up golf and bowling, while emerging as one of the nation's top backgammon players.

"Jim was a restless man with a restless mind," Kochen says.

Ax focused the bulk of his energies on math, a world that is more competitive than most realize. Mathematicians usually enter the field out of a love for numbers, structures, or models, but the real thrill often comes from being the first to make a discovery or advance. Andrew Wiles, the Princeton mathematician famous for proving the Fermat conjecture, describes mathematics as a journey through "a dark unexplored mansion," with months, or even years, spent "stumbling around." Along the way, pressures emerge. Math is considered a young person's game—those who don't accomplish something of significance in their twenties or early thirties can see their chances slip away.[1]

Even as Ax made progress in his career, anxieties and irritations built. One day, after complaining bitterly to Kochen that his office was too close to the department's bathroom and that sounds from inside were interfering with his concentration, Ax drove a boot through the wall between his office and the bathroom, leaving a gaping hole. He had successfully proved how flimsy the wall was, but Ax could now hear each toilet flush even more clearly than before. To tweak Ax, the professors preserved the opening, further riling him.

As Kochen got to know Ax and became aware of the pain of his early years, Kochen adopted a more generous attitude toward his colleague. Ax's fury stemmed from deep insecurities, Kochen argued to others, not outright cruelty, and his unhappiness often dissipated quickly. Kochen and Ax became close friends, as did their wives. Eventually, the mathematicians introduced an elegant solution to their long-running mathematical challenge, an advance that became known as the Ax-Kochen theorem. In some ways, their approach was more startling than their accomplishment; until then, no one had used the techniques of mathematical logic to solve problems in number theory.

"The methods we used were from left field," Kochen says.

In 1967, the theorem, described in three innovative papers, won Kochen and Ax the Frank Nelson Cole Prize in number theory, among the top honors in the field and an award given out just once every five years. Ax received a fair amount of acclaim, and the university promoted him to full professor in 1969. At twenty-nine, Ax was the youngest ever to hold that title at Cornell.

That was the year Ax received a call from Simons inviting him to join Stony Brook's growing mathematics department. Ax was born and raised in New York City, but he was drawn to the calm of the ocean, perhaps the result of the early upheaval in his life. At the same time, his wife, Barbara, had grown weary of Ithaca's brutal winters.

After Ax left for Stony Brook, Cornell threatened to register a protest with Governor Rockefeller if Simons raided any more of the university's faculty members, a sign of the dismay the Ivy League school felt about losing its celebrated mathematician.

Soon after arriving at Stony Brook, Ax told a colleague that mathematicians do their best work by the age of thirty, a possible indication he was feeling pressure to top his early success. Colleagues sensed that Ax was disappointed that his work with Kochen hadn't resulted in sufficient adulation. Ax's publication rate dwindled and he threw himself into poker, chess, and even fishing, searching for distractions from mathematics.

Battling clear signs of depression, Ax engaged in frequent arguments with his wife, Barbara. Like others in the department, Ax had wed at a young age, before the decade's period of sexual liberation and experimentation had begun. As Ax let his hair grow and began favoring tight-fitting jeans, rumors emerged of his infidelities. Others with two young children might have worked on their marriage for the sake of the kids, but fatherhood didn't come easily to Ax.

"I like kids," he said with a lingering Bronx accent, "once they learn algebra."

After Ax's divorce turned bitter and he lost custody of his sons, Kevin and Brian, he had little to do with the boys. Ax seemed in a perpetual dark mood. At department meetings, he interrupted colleagues so frequently that Leonard Charlap began carrying a bell, so he could ring it each time Ax cut someone off.

"What the hell are you doing?" Ax screamed one day.

When Charlap explained the bell's purpose, Ax stormed out, leaving his co-workers in laughter.

Another time, Ax got into a fistfight with an associate professor, forcing colleagues to pull him off the younger colleague. Ax's incessant needling had convinced the younger professor that Ax would block his promotion, sparking tension.

"I could have been killed!" the younger professor screamed at Ax.

Despite the interpersonal drama, Ax's reputation in the field remained such that Michael Fried, a young professor, turned down a tenured position at the University of Chicago to join Ax at Stony Brook. Ax respected Fried's abilities and seemed taken with the mathematician's natural magnetism. Fried was a muscular, six-foot athlete with wavy auburn hair and a thin mustache, the closest the math world could expect to come to the macho-man look sweeping the country in the early 1970s. At department parties, women swooned; Ax, newly divorced, seemed to take note, Fried recalls.

"It was almost as if Ax invited me there to attract women," he says.

Their relationship frayed, however, as Fried suspected Ax was appropriating his work without sharing proper credit. For his part, Ax believed Fried wasn't showing him the appropriate amount of respect around other academics. At a grievance-airing meeting with Fried, Simons, and a Stony Brook administrator, Ax got in Fried's face to deliver an ominous vow.

"I'm going to do everything I can to ruin your career, fair or foul," Ax foamed.

Stunned, Fried couldn't muster much of a comeback.

"Forget it," Fried responded.

He walked out, never to speak to Ax again.

=

When Simons first talked to Ax about joining his trading venture, in 1978, Ax viewed financial markets as a bit boring. He changed his mind after visiting Simons's office and getting a look at Baum's early trading models. Simons portrayed investing as the ultimate puzzle, promising to back Ax with his own account if he left academia to focus on trading. Eager for fresh competition and in need of a break from academia, Ax wondered if he could beat the market.

In 1979, Ax joined Simons in his strip-mall office near the pizza parlor and the women's clothing store. At first, Ax focused on the market's fundamentals, such as whether demand for soybeans would grow or a severe weather pattern would affect the supply of wheat. Ax's returns weren't remarkable, so he began developing a trading system to take advantage of his math background. Ax mined the assorted data Simons and his team had collected, crafting algorithms to predict where various currencies and commodities were headed.

His early research wasn't especially original. Ax identified slight upward trends in a number of investments and tested if their average price over the previous ten, fifteen, twenty, or fifty days was predictive of future moves. It was similar to the work of other traders, often called *trenders*, who examine *moving averages* and jump on market trends, riding them until they peter out.

Ax's predictive models had potential, but they were quite crude. The trove of data Simons and others had collected proved of little use, mostly because it was riddled with errors and faulty prices. Also, Ax's trading system wasn't in any way automated—his trades were made by phone, twice a day, in the morning and at the end of the trading day.

To gain an edge on his rivals, Ax began relying on a former professor with hidden talents soon to be revealed.

=

A native of Philadelphia, Sandor Straus earned a PhD in mathematics from Berkeley in 1972 and moved to Long Island for a teaching job in Stony Brook's math department. Outgoing and gregarious, Straus received strong reviews for his teaching and thrived among colleagues who shared his passion for mathematics and computers. Straus even looked the part of a successful academic of the era. An unabashed liberal who had met his wife, Faye, at an antiwar rally during Eugene McCarthy's presidential campaign in 1968, Straus, like many other men on campus, wore round, John Lennon–style glasses and combed his long brown hair back in a ponytail.

Over time, however, Straus began worrying about his future. He sensed he was a subpar mathematician and knew he was inept at department politics. Ill equipped to jostle with fellow mathematicians for funding for projects of interest, Straus understood he had little chance of obtaining tenure at Stony Brook or another school with a respected math department.

In 1976, Straus joined Stony Brook's computer center, where he helped Ax and other faculty members develop computer simulations. Straus was making an annual salary of less than $20,000, had little opportunity for advancement, and was unsure about his future.

"I wasn't super happy," he says.

In the spring of 1980, as Hullender prepared to leave Monemetrics, Ax recommended the firm hire Straus as its new computer specialist. Impressed with Straus's credentials and a bit desperate to fill the hole Hullender was leaving, Simons offered to double Straus's salary. Straus was torn—he was thirty-five years old, and the computer-center salary made it difficult to support his wife and one-year-old baby. But he thought if he hung on for another couple of years he might receive the equivalent of tenure at the university. Straus's father and friends gave the same advice: Don't even consider giving up a steady job to join a no-name trading firm that might fold.

Straus ignored the advice and accepted Simons's offer, but he hedged his bet, requesting a one-year leave of absence from Stony Brook rather than resigning outright. Greeting the new hire, Ax asked for help building his computer models. Ax said he wanted to invest in commodity, currency, and bond futures based on *technical analysis,* an age-old craft that aims to make forecasts based on patterns in past market data. Ax directed Straus to dig up all the historic information he could to improve his predictive models.

As Straus searched for pricing data, he ran into problems. At the time, the Telerate machines dominating trading floors didn't have an interface enabling investors to collect and analyze the information. (A few years later, a laid-off businessman named Michael Bloomberg would introduce a competing machine with those capabilities and much more.)

Piecing together a custom-built database, Straus purchased historic commodity-price data on magnetic tape from an Indiana-based firm called Dunn & Hargitt, then merged it with the historic information others in the firm already had amassed. For more recent figures, Straus got his hands on opening and closing prices for each day's session, along with high and low figures. Eventually, Straus discovered a data feed that had *tick* data, the intraday fluctuations of various commodities and other futures trades. Using an Apple II computer, Straus and others wrote a program to collect and store their growing data trove.

No one had asked Straus to track down so much information. Opening and closing prices seemed sufficient to Simons and Ax. They didn't even have a way to use all the data Straus was gathering, and with computer-processing power still limited, that didn't seem likely to change. But Straus figured he'd continue collecting the information in case it came in handy down the road.

Straus became somewhat obsessive in his quest to locate pricing data before others realized its potential value. Straus even collected information on stock trades, just in case Simons's team wanted it at some point in the future. For Straus, gathering data became a matter of personal pride.

Looking over his mounds of data, though, Straus became concerned. Over long stretches of time, some commodity prices didn't seem to move. That didn't seem to make sense—twenty minutes and not a single trade? There was even an odd gap, years earlier, when there was no futures trading in Chicago over a period of a couple of days, even though there was activity in other markets during that time. (It turned out a major flood had suspended Chicago trading.)

The inconsistencies bothered Straus. He hired a student to write computer programs to detect unusual spikes, dips, or gaps in their collection of prices. Working in a small, windowless office next to Ax and down a spiral staircase from Simons, Straus began the painstaking work of checking his prices against yearbooks produced by commodity exchanges, futures tables, and archives of the *Wall Street Journal* and other newspapers, as well as other sources. No one had told Straus to worry so much about the prices, but he had transformed into a data purist, foraging and cleaning data the rest of the world cared little about.

Some people take years to identify a profession for which they are naturally suited; others never make the discovery. Straus had certain gifts that were only now being revealed. In almost any other trading firm or previous era, his fixation on accurate pricing information would have seemed out of place, maybe even a bit kooky. But Straus saw himself as an explorer on the trail of untold riches with almost no one in pursuit. Some other traders were gathering and cleaning data, but no one collected as much as Straus, who was becoming something of a data guru. Energized by the challenge and opportunity, he came to an obvious career decision.

I'm not going back to that computer center.

═

Straus's data helped Ax improve his trading results, putting him in rare spirits as he became increasingly optimistic about their methods. Ax still gambled, played in a racquetball league, and bowled, mind you. He also traveled to Las Vegas, where he captured third place in backgammon's World Amateur Championship, earning a mention in the *New York Times* along the way.

"He had to have competition, and he had to win," says Reggie Dugard, another programmer.

But Ax had discovered trading to be as absorbing and stimulating as any challenge he had encountered. He and Straus programmed past price moves into their trading model, hoping to predict the future.

"There's something here," Simons told Ax, encouraging their new approach.

Searching for additional help, Simons asked Henry Laufer, a well-regarded Stony Brook mathematician, to spend one day a week helping out. Laufer and Ax had complementary mathematical skills—Ax was a number theorist, while Laufer explored functions of complex numbers—suggesting a partnership might work. They had distinct personalities, though. Taking over Lenny Baum's old office, Laufer sometimes brought his infant into the office in a car seat, as Ax looked on askance.

Laufer created computer simulations to test whether certain strategies should be added to their trading model. The strategies were often based on the idea that prices tend to revert after an initial move higher or lower. Laufer would buy futures contracts if they opened at unusually low prices compared with their previous closing price, and sell if prices began the day much higher than their previous close. Simons made his own improvements to the evolving system, while insisting that the team work together and share credit. Ax sometimes had difficulty with the request, stressing out over recognition and compensation.

"Henry is overstating his role," Ax complained to Simons one day.

"Don't worry about it. I'll treat you both equally."

Simons's response did little to appease Ax. For the next six months, he refused to speak to Laufer, though Laufer was so caught up in his work he barely noticed.

Around the office, Ax pushed conspiracy theories, especially those involving the Kennedy assassination. He also demanded that staffers refer to him as "Dr. Ax," out of respect for his PhD. (They refused.) Once, Ax asked Penny Alberghine to tell a driver in an adjoining parking lot to move his car because the sun glare was bothering him. (Alberghine pretended she couldn't find the car's owner.)

"He had no personal self-confidence and always took things the wrong way," Alberghine says. "I would pray that I wouldn't upset him or aggravate him."

Ax and his team were making money, but there were few hints their efforts would lead to anything special. It wasn't even clear Simons would keep the trading effort going. When one employee received a job offer from Grumman, Straus supported his decision to leave. The defense contractor was a stable company—it even offered a signing bonus of a free turkey. Leaving seemed like a no-brainer.

===

In 1985, Ax surprised Simons with the news that he was moving. Ax wanted to be in a warmer climate so he could sail, surf, and play racquetball year-round. Straus also wanted to flee the cold of the Northeast. Given little choice, Simons agreed to let them move the trading business to the West Coast.

Settling in Huntington Beach, California, thirty-seven miles from Los Angeles, Ax and Straus established a new company called Axcom Limited. Simons received 25 percent of the new entity's profits, while agreeing to provide trading help and communicate with the new firm's clients. Ax and Straus would manage the investments and split the remaining 75 percent ownership. Laufer, who had no desire to move west, returned to teach at Stony Brook, though he continued to trade with Simons in his spare time.

Ax had another impetus for his move that he didn't share with Simons: He was dealing with enduring sadness from his divorce, which he continued to blame on his ex-wife. Once he left New York, Ax abandoned his children, much as his own father had vanished from his life years earlier. Ax wouldn't speak to his boys again for more than fifteen years.

=

The Huntington Beach office, located on the top floor of a two-story office park owned by a subsidiary of oil giant Chevron, was about the last place one would expect to find a cutting-edge trading firm. Oil wells pumped away in the parking lot, and the smell of crude oil permeated the entire neighborhood. The building didn't have an elevator, so Straus and a crew of workers used a stair crawler to get a hulking VAX-11/750, with 300 megabytes of disk storage, into the office. An immense Gould superminicomputer, which had 900 megabytes of storage and was the size of a large refrigerator, had to be moved off a truck onto a forklift, which deposited it in the office via a second-floor balcony.

By 1986, Axcom was trading twenty-one different futures contracts, including the British pound, Swiss franc, deutsch mark, Eurodollars, and commodities including wheat, corn, and sugar. Mathematical formulas developed by Ax and Straus generated most of the firm's moves, though a few decisions were based on Ax's judgment calls. Before the beginning of trading each day, and just before the end of trading in the late afternoon, a computer program would send an electronic message to Greg Olsen, their broker at an outside firm, with an order and some simple conditions. One example: "If wheat opens above $4.25, sell 36 contracts."

Olsen would buy and sell futures contracts the old-fashioned way: calling floor brokers at various commodity and bond exchanges. Sometimes the results of this partially automated system were impressive; often, they left the team frustrated. One big problem: Neither Simons nor the team in the Huntington Beach office were unearthing new ways to make money or improve their existing strategies, some of which their rivals had caught on to.

Simons considered the possible influence of sunspots and lunar phases on trading, but few reliable patterns resulted. Straus had a cousin who worked at AccuWeather, the weather forecasting company, so he made a deal to review Brazilian weather history to see if it could predict coffee prices, another effort that proved a waste of time. Data on public sentiment and the holdings of fellow futures traders also yielded few dependable sequences.

Ax spent time searching for fresh algorithms, but he was also playing a lot of racquetball, learning how to windsurf, and generally attending to an emerging midlife crisis. With his broad shoulders, muscular build, and wavy brown hair, Ax had the look of a chilled-out surfer, but he was anything but relaxed, even in California.

Ax began staging intense weight-loss competitions and became determined to trounce his officemates. Once, just before the initial weigh-in, Ax packed on several pounds gorging on melon, calculating that he'd quickly shed the new weight, since melon is laden with water. Another time, Ax furiously biked to work in the sun, hoping to lose weight, arriving so drenched in perspiration that he placed his underwear in an office microwave to dry; minutes later, the microwave burst into flames as a staffer ran for a fire extinguisher.

Several times a year, Simons flew to California to discuss potential trading approaches, but his visits produced more misery than breakthroughs. Now that they lived in California, some of the staff embraced health-conscious lifestyles. Simons was still chain-smoking three packs of Merits a day.

"No one wanted to be with him as he smoked in the office," says an employee at the time, "so we'd go out for lunch and try to get him to work outside as long as we could."

When lunch was over, Simons would suggest they return to the office, but the team so dreaded being cooped up with his smoke that they'd manufacture excuses to stay away.

"You know what, Jim, it's nice out here," a colleague told Simons after one of their lunches.

"Yeah, let's just stay and work outside," another Axcom member chimed in.

Simons agreed, oblivious to the true reason staffers were dragging their feet about heading back inside.

Eventually, Ax decided they needed to trade in a more sophisticated way. They hadn't tried using more-complex math to build trading formulas, partly because the computing power didn't seem sufficient. Now Ax thought it might be time to give it a shot.

Ax had long believed financial markets shared characteristics with Markov chains, those sequences of events in which the next event is only dependent on the current state. In a Markov chain, each step along the way is impossible to predict with certainty, but future steps can be predicted with some degree of accuracy if one relies on a capable model. When Simons and Baum developed their hypothetical trading model at the IDA, a decade prior, they, too, had described the market as a Markov-like process.

To improve their predictive models, Ax concluded it was time to bring in someone with experience developing stochastic equations, the broader family of equations to which Markov chains belong. Stochastic equations model *dynamic* processes that evolve over time and can involve a high level of uncertainty. Straus had recently read academic literature suggesting that trading models based on stochastic equations could be valuable tools. He agreed that Axcom needed to recruit additional mathematical firepower.

A bit later, René Carmona, a professor at nearby University of California, Irvine, got a call from a friend.

"There's a group of mathematicians doing stochastic differential equations who are looking for help," the friend said. "How well do you know that stuff?"

A forty-one-year-old native of France who later became a professor at

Princeton University, Carmona didn't know much about markets or investing, but stochastic differential equations were his specialty. These equations can make predictions using data that appears random; weather-forecasting models, for example, use stochastic equations to generate reasonably accurate estimates. Members of Axcom's team viewed investing through a math prism and understood financial markets to be complicated and evolving, with behavior that is difficult to predict, at least over long stretches—just like a stochastic process.

It's easy to see why they saw similarities between stochastic processes and investing. For one thing, Simons, Ax, and Straus didn't believe the market was truly a "random walk," or entirely unpredictable, as some academics and others argued. Though it clearly had elements of randomness, much like the weather, mathematicians like Simons and Ax would argue that a probability distribution could capture futures prices as well as any other stochastic process. That's why Ax thought employing such a mathematical representation could be helpful to their trading models. Perhaps by hiring Carmona, they could develop a model that would produce a range of likely outcomes for their investments, helping to improve their performance.

Carmona was eager to lend a hand—he was consulting for a local aerospace company at the time and liked the idea of picking up extra cash working for Axcom a few days a week. The challenge of improving the firm's trading results also intrigued him.

"The goal was to invent a mathematical model and use it as a framework to infer some consequences and conclusions," Carmona says. "The name of the game is not to *always* be right, but to be right often enough."

Carmona wasn't certain the approach would work, or even that it was much better than the less-quantitative investment strategies embraced by most others at the time.

"If I had a better understanding of psychology or traders on the floor of the exchange, maybe we would do that," Carmona says.

Early on, Carmona used Straus's data to try to improve Axcom's existing mathematical models, but his work didn't lead to many useful advances. Although Carmona's models were more sophisticated than those Axcom previously employed, they didn't seem to work much better. Later, Renaissance would fully embrace stochastic differential equations for risk management and options pricing, but, for now, they couldn't find a way to profit from these techniques, frustrating Carmona.

=

By 1987, Carmona was plagued by guilt. His pay came from a portion of Ax's personal bonus, yet Carmona was contributing next to nothing to the company. He decided to spend that summer working full-time at Axcom, hoping more time devoted to the models would lead to greater success. Carmona made little headway, further aggravating him. Ax and Straus didn't seem to mind, but Carmona felt awful.

"I was taking money from them and nothing was really working," he says.

One day, Carmona had an idea. Axcom had been employing various approaches to using their pricing data to trade, including relying on *breakout* signals. They also used simple linear regressions, a basic forecasting tool relied upon by many investors that analyzes the relationships between two sets of data or variables under the assumption those relationships will remain linear. Plot crude-oil prices on the *x*-axis and the price of gasoline on the *y*-axis, place a straight *regression line* through the points on the graph, extend that line, and you usually can do a pretty good job predicting prices at the pump for a given level of oil price.

Market prices are sometimes all over the place, though. A model dependent on running simple linear regressions through data points generally does a poor job predicting future prices in complex, volatile markets marked by freak snowstorms, panic selling, and turbulent geopolitical events, all of which can play havoc with commodity and other prices. At the same time,

Straus had collected dozens of data sets with closing prices of commodities from various historical periods. Carmona decided they needed regressions that might capture nonlinear relationships in market data.

He suggested a different approach. Carmona's idea was to have computers search for relationships in the data Straus had amassed. Perhaps they could find instances in the remote past of similar trading environments, then they could examine how prices reacted. By identifying comparable trading situations and tracking what subsequently happened to prices, they could develop a sophisticated and accurate forecasting model capable of detecting hidden patterns.

For this approach to work, Axcom needed *a lot* of data, even more than Straus and the others had collected. To solve the problem, Straus began to *model* data rather than just collect it. In other words, to deal with gaps in the historical data, he used computer models to make educated guesses as to what was missing. They didn't have extensive cotton pricing data from the 1940s, for example, but maybe *creating* the data would suffice. Just as one can infer what a missing jigsaw puzzle piece might look like by observing pieces already in place, the Axcom team made deductions about the missing information and inputted it into its database.

Carmona suggested letting the model run the show by digesting all the various pieces of data and spitting out buy-and-sell decisions. In a sense, he was proposing an early machine-learning system. The model would generate predictions for various commodity prices based on complex patterns, clusters, and correlations that Carmona and the others didn't understand themselves and couldn't detect with the naked eye.

Elsewhere, statisticians were using similar approaches—called *kernel* methods—to analyze patterns in data sets. Back on Long Island, Henry Laufer was working on similar machine-learning tactics in his own research and was set to share it with Simons and others. Carmona wasn't aware of this work. He was simply proposing using sophisticated algorithms to give Ax and Straus the framework to identify patterns in current prices that seemed similar to those in the past.

"You should use this," Carmona urged his colleagues.

When they shared the approach with Simons, he blanched. The linear equations they had been relying on generated trade ideas and an allocation of capital that Simons could understand. By contrast, it wasn't clear why Carmona's program produced its results. His method wasn't based on a model Simons and his colleagues could reduce to a set of standard equations, and that bothered him. Carmona's results came from running a program for hours, letting computers dig through patterns and then generate trades. To Simons, it just didn't *feel* right.

"I can't get comfortable with what this is telling me," Simons told the team one day. "I don't understand why [the program is saying to buy and not sell]."

Later, Simons became more exasperated.

"It's a black box!" he said with frustration.

Carmona agreed with Simons's assessment, but he persisted.

"Just follow the data, Jim," he said. "It's not me, it's the data."

Ax, who was developing a friendship with Carmona, became a believer in the approach, defending it to Simons.

"It works, Jim," Ax said to Simons. "And it makes rational sense . . . humans can't forecast prices."

Let computers do it, Ax urged. It was exactly what Simons originally had hoped to do. Yet, Simons still wasn't convinced of the radical approach. In his head, Simons was all-in on the concept of relying on models. His heart wasn't quite there yet, it appeared.

"Jim liked to figure out what the model was doing," Straus recalls. "He wasn't super fond of the kernel."

Over time, Straus and his colleagues created and discovered additional historical pricing data, helping Ax develop new predictive models relying on

Carmona's suggestions. Some of the weekly stock-trading data they'd later find went back as far as the 1800s, reliable information almost no one else had access to. At the time, the team couldn't do much with the data, but the ability to search history to see how markets reacted to unusual events would later help Simons's team build models to profit from market collapses and other unexpected events, helping the firm trounce markets during those periods.

When the Axcom team started testing the approach, they quickly began to see improved results. The firm began incorporating *higher dimensional* kernel regression approaches, which seemed to work best for *trending* models, or those predicting how long certain investments would keep moving in a trend.

Simons was convinced they could do even better. Carmona's ideas helped, but they weren't enough. Simons called and visited, hoping to improve Axcom's performance, but he mostly served as the *pool operator*, finding wealthy investors for the fund and keeping them happy, while attending to the various technology investments that made up about half of the $100 million assets now held by the firm.

Seeking even more mathematical firepower, Simons arranged for a well-respected academic to consult with the firm. That move would lay the groundwork for a historic breakthrough.

CHAPTER FIVE

> I strongly believe, for all babies and a significant number of grownups, curiosity is a bigger motivator than money.
>
> Elwyn Berlekamp

For much of his life, the suggestion that Elwyn Berlekamp might help revolutionize the world of finance would have sounded like someone's idea of a bad joke.

Growing up in Fort Thomas, Kentucky, on the southern bank of the Ohio River, Berlekamp devoted himself to church life, math games, and staying as far away from athletics as possible. Berlekamp's father was a minister in the Evangelical and Reformed Church, now known as the United Church of Christ, one of the largest and most liberal Protestant denominations in the country. Waldo Berlekamp was a gentle and compassionate ecumenical leader who arranged joint services with different Protestant churches and Catholic congregations, gaining a loyal following for his captivating sermons and engaging personality. When the family moved, 450 congregants came to a going-away party. They presented Waldo with a new DeSoto automobile, a sign of their affection and appreciation.

As a boy in Fort Thomas, a 10,000-person Cincinnati suburb proud of its abolitionist history, Elwyn developed a strong anti-Southern bias and the conviction to pursue his interests, no matter how unpopular. While others in grade school were tackling, throwing, and wrestling on the playground, Berlekamp, serious and slim, was inside a classroom competing in a different way. Berlekamp and a few friends liked to grab pencils and paper to create boards of dots. They'd take turns adding lines, linking dots, and closing squares, playing dots and boxes, a century-old strategy game popular at the time in the Midwest. Some viewed the game as simple child's play, but dots and boxes has surprising complexity and mathematical underpinnings, something Berlekamp came to appreciate later in life.

"It was an early education in game theory," Berlekamp says.

By the time Berlekamp entered Fort Thomas Highlands High School, in 1954, he was a wiry five-foot-ten-inch young man with a good idea of what he enjoyed inside and outside the classroom. In school, it was mostly math and science. Detecting an intelligence that stood out from others, his classmates elected Berlekamp class president. He had curiosity about other subjects, too, though a passion for literature was mostly extinguished by a teacher who insisted on spending half the semester analyzing the novel *Gone With the Wind*.

Sports didn't register anywhere on Berlekamp's list of interests, yet he felt pressure to participate.

"Nerds were unpopular, and school spirit was greatly emphasized," he says, "so I went with the flow and decided to join a team."

Berlekamp did the math and realized his best odds were in swimming.

"The swim team didn't have as many people as they needed, so I at least knew I wouldn't be cut."

Each night, the boys swam in the nude in a pool at the local YMCA filled with so much chlorine that it took hours to wash it all off, a likely reason the team was so unpopular. It also could have been the coach, who screamed at the boys throughout the practice. Berlekamp, the slowest and weakest swimmer, usually bore the brunt of the abuse.

"Come on, Berlekamp!" the coach bellowed. "Get the lead out of your pants!"

The idiom struck the young man as especially inane since he was naked at the time.

Berlekamp was both slow and out of shape. In the few meets where he managed to finish second and capture a medal, only one other competitor had registered for his races.

There was a mix-up at a state competition in 1957, and Berlekamp was forced to swim in a relay race against a group of much stronger swimmers. Luckily, his teammates handed Berlekamp a huge lead that even he couldn't blow. His team took gold, Berlekamp's one shining athletic moment, teaching him a valuable life lesson.

"Try to get on a great team," he says.

(Decades later, the relay team's anchor, Jack Wadsworth Jr., then working as an investment banker, led the initial public offering for an upstart company called Apple Computer.)

When applying to college, Berlekamp had two requirements: world-class academics and a weak sports program. He had decided that sports was overemphasized in society, and he was no longer going to pretend to care.

The Massachusetts Institute of Technology became an obvious choice. "When I heard MIT didn't have a football team, I knew it was the school for me," he says.

Moving to Cambridge, Massachusetts, Berlekamp dabbled in physics, economics, computers, and chemistry. As a freshman, he was selected to participate in an advanced calculus class taught by John Nash, the game theorist and mathematician who later would be immortalized in Sylvia Nasar's book *A Beautiful Mind.* One day, in early 1959, Nash was lecturing at the chalkboard when a student raised his hand to ask a question. Nash turned to him and stared intensely. After several minutes of awkward silence, Nash pointed a finger at the student, berating him for having the temerity to interrupt his lecture.

"He looked mad," Berlekamp recalls.

It was one of the first public hints of Nash's developing mental illness. A few weeks later, Nash resigned from MIT and was admitted to a local hospital for treatment of schizophrenia.

Berlekamp had little trouble navigating most of his classes. One year, he received eight As in a single semester and a 4.9 grade point average (on a 5.0 scale), weighed down by a single C in humanities. After winning a prestigious mathematics competition in his senior year to become a Putnam Fellow, Berlekamp began a PhD program at MIT. He focused on electrical engineering, studying with Peter Elias and Claude Shannon. Elias and Shannon were pioneers of information theory, the groundbreaking approach to quantifying, encoding, and transmitting telephone signals, text, pictures, and other kinds of information that would provide the underpinnings for computers, the internet, and all digital media.

One afternoon, Shannon passed Berlekamp in the school's hallway. The thin, five-foot-ten-inch professor was a notorious introvert, so Berlekamp had to think fast to try to grab his attention.

"I'm going to the library to check out one of your papers," Berlekamp blurted.

Shannon grimaced.

"Don't do that—you learn more if you try to work it out yourself," Shannon insisted.

He pulled Berlekamp aside, as if to share a secret.

"It's not a good time to invest in the market," Shannon said.

Shannon hadn't told many others, but he had begun building mathematical formulas to try to beat the stock market. At that point, his formulas were flashing signs of caution. Berlekamp tried hard not to laugh; he had virtually nothing in the bank, so Shannon's warnings meant nothing to him. Besides, Berlekamp held a dismissive view of finance.

"My impression was that it was a game in which rich people play around with each other, and it doesn't do the world much good," Berlekamp says. "It *still* is my impression."

The fact that someone Berlekamp admired was trading stocks came as something of a shock to the young man.

"That was really news," he says.

During the summers of 1960 and 1962, Berlekamp spent time as a research assistant at the prestigious Bell Laboratories research center in Murray Hill, New Jersey. There, Berlekamp worked for John Larry Kelly Jr., a handsome physicist with a thick Texan drawl and a range of interests and habits, many of which Berlekamp didn't initially appreciate. Kelly, who had spent four years as a pilot in the US Navy during World War II, mounted a huge rifle on his living room wall, smoked six packs of cigarettes a day, and was passionate about professional and college football, even introducing a novel betting system to predict game scores.

When Kelly became frustrated with his work, he used language that his young assistant was unaccustomed to hearing.

"Mother*fucking* integrals," Kelly cried out one day, startling Berlekamp.

Despite the sometimes-crude exterior, Kelly was the most brilliant scientist Berlekamp had ever met.

"To my shock, all his math was right," Berlekamp says. "I used to think of Southerners as dumb—Kelly changed my view."

Several years earlier, Kelly had published a paper describing a system he'd developed to analyze information transmitted over networks, a strategy that also worked for making various kinds of wagers. To illustrate his ideas,

Kelly developed a method he had devised to profit at the racetrack. Kelly's system proposed ideal bets if one somehow obtained enough information to disregard the posted odds and could instead rely on a more accurate set of probabilities—the "true odds" for each race.

Kelly's formula had grown out of Shannon's earlier work on information theory. Spending evenings at Kelly's home playing bridge and discussing science, math, and more, Berlekamp came to see the similarities between betting on horses and investing in stocks, given that chance plays a huge role in both. They also discussed how accurate information and properly sized wagers can provide one with an advantage.

Kelly's work underscored the importance of sizing one's bets, a lesson Berlekamp would draw on later in life.

"I had zero interest in finance, but here was Kelly doing all this portfolio theory," Berlekamp says.

Slowly, Berlekamp began to appreciate the intellectual challenges—and financial rewards—stemming from finance.

=

In 1964, Berlekamp found himself in a deep rut. A young woman he had been dating broke up with him, and he was wallowing in self-pity. When the University of California, Berkeley, asked if he'd fly to the West Coast to interview for a teaching job, Berlekamp jumped at the opportunity.

"It was snowing and freezing, and I needed a break," he says.

Berlekamp eventually accepted the job and completed his doctoral thesis at Berkeley, becoming an assistant professor in electrical engineering. One day, while juggling in his apartment, Berlekamp heard a rapping from the floor below. The noise he was making was disturbing the two women who lived below him. Berlekamp's apology led to an introduction to a student from England named Jennifer Wilson, whom he married in 1966.[1]

Berlekamp became an expert in decoding digital information, helping NASA decipher images coming back from satellites exploring Mars, Venus, and other parts of the solar system. Employing principles he had developed studying puzzles and games, like dots and boxes, Berlekamp cofounded a branch of mathematics called *combinatorial game theory* and wrote a book called *Algebraic Coding Theory*, a classic in the field. He also constructed an algorithm, appropriately named Berlekamp's algorithm, for the factorization of polynomials over finite fields, which became a crucial tool in cryptography and other fields.

Berlekamp wasn't nearly as capable at navigating campus politics, as he soon found himself caught in a raging turf war between departments in Berkeley's College of Letters and Science.

"I got criticized for having lunch with the wrong people," he recalls.

Berlekamp came to realize that much of human interaction is colored by shades of gray that he sometimes found difficult to discern. Mathematics, by contrast, elicits objective, unbiased answers, results he found calming and reassuring.

"Truth in life is broad and nuanced; you can make all kinds of arguments, such as whether a president or person is fantastic or awful," he says. "That's why I love math problems—they have clear answers."

By the late 1960s, Berlekamp's work on coding theory had gained the attention of the Institute for Defense Analyses, the nonprofit corporation that also employed Simons. Berlekamp began doing classified work for the IDA in 1968, spending years on various projects in Berkeley and in Princeton. During that time, a colleague introduced him to Simons, but the two didn't hit it off, despite sharing a love of math and time spent at MIT, Berkeley, and the IDA.

"His mathematics were different from mine," Berlekamp says. "And Jim had an insatiable urge to do finance and make money. He likes action. . . .

He was always playing poker and fussing around with the markets. I've always viewed poker as a digression, of no more interest to me than baseball or football—which is to say hardly any."

Berlekamp returned to Berkeley as a professor of electrical engineering and mathematics around the same time Simons built his Stony Brook department. In 1973, when Berlekamp became part owner of a cryptography company, he thought Simons might want a stake. Simons couldn't afford the $4 million investment, but he served on the company's board of directors. Berlekamp noticed Simons was a good listener at board meetings and made sensible recommendations, though he often interrupted the gatherings to take smoking breaks.

In 1985, Eastman Kodak acquired a company Berlekamp had founded that worked with block codes for space and satellite communications. The resulting windfall of several million dollars brought new challenges to his marriage.

"My wife wanted a bigger house; I wanted to travel," he says.

Determined to protect his newfound wealth, Berlekamp bought top-rated municipal bonds, but a rumor in the spring of 1986 that Congress might remove the tax-free status of those investments crushed their value. Congress never acted, but the experience taught Berlekamp that investors sometimes act irrationally. He considered investing his money in stocks, but a former college roommate warned him that corporate executives "lie to shareholders," rendering most shares dicey prospects.

"You should look at commodities," the college friend said.

Berlekamp knew commodities trading entailed complicated futures contracts, so he called Simons, the one person he knew who had some understanding of the area, asking for advice.

Simons seemed thrilled to receive the phone call.

"I have just the opportunity for you," he said.

Simons invited Berlekamp to fly to Huntington Beach a couple times a month to learn to trade for himself and see if his expertise in statistical information theory might be useful to Axcom.

"You really should go down and talk to Jim Ax," Simons told Berlekamp. "He could benefit from someone like you."

Earlier in life, Berlekamp had been contemptuous of the trading business; now he was intrigued by the idea of a new challenge. He flew to the Huntington Beach office in 1988, with eager anticipation. Before Berlekamp could settle into his desk, however, Ax approached with a look of annoyance on his face.

"If Simons wants you to work for us, he'll have to pay for you," Ax told Berlekamp by way of introduction. "I know *I'm* not."

Berlekamp was taken aback. Ax wanted him out of the office *right away.* Berlekamp had flown all the way from Berkeley, and he didn't want to turn around and go home so quickly. He decided to stick around a bit, but to stay out of Ax's way, much as George Costanza returned to work after getting fired in a classic episode of the television show *Seinfeld.*

Soon, Berlekamp learned that Ax and Simons were in the midst of a bitter, long-running feud centered on who should pay Axcom's mounting expenses, a battle Simons had neglected to mention to Berlekamp.

For all the brainpower the team was employing, and the help they were receiving from Carmona and others, Axcom's model usually focused on two simple and commonplace trading strategies. Sometimes, it *chased prices,* or bought various commodities that were moving higher or lower on the assumption that the trend would continue. Other times, the model wagered that a price move was petering out and would reverse, a *reversion* strategy.

Ax had access to more extensive pricing information than his rivals, thanks to Straus's growing collection of clean, historic data. Since price movements often resembled those of the past, that data enabled the firm to more accurately determine when trends were likely to continue and when they were ebbing. Computing power had improved and become cheaper, allowing the team to produce more sophisticated trading models, including Carmona's kernel methods—the early, machine-learning strategy that had made Simons so uncomfortable. With those advantages, Axcom averaged annual gains of about 20 percent, topping most rivals.

Yet Simons kept asking why returns weren't better. Adding to the tension, their rivals were multiplying. A veteran analyst at Merrill Lynch named John Murphy had published a book called *Technical Analysis of the Financial Markets*, explaining, in simple terms, how to track and trade price trends.

Buying investments as they became more expensive and selling them as they fell in value was at odds with leading academic theory, which recommended buying when prices cheapened and taking money off the table when prices richened. Warren Buffett and other big-name investors embraced that *value* style of investing. Still, some aggressive traders, including hedge-fund manager Paul Tudor Jones, had adopted *trend following* strategies similar to those Simons's team relied on. Simons needed new approaches to stay a step ahead of the pack.

Berlekamp began sharing his suggestions. He told Ax that Axcom's trading models didn't seem to size trades properly. They should buy and sell larger amounts when their model suggested a better chance of making money, Berlekamp argued, precepts he had learned from Kelly. "We ought to be loading up here," Berlekamp said one day.

Ax didn't seem impressed.

"We'll get to that," Ax replied, halfheartedly.

Berlekamp discovered other problems with Axcom's operations. The firm traded gold, silver, copper, and other metals, as well as hogs and other meats, and grains and other commodities. But their buy-and-sell orders were still placed through emailed instructions to their broker, Greg Olsen, at the open and close of trading each day, and Axcom often held on to investments for weeks or even months at a time.

That's a dangerous approach, Berlekamp argued, because markets can be volatile. Infrequent trading precluded the firm from jumping on new opportunities as they arose and led to losses during extended downturns. Berlekamp urged Ax to look for smaller, short-term opportunities—get in and get out. Ax brushed him off again, this time citing the cost of doing rapid trading. Besides, Straus's intraday price data was riddled with inaccuracies—he hadn't fully "cleaned" it yet—so they couldn't create a reliable model for short-term trades.

Ax consented to giving Berlekamp a few research assignments, but each time Berlekamp visited, he realized Ax had mostly ignored his recommendations—calling them mere "tinkering"—or they had been poorly implemented. It hadn't been Ax's idea for Berlekamp to pop in to share his opinions, and he wasn't going to be bothered with the theories and suggestions of a professor just beginning to understand the trading game.

Ax didn't seem to need much help. The previous year, 1987, Axcom had scored double-digit returns, sidestepping a crash in October that sent the Dow Jones Industrial Average plummeting 22.6 percent in a day. Ignoring the trading model, Ax had presciently purchased Eurodollar futures, which soared as stocks plummeted, helping Axcom offset other losses.

Word was beginning to get out that Simons had math wizards attempting a new strategy, and a few individuals showed interest in investing in Axcom, including Edward Thorp, the pioneering quantitative trader. Thorp made an appointment to meet Simons in New York but canceled it after doing some due diligence. It wasn't Simons's strategies that most concerned him.

"I learned Simons was a chain-smoker and going to their offices was like walking into a giant ashtray," said Thorp, who had moved to Newport Beach, California.

Clients had other issues with Axcom. Some didn't have faith in Simons's venture-capital adventures and didn't want a fund with those kinds of investments. To keep those investors in the fold, Simons shut down Limroy in March 1988, selling off the venture investments to launch, together with Ax, an offshore hedge fund focused solely on trading. They named their hedge fund Medallion, in honor of the prestigious math awards each had received.

Within six months, Medallion was suffering. Some of the losses could be traced to a shift in Ax's focus.

=

After moving to California, Ax had rented a quiet home with a boat slip in nearby Huntington Harbor, five miles down Pacific Coast Highway from the office. Soon, Ax was searching for a more isolated spot, eventually renting a seaside estate in Malibu.

Ax never truly enjoyed the company of others, especially his co-workers. Now he became even more detached from those around him, managing nearly a dozen employees in the Huntington office remotely. He went into the office just once a week. Sometimes, Berlekamp flew in for a meeting only to discover Ax hadn't budged from Malibu. After Ax married an accountant named Frances, he became even less inclined to travel to meet with the team. Sometimes he called to make requests entirely unrelated to their algorithms and predictive models.

"Okay, so what kind of cereal do you want me to bring?" an employee was overheard saying to Ax on the phone one day.

As Ax became more disengaged, Axcom's results deteriorated.

"The research wasn't as aggressive," Carmona says. "When the boss isn't present, the dynamics aren't the same."

Berlekamp puts it this way: "Ax was a competent mathematician but an incompetent research manager."

Looking for still more seclusion, Ax purchased a spectacular home on a cliff in Pacific Palisades atop a hill overlooking the Santa Monica Mountains. Carmona drove there once a week to bring Ax food, books, and other necessities. They'd engage in grueling paddle tennis matches as Carmona patiently listened to Ax's latest conspiracy theories. Colleagues came to see Ax as something of a hermit, theorizing that he kept choosing homes near the coast so he wouldn't have to deal with anyone on at least one side of his house. After a staffer agreed to come install a salt lick in Ax's yard, so he could attract deer and other animals, Ax spent long stretches staring at the scene from a window.

Ax relied on his instincts for a portion of the portfolio, edging away from trading based on the sophisticated models he and Straus had developed, much as Baum had drifted toward traditional trading years earlier and Simons was initially uncomfortable with Carmona's "kernels." It seemed quantitative investing didn't come naturally, even to math professors. Ax figured out that West Coast copies of the *New York Times* were printed in the city of Torrance, about forty miles away, and arranged for the next day's paper to be delivered to his home just after midnight. Ax proceeded to make trades in overnight, international markets based on comments from government officials and others he had read in the paper, hoping to get a step on competitors. He also installed enormous television screens throughout his home to monitor the news and communicate with colleagues through a video connection he had established.

"He became infatuated with technology," Berlekamp says.

Ax drove a white Jaguar, played a lot of racquetball, and spent time on his mountain bike in the nearby hills, at one point falling headfirst, prompting emergency brain surgery. The firm's results remained strong during the first half of 1988, but then losses hit. Ax was confident a rebound was imminent, but Simons grew concerned. Soon, he and Ax were squabbling once again. Ax wanted to upgrade the firm's computers, so the trading system could run faster, but there was no way he was going to pay for the improvements. Simons also resisted writing any checks. As tensions grew, Ax complained that Simons wasn't meeting his share of the responsibilities.

"Let Simons pay for everything," Ax told a colleague when a bill arrived.

By the spring of 1989, Ax had developed a healthy respect for Berlekamp, a fellow world-class mathematician who shared his competitive streak. Ax still wasn't implementing Berlekamp's trading suggestions, mind you, but he realized he was in a bind, and there were few others around to listen to his complaints about Simons.

"I'm doing all the trading, and he's just dealing with the investors," Ax told Berlekamp, who tried to be sympathetic.

One day, when Berlekamp visited, Ax looked somber. Their fund had been losing money for months and was now down nearly 30 percent from the middle of the previous year, a staggering blow. Axcom's soybean-futures holdings had collapsed in value when an attempt by an Italian conglomerate to corner the market came undone, sending prices plummeting. Mounting competition from other trend followers was also having an effect.

Ax showed Berlekamp a letter he'd received from Simons's accountant, Mark Silber, ordering Axcom to halt all trading that was based on the firm's struggling, longer-term predictive signals until Ax and his team produced a plan to revamp and improve its trading operations. Simons would only allow Axcom to do short-term trading, a style that represented just 10 percent of its activity.

Ax was furious. He was in charge of trading; Simons's job was handling their investors.

"How can he stop me from trading?" Ax said, his voice rising. "He *can't* close me down!"

Ax remained certain the fund's performance would rebound. Trending strategies require an investor to live through tough periods, when trends ebb or they can't be identified, because new ones are often around the bend. Simons's trading halt had violated their partnership agreement. Ax was going to sue Simons.

"He's been bossing me around too long!" Ax bellowed.

Berlekamp tried to calm Ax down. A lawsuit wasn't the brightest idea, Berlekamp said. It would be costly, take forever, and ultimately might not succeed. Besides, Simons had a good argument: Technically, Axcom was trading for a general partnership controlled by Simons, so he had the legal right to determine the firm's future.

Ax didn't realize it, but Simons was dealing with his own pressures. Old friends and investors were calling, worried about the steep losses. Some couldn't take the pain and withdrew their cash. When Simons dealt with Straus and others at the office, he was curt. They all could see the losses mounting, and the mood within the firm soured.

Simons decided Ax's strategies were much too simple. He told Ax the only way he could prevent clients from bailing and keep the firm alive was to curtail their long-term trades, which were causing all their losses, while reassuring investors that they'd develop new and improved tactics.

Ax didn't want to hear it. He set out for Huntington Beach to elicit the support of his colleagues. He had little luck. Straus didn't want to pick sides, he told Ax, and was uncomfortable being in the middle of an escalating battle jeopardizing both his firm and his career. Ax became enraged.

"How can you be so disloyal!" he screamed at Straus.

Straus didn't know how to respond.

"I sat there feeling stupid," he says.

Simons had spent more than a decade backing various traders and attempting a new approach to investing. He hadn't made much headway. Baum had flamed out, Henry Laufer wasn't around much, and now his fund with Ax and Straus was down to $20 million amid mounting losses. Simons was spending more time on his various side businesses than he was on trading; his heart didn't seem to be in the investment business. Straus and his colleagues became convinced Simons might shutter the firm.

"It wasn't clear Jim had any faith," he says. "And it wasn't clear if we would survive or fold."

Returning home at night, Straus and his wife spent hours preparing for the worst, calculating their spending habits and tallying their accumulated wealth as their two young children played nearby in their den. They discussed where they might move if Simons closed Axcom and gave up trading.

Back in the office, the bickering between Simons and Ax continued. Straus listened as Ax screamed over the phone at Simons and Silber. It all became too much.

"I'm going on vacation," Straus finally told Ax. "You guys work this out."

=

By the summer of 1989, Ax felt boxed in. He was using second-tier lawyers who worked on contingency fees while Simons employed top-flight New York attorneys. It was becoming obvious that Simons would outlast him in a legal fight.

One day, Berlekamp presented Ax with an idea.

"Why don't I buy your stake in the firm?"

Privately, Berlekamp was beginning to think he might be able to turn Axcom around. He was only spending a day or two each month at the firm, and he wondered how it might fare if he focused his full attention on improving the trading system. No one had figured out how to build a computer system to score huge gains; maybe Berlekamp could be the one to help do it.

"I was hooked on the intellectual exercise," Berlekamp says.

Ax decided he didn't have a better option, so he agreed to sell most of his Axcom shares to Berlekamp. After the deal was completed, Berlekamp owned 40 percent of the firm, leaving Straus and Simons with 25 percent each, while Ax retained 10 percent.

Ax holed up in his home for months, speaking to his wife and few others. Eventually, he began a slow and remarkable transformation. Ax and his wife moved to San Diego, where he finally learned to relax just a bit, writing poetry and enrolling in screenwriting classes. He even completed a science-fiction thriller called *Bots*.

Ax went online and read an academic paper about quantum mechanics written by Simon Kochen and decided to reconnect with his former colleague, who still taught at Princeton. Soon, they were collaborating on academic papers about mathematical aspects of quantum mechanics.[2]

There remained an emptiness in Ax's life. He tracked down the whereabouts of his younger son, Brian. One day, he picked up the phone to call Brian in his dormitory room at Brown University in Providence, Rhode Island. They hadn't spoken in more than fifteen years.

"Hi," he began, tentatively. "This is James Ax."

They spoke for hours that evening, the first of a series of lengthy and intense conversations between Ax and his two sons. Ax shared his regrets about how he had abandoned his boys and acknowledged the damage his anger had caused. The boys forgave Ax, eager to have their father back in their lives. Over time, Ax and his sons forged close relationships. In 2003, after Ax became a grandfather, he and Barbara, his ex-wife, reunited and established their own unlikely friendship.

Three years later, at the age of sixty-nine, Ax died of colon cancer. On his tombstone, his sons engraved a formula representing the Ax-Kochen theorem.

were shoved into a train [illegible] [illegible]
[illegible]
[illegible]

[illegible]
[illegible] and [illegible]
[illegible]
[illegible]

[illegible]
[illegible]
[illegible]
[illegible] in more than fifteen [illegible]

[illegible]

[illegible]
[illegible]
[illegible]
[illegible]
[illegible]
[illegible]
[illegible]

[illegible]
[illegible]
[illegible]

CHAPTER SIX

Scientists are human, often all too human.
When desire and data are in collision,
evidence sometimes loses out to emotion.

Brian Keating, cosmologist, *Losing the Nobel Prize*

Elwyn Berlekamp took the reins of the Medallion fund during the summer of 1989, just as the investment business was heating up. A decade earlier, financial companies claimed about 10 percent of all US profits. Now they were on their way to more than doubling that figure in an era that became known for greed and self-indulgence, as captured by novels like *Bright Lights, Big City* and songs like Madonna's "Material Girl."

The unquenchable thirst of traders, bankers, and investors for market-moving financial news unavailable to the general public—known as an *information advantage*—helped fuel Wall Street's gains. Tips about imminent corporate-takeover offers, earnings, and new products were coin of the realm in the twilight of the Reagan era. Junk-bond king Michael Milken pocketed over one billion dollars in compensation between 1983 and 1987 before securities violations related to an insider trading investigation landed him in jail. Others joined him, including investment banker Martin Siegel and trader Ivan Boesky, who exchanged both takeover information and briefcases packed with hundreds of thousands of dollars in neat stacks of $100 bills.[1] By 1989, Gordon Gekko, the protagonist in the movie *Wall Street*, had come to define the business's aggressive, cocksure professionals, who regularly pushed for an unfair edge.

Berlekamp was an anomaly in this testosterone-drenched period, an academic with little use for juicy rumors or hot tips. He barely knew how various companies earned their profits and had zero interest in learning.

Approaching his forty-ninth birthday, Berlekamp also bore little physical resemblance to the masters of the universe reaping Wall Street's mounting spoils. Berlekamp had come to value physical fitness, embracing a series of extreme and unsafe diets and grueling bicycle rides. At one point, he lost so much weight that he looked emaciated, worrying colleagues. Balding and bespectacled, with a neat, salt-and-pepper beard, Berlekamp rarely wore ties and stored as many as five multicolored BIC pens in his front pocket.

Even among the computer nerds gaining some prominence in corners of the business world, Berlekamp stood out. When he traveled to a conference in Carmel, California, in 1989, to study how machines could build better predictive models, Berlekamp seemed the most absentminded professor of them all.

"Elwyn was a little disheveled, his shirttail out and wrinkled, and his eyes darting around when he was thinking hard," says Langdon Wheeler, who met Berlekamp at the conference and later became his friend. "But he was so smart, I saw past the quirks and wanted to learn from him."

Around the office at Axcom, Berlekamp favored lengthy tangents and digressions, causing rounds of hand-wringing among employees. Berlekamp once said he liked to do 80 percent of the talking in a conversation; those who knew him viewed the estimate as a bit conservative. But Berlekamp's reputation as a mathematician earned him respect, and his confidence that Medallion could improve its performance bred optimism.

Berlekamp's first plan of action was to move the firm closer to his home in Berkeley, a decision Straus and his wife came to support. In September 1989, Straus leased offices on the ninth floor of the historic, twelve-story Wells Fargo Building, the city's first high-rise, a short walk from the campus of UC Berkeley. The office's existing hardwire lines couldn't deliver accurate prices at a fast-enough speed, so a staffer arranged to use a satellite receiver atop the Tribune Tower in nearby Oakland to transmit up-to-the-minute futures prices. A month later, the San Francisco area was rocked by the Loma Prieta earthquake, which killed sixty-three people. Axcom's new office didn't suffer serious damage, but shelves and desks collapsed, books and equipment were damaged, and the satellite receiver toppled, an inauspicious start for a trading operation desperate to revive itself.

The team forged ahead, with Berlekamp focused on implementing some of the most promising recommendations Ax had ignored. Simons, exhausted from months of bickering with Ax, supported the idea.

"Let's bank some sure things," Berlekamp told Simons.

Ax had resisted shifting to a more frequent, short-term trading strategy, partly because he worried brokerage commissions and other costs resulting from a fast-paced, higher-frequency approach would offset possible profits. Ax had also been concerned that rapid trading would push prices enough to cut into any gains, a cost called *slippage*, which Medallion couldn't measure with any accuracy.

These were legitimate concerns that had led to something of an unwritten rule on Wall Street: Don't trade too much. Beyond the costs, short-term moves generally yield tiny gains, exciting few investors. What's the point of working so hard and trading so frequently if the upside is so limited?

"Like with baseball, motherhood, and apple pie, you just didn't question that view," Berlekamp says.

Berlekamp hadn't worked on Wall Street and was inherently skeptical of long-held dogmas developed by those he suspected weren't especially sophisticated in their analysis. He advocated for more short-term trades. Too many of the firm's long-term moves had been duds, while Medallion's short-term trades had proved its biggest winners, thanks to the work of Ax, Carmona, and others. It made sense to try to build on that success. Berlekamp also enjoyed some good timing—by then, most of Straus's intraday data had been cleaned up, making it easier to develop fresh ideas for shorter-term trades.

Their goal remained the same: scrutinize historic price information to discover sequences that might repeat, under the assumption that investors will exhibit similar behavior in the future. Simons's team viewed the approach as sharing some similarities with *technical trading*. The Wall Street establishment generally viewed this type of trading as something of a dark art, but Berlekamp and his colleagues were convinced it could work, if done in a sophisticated and scientific manner—but only if their trading focused on short-term shifts rather than longer-term trends.

Berlekamp also argued that buying and selling infrequently magnifies the consequences of each move. Mess up a couple times, and your portfolio could be doomed. Make a lot of trades, however, and each individual move is less important, reducing a portfolio's overall risk.

Berlekamp and his colleagues hoped Medallion could resemble a gambling casino. Just as casinos handle so many daily bets that they only need to profit from a bit more than half of those wagers, the Axcom team wanted their fund to trade so frequently that it could score big profits by making money on a bare majority of its trades. With a slight statistical edge, the law of large numbers would be on their side, just as it is for casinos.

"If you trade a lot, you only need to be right 51 percent of the time," Berlekamp argued to a colleague. "We need a smaller edge on each trade."

As they scrutinized their data, looking for short-term trading strategies to add to Medallion's trading model, the team began identifying certain intriguing oddities in the market. Prices for some investments often fell just before key economic reports and rose right after, but prices didn't *always* fall before the reports came out and didn't *always* rise in the moments after. For whatever reason, the pattern didn't hold for the US Department of Labor's employment statistics and some other data releases. But there was enough data to indicate when the phenomena were most likely to take place, so the model recommended purchases just before the economic releases and sales almost immediately after them.

Searching for more, Berlekamp got on the phone with Henry Laufer, who had agreed to spend more time helping Simons turn Medallion around after Ax quit. Laufer was in the basement of Simons's office on Long Island with a couple of research assistants from the Stony Brook area trying to revamp Medallion's trading model, just as Berlekamp and Straus were doing in Berkeley.

Sifting through Straus's data, Laufer discovered certain recurring trading sequences based on the day of the week. Monday's price action often followed Friday's, for example, while Tuesday saw *reversions* to earlier trends. Laufer also uncovered how the previous day's trading often can predict the next day's activity, something he termed the *twenty-four-hour effect*. The Medallion model began to buy late in the day on a Friday if a clear up-trend existed, for instance, and then sell early Monday, taking advantage of what they called the *weekend effect*.

Simons and his researchers didn't believe in spending much time proposing and testing their own intuitive trade ideas. They let the data point them to the anomalies signaling opportunity. They also didn't think it made sense to worry about why these phenomena existed. All that mattered was that they happened frequently enough to include in their updated trading system, and that they could be tested to ensure they weren't statistical flukes.

They did have theories. Berlekamp and others developed a thesis that *locals*, or floor traders who buy or sell commodities and bonds to keep the market functioning, liked to go home at the end of a trading week holding few or no futures contracts, just in case bad news arose over the weekend that might saddle them with losses. Similarly, brokers on the floors of commodity exchanges seemed to trim futures positions ahead of the economic reports to avoid the possibility that unexpected news might cripple their holdings.

These traders got right back into their positions after the weekend, or subsequent to the news releases, helping prices rebound. Medallion's system would buy when these brokers sold, and sell the investments back to them as they became more comfortable with the risk.

"We're in the insurance business," Berlekamp told Straus.

Oddities in currency markets represented additional attractive trades. Opportunity seemed especially rich in the trading of deutsche marks. When the currency rose one day, it had a surprising likelihood of climbing the next day, as well. And when it fell, it often dropped the next day, too. It didn't seem to matter if the team looked at the month-to-month, week-to-week, day-to-day, or even hour-to-hour correlations; deutsche marks showed an unusual propensity to trend from one period to the next, trends that lasted longer than one might have expected.

When you flip a coin, you have a 25 percent chance of getting heads twice in a row, but there is no correlation from one flip to the next. By contrast, Straus, Laufer, and Berlekamp determined the correlation of price moves in deutsche marks between any two consecutive time periods was as much as 20 percent, meaning that the sequence repeated more than half of the time. By comparison, the team found a correlation between consecutive periods of 10 percent or so for other currencies, 7 percent for gold, 4 percent for hogs and other commodities, and just 1 percent for stocks.

"The time scale doesn't seem to matter," Berlekamp said to a colleague one day, with surprise. "We get the same statistical anomaly."

Correlations from one period to the next shouldn't happen with any frequency, at least according to most economists at the time who had embraced the *efficient market* hypothesis. Under this view, it's impossible to beat the market by taking advantage of price irregularities—they shouldn't exist. Once irregularities are discovered, investors should step in to remove them, the academics argued.

The sequences witnessed in the trading of deutsche marks—and even stronger correlations found in the yen—were so unexpected that the team felt the need to understand why they might be happening. Straus found academic papers arguing that global central banks have a distaste for abrupt currency moves, which can disrupt economies, so they step in to slow sharp moves in either direction, thereby extending those trends over longer periods of time. To Berlekamp, the slow pace at which big companies like Eastman Kodak made business decisions suggested that the economic forces behind currency shifts likely played out over many months.

"People persist in their habits longer than they should," he says.

The currency moves were part of Medallion's growing mix of *tradeable effects*, in their developing parlance. Berlekamp, Laufer, and Straus spent months poring over their data, working long hours glued to their computers, examining how prices reacted to tens of thousands of market events. Simons checked in daily, in person or on the phone, sharing his own ideas to improve the trading system while encouraging the team to focus on uncovering what he called "subtle anomalies" others had overlooked.

Beyond the repeating sequences that seemed to make sense, the system Berlekamp, Straus, and Laufer developed spotted barely perceptible patterns in various markets that had no apparent explanation. These trends and oddities sometimes happened so quickly that they were unnoticeable to most investors. They were so faint, the team took to calling them *ghosts*, yet they kept reappearing with enough frequency to be worthy additions to their mix of trade ideas. Simons had come around to the view that the *whys* didn't matter, just that the trades worked.

As the researchers worked to identify historic market behavior, they wielded a big advantage: They had more accurate pricing information than their rivals. For years, Straus had collected the *tick* data featuring intraday volume and pricing information for various futures, even as most investors ignored such granular information. Until 1989, Axcom generally relied on opening and closing data, like most other investors; to that point, much of the intraday data Straus had collected was pretty much useless. But the more modern and powerful MIPS (million instructions per second) computers in their new offices gave the firm the ability to quickly parse all the pricing data in Straus's collection, generating thousands of statistically significant observations within the trading data to help reveal previously undetected pricing patterns.

"We realized we had been saving intraday data," Straus says. "It wasn't super clean, and it wasn't all the tick data," but it was more reliable and plentiful than what others were using.

=

By late 1989, after about six months of work, Berlekamp and his colleagues were reasonably sure their rebuilt trading system—focused on commodity, currency, and bond markets—could prosper. Some of their anomalies and trends lasted days, others just hours or even minutes, but Berlekamp and Laufer were confident their revamped system could take advantage of them. The team found it difficult to pinpoint reliable trends for stocks, but that didn't seem to matter; they'd found enough trading oddities in other markets.

Some of the trading signals they identified weren't especially novel or sophisticated. But many traders had ignored them. Either the phenomena took place barely more than 50 percent of the time, or they didn't seem to yield enough in profit to offset the trading costs. Investors moved on, searching for juicier opportunities, like fishermen ignoring the guppies in their nets, hoping for bigger catch. By trading frequently, the Medallion team figured it would be worthwhile to hold on to all the guppies they were collecting.

The firm implemented its new approach in late 1989 with the $27 million Simons still managed. The results were almost immediate, startling nearly everyone in the office. They did more trading than ever, cutting Medallion's average holding time to just a day and a half from a week and a half, scoring profits almost every day.

Just as suddenly, problems arose. Whenever Medallion traded Canadian dollars, the fund seemed to lose money. Almost every trade was a dud. It didn't seem to make sense—the model said Medallion should be racking up money, but they were losing, over and over, every day.

One afternoon, Berlekamp shared his frustrations with Simons, who called a trader on the floor of the Chicago Board of Trade to get his take on their problems.

"Don't you know, Jim?" the trader told him, with a chuckle. "Those guys are crooks."

Only three traders on the exchange focused on Canadian dollar futures, and they worked hand-in-hand to take advantage of customers naive enough to transact with them. When Simons's team placed a buy order, the brokers shared the information, and the traders immediately purchased Canadian dollar contracts for themselves, pushing the price up just a tad, before selling to Simons and pocketing the difference as profit. They'd do the opposite if Medallion was selling; the small differences in price were enough to turn the Canadian dollar trades into losers. It was one of Wall Street's oldest tricks, but Berlekamp and his fellow academics were oblivious to the practice. Simons immediately eliminated Canadian dollar contracts from Medallion's trading system.

A few months later, in early 1990, Simons called Berlekamp with even more unsettling news.

"There's a rumor Stotler is in trouble," Simons said, anxiety in his voice.

Berlekamp was stunned. Every single one of Medallion's positions was held in accounts at the Stotler Group, a commodity-trading firm run by Karsten Mahlmann, the top elected official at the Chicago Board of Trade. Berlekamp and others had viewed Stotler as the safest and most reliable brokerage firm in Chicago. If Stotler went under, their account would be frozen. In the weeks it would likely take to sort out, tens of millions of dollars of futures contracts would be in limbo, likely leading to devastating losses. Straus's sources at the exchange confided that Stotler was struggling with heavy debt, adding to the nervousness.

These were just rumors, though. Shifting all of their trades and accounts to other brokers would be cumbersome, time-consuming, and cost Medallion money just as it was turning things around. Stotler had long been among the most powerful and prestigious firms in the business, suggesting it could survive any setback. Berlekamp told Simons he was unsure what to do.

Simons couldn't understand his indecision.

"Elwyn, when you smell smoke, you get the *hell* out!" Simons told him.

Straus closed the brokerage account and shifted their trades elsewhere. Months later, Mahlmann resigned from Stotler and the Chicago Board of Trade; two days later, Stotler filed for bankruptcy. Eventually, regulators charged the firm with fraud.

Simons and his firm had narrowly escaped a likely death blow.

=

For much of 1990, Simons's team could do little wrong, as if they had discovered a magic formula after a decade of fumbling around in the lab. Rather than transact only at the open and close of trading each day, Berlekamp, Laufer, and Straus traded at noon, as well. Their system became mostly short-term moves, with long-term trades representing about 10 percent of activity.

One day, Axcom made more than $1 million, a first for the firm. Simons rewarded the team with champagne, much as the IDA's staff had passed around flutes of bubbly after discovering solutions to thorny problems. The one-day gains became so frequent that the drinking got a bit out of hand; Simons had to send word that champagne should be handed out only if returns rose 3 percent in a day, a shift that did little to dampen the team's giddiness.

For all the gains, few outside the office shared the same regard for the group's approach. When Berlekamp explained his firm's methods to business students on Berkeley's campus, some mocked him.

"We were viewed as flakes with ridiculous ideas," Berlekamp says.

Fellow professors were polite enough not to share their criticism and skepticism, at least within earshot. But Berlekamp knew what they were thinking.

"Colleagues avoided or evaded commenting," he says.

Simons didn't care about the doubters; the gains reinforced his conviction that an automated trading system could beat the market.

"There's a real opportunity here," he told Berlekamp, his enthusiasm growing.

Medallion scored a gain of 55.9 percent in 1990, a dramatic improvement on its 4 percent loss the previous year. The profits were especially impressive because they were over and above the hefty fees charged by the fund, which amounted to 5 percent* of all assets managed and 20 percent of all gains generated by the fund.

Just a year or so earlier, Simons had been as involved in his side businesses as he was in the hedge fund. Now he was convinced the team was

*The 5 percent management fee had been determined in 1988, when Straus told Simons he needed about $800,000 to run the firm's computer system and pay for other operational costs—a figure that amounted to 5 percent of the $16 million managed at the time. The fee seemed about right to Simons, who kept it as the firm grew.

finally on to something special and wanted to be a bigger part of it. Simons dialed Berlekamp, over and over, almost every day.

In early August of that year, after Iraq invaded Kuwait, sending gold and oil prices soaring, Simons called Berlekamp, encouraging him to add gold and oil futures contracts to the system's mix.

"Elwyn, have you looked at gold?"

It turned out that Simons still did some trading on his own, charting the technical patterns of various commodities. He wanted to share the bullish insights he had developed about various gold investments.

Berlekamp listened to the advice politely, as usual, before telling Simons it would be best to let the model run the show and avoid adjusting algorithms they had worked so hard to perfect.

"Okay, go back to what you were doing," Simons said.

A bit later, as gold shot even higher, he phoned again: "It went up more, Elwyn!"

Berlekamp was baffled. It was Simons who had pushed to develop a computerized trading system free of human involvement, and it was Simons who wanted to rely on the scientific method, testing overlooked anomalies rather than using crude charts or gut instinct. Berlekamp, Laufer, and the rest of the team had worked diligently to remove humans from the trading loop as much as possible. Now Simons was saying he had a good feeling about gold prices and wanted to tweak the system?

"Jim believed the fund should be managed systematically, but he was fussing around when he had time, five to ten hours a week, trading gold or copper, thinking he was learning something," Berlekamp says.

Much like Baum and Ax before him, Simons couldn't help reacting to the news.

Berlekamp pushed back.

"Like I said, Jim, we're not going to adjust our positions," a peeved Berlekamp told Simons one day.

Hanging up, Berlekamp turned to a colleague: "*The system* will determine what we trade."

Simons never ordered any major trades, but he did get Berlekamp to buy some oil call options to serve as "insurance" in case crude prices kept rising as the Gulf War began, and he scaled the fund's overall positions back by a third as Middle East hostilities continued to flare.

Simons felt a need to explain the adjustments to his clients.

"We must still rely on human judgment and manual intervention to cope with a drastic, sudden change," he explained in a letter that month.

Simons kept on calling Berlekamp, who grew increasingly exasperated.

"One day he called me four times," he says. "It was annoying."

Simons phoned again, this time to tell Berlekamp he wanted the research team moved to Long Island. Simons had lured Laufer back as a full-time member of the team, and Simons wanted to play a larger role running the trading effort. On Long Island, he argued, they could all be together, an idea that Berlekamp and Straus resisted.

As the year wore on, Simons began telling Berlekamp how much better the fund, which now managed nearly $40 million, should be doing. Simons was enthusiastic about the model's most recent tweaks and convinced Medallion was on the verge of remarkable success.

"Let's work on the system," Simons said one day. "Next year we should get it up to 80 percent."

Berlekamp could not believe what he was hearing.

"We're lucky in some respects, Jim," Berlekamp told Simons, hoping to rein in his exuberance.

Hanging up, Berlekamp shook his head in frustration. Medallion's gains already were staggering. He doubted the hedge fund could keep its hot streak going at the same pace, let alone improve on its performance.

Simons made still more requests. He wanted to expand the team, purchase additional satellite dishes for the roof, and spend on other infrastructure that would allow them to upgrade Medallion's computerized trading system. He asked Berlekamp to chip in to pay for the new expenses.

The pressures wore on Berlekamp. He had remained a part-time professor at Berkeley and found himself enjoying his classes more than ever, likely because they didn't involve someone looking over his shoulder at all hours.

"Jim was calling a lot, and I was having more fun teaching," Berlekamp explains.

It became more than he could bear. Finally, Berlekamp phoned Simons with an offer.

"Jim, if you think we're going to be up 80 percent, and I think we can do 30 percent, you must think the company is worth a lot more than I do," Berlekamp said. "So why don't you buy me out?"

Which is exactly what Simons did. In December 1990, Axcom was disbanded; Simons purchased Berlekamp's ownership interest for cash, while Straus and Ax traded their Axcom stakes for shares in Renaissance, which began to manage the Medallion fund. Berlekamp returned to Berkeley to teach and do full-time math research, selling his Axcom shares at a price that amounted to six times what he had paid just sixteen months earlier, a deal he thought was an absolute steal.

"It never occurred to me that we'd go through the roof," Berlekamp says.

Later, Berlekamp started an investment firm, Berkeley Quantitative, which did its own trading of futures contracts and, at one point, managed over $200 million. It closed in 2012 after recording middling returns.

"I was always motivated more by curiosity," Berlekamp says. "Jim was focused on money."

In the spring of 2019, Berlekamp died from complications of pulmonary fibrosis at the age of seventy-eight.

═

Berlekamp, Ax, and Baum had all left the firm, but Simons wasn't especially concerned. He was sure he had developed a surefire method to invest in a *systematic* way, using computers and algorithms to trade commodities, bonds, and currencies in a manner that can be seen as a more scientific and sophisticated version of technical trading, one that entailed searching for overlooked patterns in the market.

Simons was a mathematician with a limited understanding of the history of investing, however. He didn't realize his approach wasn't as original as he believed. Simons also wasn't aware of how many traders had crashed and burned using similar methods. Some traders employing similar tactics even had substantial head starts on him.

To truly conquer financial markets, Simons would have to overcome a series of imposing obstacles that he didn't even realize were in his way.

CHAPTER SEVEN

What had Jim Simons so excited in late 1990 was a straightforward insight: Historic patterns can form the basis of computer models capable of identifying overlooked and ongoing market trends, allowing one to divine the future from the past. Simons had long held this view, but his recent big gains convinced him the approach was a winner.

Simons hadn't spent much time delving into financial history, though. Had he done so, Simons might have realized that his approach wasn't especially novel. For centuries, speculators had embraced various forms of pattern recognition, relying on methods that bore similarity to some of the things Renaissance was doing. The fact that many of these colorful characters had failed miserably, or were outright charlatans, didn't augur well for Simons.

The roots of Simons's investing style reached as far back as Babylonian times, when early traders recorded the prices of barley, dates, and other crops on clay tablets, hoping to forecast future moves. In the middle of the sixteenth century, a trader in Nuremberg, Germany, named Christopher Kurz won acclaim for his supposed ability to forecast twenty-day prices of cinnamon, pepper, and other spices. Like much of society at the time, Kurz relied on astrological signs, but he also tried to back-test his signals, deducing certain credible principles along the way, such as the fact that prices often move in long-persisting trends.

An eighteenth-century Japanese rice merchant and speculator named Munehisa Homma, known as the "god of the markets," invented a charting method to visualize the open, high, low, and closing price levels for the country's rice exchanges over a period of time. Homma's charts, including the classic *candlestick* pattern, resulted in an early and reasonably sophisticated reversion-to-the-mean trading strategy. Homma argued that markets are governed by emotions, and that "speculators should learn to take losses quickly and let their profits run"—tactics embraced by future traders.[1]

In the 1830s, British economists sold sophisticated price charts to investors. Later that century, an American journalist named Charles Dow, who devised the Dow Jones Industrial Average and helped launch the *Wall Street Journal*, applied a level of mathematical rigor to various market hypotheses, birthing modern technical analysis, which relies on the charting of distinct price trends, trading volume, and other factors.

In the early twentieth century, a financial prognosticator named William D. Gann gained a rabid following despite the dubious nature of his record. Legend has it that Gann was born to a poor Baptist family on a cotton ranch in Texas. He quit grammar school to help his family members in the fields, gaining his only financial education at a local cotton warehouse. Gann ended up in New York City, where he opened a brokerage firm in 1908, developing a reputation for skillfully reading price charts, pinpointing and anticipating cycles and retracements.

A line from Ecclesiastes guided Gann's moves: "That which has been is that which shall be . . . there is nothing new under the sun." To Gann, the phrase suggested that historic reference points are the key to unlocking trading profits. Gann's renown grew, based partly on a claim that, in a single month, he turned $130 into $12,000. Loyalists credited Gann with predicting everything from the Great Depression to the attack on Pearl Harbor.

Gann concluded that a universal, natural order governed all facets of life—something he called the *Law of Vibration*—and that geometric sequences and angles could be used to predict market action. To this day, *Gann analysis* remains a reasonably popular branch of technical trading.

Gann's investing record was never substantiated, however, and his fans tended to overlook some colossal bloopers. In 1936, for example, Gann said, "I am confident the Dow Jones Industrial Average will never sell at 386 again," meaning he was sure the Dow wouldn't again reach that level, a prediction that didn't quite stand the test of time. The fact that Gann wrote eight books and penned a daily investment newsletter, yet managed to share few details of his trading approach and, by some accounts, died with a net worth of only $100,000 raises other questions.[2]

"He was a financial astrologer of sorts," concludes Andrew Lo, a professor at the MIT Sloan School of Management.

Decades later, Gerald Tsai Jr. used technical analysis, among other tactics, to become the most influential investor of the raging late 1960s. Tsai gained prominence at Fidelity Investments, where he rode momentum stocks to fortune, becoming the first growth-fund manager. Later, Tsai launched his own firm, the Manhattan Fund, a much-hyped darling of the era. Tsai built a war room featuring sliding and rotating charts tracking hundreds of averages, ratios, and oscillators. He kept the room a frigid fifty-five degrees, trying to ensure that the three full-time staff members tasked with updating the figures remained fully alert and attentive.

The Manhattan Fund was crushed in the 1969–70 bear market, its performance and methods ridiculed. By then, Tsai had sold out to an insurance company and was busy helping turn financial-services company Primerica into a key building block for the banking power that became Citigroup.[3]

Over time, technical traders became targets of derision, their strategies viewed as simplistic and lazy at best, voodoo science at worst. Despite the ridicule, many investors continue to chart financial markets, tracing *head and shoulders* formations and other common configurations and patterns. Some top, modern traders, including Stanley Druckenmiller, consult charts to confirm existing investment theses. Professor Lo and others argue that technical analysts were the "forerunners" of quantitative investing. However, their methods were never subjected to independent and thorough testing, and most of their rules arose from a mysterious combination of human pattern recognition and reasonable-sounding rules of thumb, raising questions about their efficacy.[4]

Like the technical traders before him, Simons practiced a form of pattern analysis and searched for telltale sequences and correlations in market data. He hoped to have a bit more luck than investors before him by doing his trading in a more scientific manner, however. Simons agreed with Berlekamp that technical indicators were better at guiding short-term trades than long-term investments. But Simons hoped rigorous testing and sophisticated predictive models, based on statistical analysis rather than eyeballing price charts, might help him escape the fate of the chart adherents who had crashed and burned.

But Simons didn't realize that others were busy crafting similar strategies, some using their own high-powered computers and mathematical algorithms. Several of these traders already had made enormous progress, suggesting that Simons was playing catch-up.

Indeed, as soon as the computer age dawned, there were investors, up bright and early, using computers to solve markets. As early as 1965, *Barron's* magazine spoke of the "immeasurable" rewards computers could render investors, and how the machines were capable of relieving an analyst of "dreary labor, freeing him for more creative activity." Around the same time, the *Wall Street Journal* gushed about how computers could rank and filter large numbers of stocks almost instantaneously. In *The Money Game,* the classic finance book of the period, author George Goodman, employing the pseudonym Adam Smith, mocked the "computer people" beginning to invade Wall Street.

While a segment of the investment world used machines to guide their investing and other tasks, the technology wasn't yet available to do even mildly challenging statistical analysis, nor was there much need for models with any level of sophistication, since finance wasn't especially mathematical at the time. Still, a Chicago-based trader named Richard Dennis managed to build a trading system governed by specific, preset rules aimed at removing emotions and irrationality from his trades, not unlike the approach Simons was so excited about. As Renaissance staffers struggled to improve their model throughout the 1980s, they kept hearing about Dennis's successes. At the age of twenty-six, he already was a distinctive presence on the floor of the Chicago Board of Trade, enough so to warrant a sobriquet: the "Prince of the Pit." Dennis had thick, gold-framed glasses, a stomach that protruded over his belt, and thinning, frizzy hair that fell "like a beagle's ears around his face," in the words of an interviewer at the time.

Dennis was so confident in his system, which chased market trends, that he codified its rules and shared them with twenty or so recruits he called "turtles." He staked his newbies with cash and sent them off to do their own trading, hoping to win a long-running debate with a friend that his tactics were so foolproof they could help even the uninitiated become market mavens. Some of the turtles saw striking success. Dennis himself is said to have made $80 million in 1986 and managed about $100 million a year later. He was crushed in 1987's market turbulence, however, the latest trader with a style that bore a resemblance to Simons's to crash and burn. After squandering about half his cash, Dennis took a break from trading to focus on liberal political causes and the legalization of marijuana, among other things.

"There is more to life than trading," he told an interviewer at the time.[5]

Throughout the 1980s, applied mathematicians and ex-physicists were recruited to work on Wall Street and in the City of London. They usually were tasked with building models to place values on complicated derivatives and mortgage products, analyze risk, and *hedge*, or protect, investment positions, activities that became known as forms of *financial engineering*.

It took a little while for the finance industry to come up with a nickname for those designing and implementing these mathematical models. At first, they were called *rocket scientists* by those who assumed rocketry was the most advanced branch of science, says Emanuel Derman, who received a PhD in theoretical physics at Columbia University before joining a Wall Street firm. Over time, these specialists became known as *quants*, short for specialists in quantitative finance. For years, Derman recalls, senior managers at banks and investment firms, many of whom prided themselves on maintaining an ignorance of computers, employed the term as a pejorative. When he joined Goldman Sachs in 1985, Derman says, he "instantly noticed the shame involved in being numerate . . . it was bad taste for two consenting adults to talk math or UNIX or C in the company of traders, salespeople, and bankers.

"People around you averted their gaze," Derman writes in his autobiography, *My Life as a Quant*.[6]

There were good reasons to be skeptical of the "computer people." For one thing, their sophisticated hedging didn't always work so perfectly. On October 19, 1987, the Dow Jones Industrial Average plunged 23 percent, the largest one-day decline ever, a drop blamed on the widespread embrace of *portfolio insurance*, a hedging technique in which investors' computers sold stock-index futures at the first sign of a decline to protect against deeper pain. The selling sent prices down further, of course, leading to even more computerized selling and the eventual rout.

A quarter century later, legendary *New York Times* financial columnist Floyd Norris called it, "the beginning of the destruction of markets by dumb computers. Or, to be fair to the computers, by computers programmed by fallible people and trusted by people who did not understand the computer programs' limitations. As computers came in, human judgment went out."

During the 1980s, Professor Benoit Mandelbrot—who had demonstrated that certain jagged mathematical shapes called *fractals* mimic irregularities found in nature—argued that financial markets also have fractal patterns. This theory suggested that markets will deliver more unexpected events than widely assumed, another reason to doubt the elaborate models produced by high-powered computers. Mandelbrot's work would reinforce the views of trader-turned-author Nassim Nicholas Taleb and others that popular math tools and risk models are incapable of sufficiently preparing investors for large and highly unpredictable deviations from historic patterns—deviations that occur more frequently than most models suggest.

Partly due to these concerns, those tinkering with models and machines usually weren't allowed to trade or invest. Instead, they were hired to help—and stay out of the way of—the traders and other important people within banks and investment firms. In the 1970s, a Berkeley economics professor named Barr Rosenberg developed quantitative models to track the factors influencing stocks. Rather than make a fortune trading himself, Rosenberg sold computerized programs to help other investors forecast stock behavior.

Edward Thorp became the first modern mathematician to use quantitative strategies to invest sizable sums of money. Thorp was an academic who had worked with Claude Shannon, the father of information theory, and embraced the proportional betting system of John Kelly, the Texas scientist who had influenced Elwyn Berlekamp. First, Thorp applied his talents to gambling, gaining prominence for his large winnings as well as his best-selling book, *Beat the Dealer*. The book outlined Thorp's belief in systematic, rules-based gambling tactics, as well as his insight that players can take advantage of shifting odds within games of chance.

In 1964, Thorp turned his attention to Wall Street, the biggest casino of them all. After reading books on technical analysis—as well as Benjamin Graham and David Dodd's landmark tome, *Security Analysis*, which laid the foundations for fundamental investing—Thorp was "surprised and encouraged by how little was known by so many," he writes in his autobiography, *A Man for All Markets*.[7]

Thorp zeroed in on stock warrants, which give the holder the ability to purchase shares at a certain price. He developed a formula for determining the "correct" price of a warrant, which gave him the ability to detect market mispricings instantly. Programming a Hewlett-Packard 9830 computer, Thorp used his mathematical formula to buy cheap warrants and bet against expensive ones, a tactic that protected his portfolio from jolts in the broader market.

During the 1970s, Thorp helped lead a hedge fund, Princeton/Newport Partners, recording strong gains and attracting well-known investors—including actor Paul Newman, Hollywood producer Robert Evans, and screenwriter Charles Kaufman. Thorp's firm based its trading on computer-generated algorithms and economic models, using so much electricity that their office in Southern California was always boiling hot.

Thorp's trading formula was influenced by the doctoral thesis of French mathematician Louis Bachelier, who, in 1900, developed a theory for pricing options on the Paris stock exchange using equations similar to those later employed by Albert Einstein to describe the Brownian motion of pollen particles. Bachelier's thesis, describing the irregular motion of stock prices, had been overlooked for decades, but Thorp and others understood its relevance to modern investing.

In 1974, Thorp landed on the front page of the *Wall Street Journal* in a story headlined: "Computer Formulas Are One Man's Secret to Success in Market." A year later, his fortune swelling, he was driving a new red Porsche 911S. To Thorp, relying on computer models to trade warrants, options, convertible bonds, and other so-called derivative securities was the only reasonable investing approach.

"A model is a simplified version of reality, like a street map that shows you how to travel from one part of the city to another," he writes. "If you got them right, [you] could then use the rules to predict what would happen in new situations."

Skeptics sniffed—one told the *Journal* that "the real investment world is too complicated to be reduced to a model." Yet, by the late 1980s, Thorp's fund stood at nearly $300 million, dwarfing the $25 million Simons's Medallion fund was managing at the time. But Princeton/Newport was ensnared in the trading scandal centered on junk-bond king Michael Milken in nearby Los Angeles, ending any hopes Thorp held of becoming an investment power.

Thorp never was accused of any impropriety, and the government eventually dropped all charges related to Princeton/Newport's activities, but publicity related to the investigation crippled his fund, and it closed in late 1988, a denouement Thorp describes as "traumatic." Over its nineteen-year existence, the hedge fund featured annual gains averaging more than 15 percent (after charging investors various fees), topping the market's returns over that span.

Were it not for the government's actions, "we'd be billionaires," Thorp says.

=

Gerry Bamberger had few visions of wealth or prominence in the early 1980s. A tall, trim computer-science graduate from Columbia University, Bamberger provided analytical and technical support for Morgan Stanley's stock traders, serving as an underappreciated cog in the investment bank's machine. When the traders prepared to buy and sell big chunks of shares for clients, acquiring a few million dollars of Coca-Cola, for example, they protected themselves by selling an equal amount of something similar, like Pepsi, in what is commonly referred to as a *pairs trade*. Bamberger created software to update the Morgan Stanley traders' results, though many of them bristled at the idea of getting assistance from the resident computer nerd.

Watching the traders buy big *blocks* of shares, Bamberger observed that prices often moved higher, as might be expected. Prices headed lower when Morgan Stanley's traders sold blocks of shares. Each time, the trading activity altered the gap, or *spread*, between the stock in question and the other company in the pair, even when there was no news in the market. An order to sell a chunk of Coke shares, for instance, might send that stock down a percentage point or even two, even as Pepsi barely moved. Once the effect of their Coke stock selling wore off, the spread between the shares reverted to the norm, which made sense, since there had been no reason for Coke's drop other than Morgan Stanley's activity.

Bamberger sensed opportunity. If the bank created a database tracking the historic prices of various paired stocks, it could profit simply by betting on the return of these price-spreads to their historic levels after block trades or other unusual activity. Bamberger's bosses were swayed, setting him up with half a million dollars and a small staff. Bamberger began developing computer programs to take advantage of "temporary blips" of paired shares. An Orthodox Jew and a heavy smoker with a wry sense of humor, Bamberger brought a tuna sandwich in a brown bag for lunch every single day. By 1985, he was implementing his strategy with six or seven stocks at a time, while managing $30 million, scoring profits for Morgan Stanley.[8]

Big bureaucratic companies often act like, well, big bureaucratic companies. That's why Morgan Stanley soon gave Bamberger a new boss, Nunzio Tartaglia, a perceived insult that sparked Bamberger to quit. (He joined Ed Thorp's hedge fund, where he did similar trades and eventually retired a millionaire.)

A short, wiry astrophysicist, Tartaglia managed the Morgan Stanley trading group very differently from his predecessor. A native of Brooklyn who had bounced around Wall Street, Tartaglia's edges were sharper. Once, when a new colleague approached to introduce himself, Tartaglia immediately cut him off.

"Don't try to get anything by me because I come from out there," Tartaglia said, pointing a finger at a nearby window and the streets of New York City.[9]

Tartaglia renamed his group Automated Proprietary Trading, or APT, and moved it to a forty-foot-long room on the nineteenth floor of Morgan Stanley's headquarters in a midtown Manhattan skyscraper. He added more automation to the system and, by 1987, it was generating $50 million of annual profits. Team members didn't know a thing about the stocks they traded and didn't need to—their strategy was simply to wager on the re-emergence of historic relationships between shares, an extension of the age-old "buy low, sell high" investment adage, this time using computer programs and lightning-fast trades.

New hires, including a former Columbia University computer-science professor named David Shaw and mathematician Robert Frey, improved profits. The Morgan Stanley traders became some of the first to embrace the strategy of *statistical arbitrage*, or stat arb. This generally means making lots of concurrent trades, most of which aren't correlated to the overall market but are aimed at taking advantage of statistical anomalies or other market behavior. The team's software ranked stocks by their gains or losses over the previous weeks, for example. APT would then sell *short*, or bet against, the top 10 percent of the winners within an industry while buying the bottom 10 percent of the losers on the expectation that these trading patterns would revert. It didn't always happen, of course, but when implemented enough times, the strategy resulted in annual profits of 20 percent, likely because investors often tend to overreact to both good and bad news before calming down and helping to restore historic relationships between stocks.

By 1988, APT was among the largest and most-secretive trading teams in the world, buying and selling $900 million worth of shares each day. The unit hit heavy losses that year, though, and Morgan Stanley executives slashed APT's capital by two-thirds. Senior management never had been comfortable investing by relying on computer models, and jealousies had grown about how much money Tartaglia's team was making. Soon, Tartaglia was out of a job, and the group shut down.

It wouldn't be clear for many years, but Morgan Stanley had squandered some of the most lucrative trading strategies in the history of finance.

=

Well before the APT group closed for business, Robert Frey had become anxious. It wasn't just that his boss, Tartaglia, wasn't getting along with his superiors, suggesting the bank might drop the team if losses arose. Frey, a heavyset man with a limp, the result of a fall in his youth that had shattered his leg and hip, was convinced rivals were catching on to his group's strategies. Thorp's fund was already doing similar kinds of trades, and Frey figured others were sure to follow. He had to come up with new tactics.

Frey proposed deconstructing the movements of various stocks by identifying the independent variables responsible for those moves. A surge in Exxon, for example, could be attributable to multiple factors, such as moves in oil prices, the value of the dollar, the momentum of the overall market, and more. A rise in Procter & Gamble might be most attributable to its healthy balance sheet and a growing demand for safe stocks, as investors soured on companies with lots of debt. If so, selling groups of stocks with robust balance sheets and buying those with heavy debt might be called for, if data showed the performance gap between the groups had moved beyond historic bounds. A handful of investors and academics were mulling *factor investing* around that same time, but Frey wondered if he could do a better job using computational statistics and other mathematical techniques to isolate the true factors moving shares.

Frey and his colleagues couldn't muster much interest among the Morgan Stanley brass for their innovative factor approach.

"They told me not to rock the boat," Frey recalls.

Frey quit, contacting Jim Simons and winning his financial backing to start a new company, Kepler Financial Management. Frey and a few others set up dozens of small computers to bet on his statistical-arbitrage strategy. Almost immediately, he received a threatening letter from Morgan Stanley's lawyers. Frey hadn't stolen anything, but his approach had been developed working for Morgan Stanley. Frey was in luck, though. He remembered that Tartaglia hadn't allowed him or anyone else in his group to sign the bank's nondisclosure or noncompete agreements. Tartaglia had wanted the option of taking his team to a rival if their bonuses ever disappointed. As a result, Morgan Stanley didn't have strong legal grounds to stop Frey's trading. With some trepidation, he ignored Morgan Stanley's continuing threats and began trading.

=

By 1990, Simons had high hopes Frey and Kepler might find success with their stock trades. He was even more enthused about his own Medallion fund and its quantitative-trading strategies in bond, commodity, and currency markets. Competition was building, however, with some rivals embracing similar trading strategies. Simons's biggest competition figured to come from David Shaw, another refugee of the Morgan Stanley APT group. After leaving the bank in 1988, the thirty-six-year-old Shaw, who had received his PhD from Stanford University, was courted by Goldman Sachs and was unsure whether to accept the job offer. To discuss his options, Shaw turned to hedge-fund manager Donald Sussman, who took Shaw sailing on Long Island Sound. One day on Sussman's forty-five-foot sloop turned into three, as the pair debated what Shaw should do.

"I think I can use technology to trade securities," Shaw told Sussman.

Sussman suggested that Shaw start his own hedge fund, rather than work for Goldman Sachs, offering a $28 million initial *seed* investment. Shaw was swayed, launching D. E. Shaw in an office space above Revolution Books, a communist bookstore in a then-gritty part of Manhattan's Union Square area. One of Shaw's first moves was to purchase two ultrafast and expensive Sun Microsystems computers.

"He needed Ferraris," Sussman says. "We bought him Ferraris."[10]

Shaw, a supercomputing expert, hired math and science PhDs who embraced his scientific approach to trading. He also brought on whip-smart employees from different backgrounds. English and philosophy majors were among Shaw's favorite hires, but he also hired a chess master, stand-up comedians, published writers, an Olympic-level fencer, a trombone player, and a demolitions specialist.

"We didn't want anyone with preconceived notions," an early executive says.[11]

Unlike the boisterous trading rooms of most Wall Street firms, Shaw's offices were quiet and somber, reminding visitors of the research room of the Library of Congress, even as employees wore jeans and T-shirts. These were the early days of the internet, and academics were the only ones using email at the time, but Shaw gushed to one of his programmers about the new era's possibilities.

"I think people will buy things on the internet," Shaw told a colleague. "Not only will they shop, but when they buy something . . . they're going to say, 'this pipe is good,' or 'this pipe is bad,' and they're going to post reviews."

One programmer, Jeffrey Bezos, worked with Shaw a few more years before piling his belongings into a moving van and driving to Seattle, his then-wife MacKenzie behind the wheel. Along the way, Bezos worked on a laptop, pecking out a business plan for his company, Amazon.com. (He originally chose "Cadabra" but dropped the name because too many people mistook it for "Cadaver.")[12]

Almost as soon as he started the engines of his Ferraris, Shaw's hedge fund minted money. Soon, it was managing several hundred million dollars, trading an array of equity-related investments, and boasting over one hundred employees.

Jim Simons didn't have a clear understanding of the kind of progress Shaw and a few others were making. He did know, if he was going to build something special to catch up with those who had a jump on him, he'd need some help. Simons called Sussman, the financier who had given David Shaw the support he needed to start his own hedge fund, hoping for a similar boost.

CHAPTER EIGHT

Jim Simons's pulse quickened as he approached Sixth Avenue.

It was a sultry summer afternoon, but Simons wore a jacket and tie, hoping to impress. He had his work cut out for him. By 1991, David Shaw and a few other upstarts were using computer models to trade stocks. Those few members of the Wall Street establishment aware of the approach mostly scoffed at it, however. Relying on inscrutable algorithms, as Simons was doing, seemed ludicrous, even dangerous. Some called it *black box* investing—hard to explain and likely masking serious risk. Huge sums of money were being made the old-fashioned way, blending thoughtful research with honed instincts. Who needed Simons and his fancy computers?

Awaiting Simons in a tall midtown Manhattan office tower was Donald Sussman, a forty-five-year-old Miami native who was something of a heretic on Wall Street. More than two decades earlier, as an undergraduate at Columbia University, Sussman took a leave of absence to work in a small brokerage firm. There, he stumbled upon an obscure strategy to trade convertible bonds, a particularly knotty investment. Sussman convinced his bosses to shell out $2,000 for an early-generation electronic calculator so he could quickly determine which bond was most attractive. Calculator in hand,

Sussman made the firm millions of dollars in profits, a windfall that opened his eyes to how technology could render an advantage.

Now the six-foot-three, broad-shouldered, mustachioed Sussman ran a fund called Paloma Partners that was backing Shaw's rapidly expanding hedge-fund firm, D. E. Shaw. Sussman suspected mathematicians and scientists might one day rival, or even best, the largest trading firms, no matter the conventional wisdom in the business. Word was out that he was open to investing in additional computer-focused traders, giving Simons hope he might gain Sussman's support.

Simons had discarded a thriving academic career to do something special in the investing world. But, after a full decade in the business, he was managing barely more than $45 million, a mere quarter the assets of Shaw's firm. The meeting had import—backing from Sussman could help Renaissance hire employees, upgrade technology, and become a force on Wall Street.

Sussman had been one of Simons's earliest investors, but he suffered losses and withdrew his money, an experience that suggested Sussman might be skeptical of his visitor. Simons's trading algorithms had recently been revamped, however, and he was bursting with confidence. He strode into Sussman's building, a block from Carnegie Hall, rode an elevator to the thirty-first floor, and stepped into an expansive conference room with panoramic views of Central Park and a large whiteboard for visiting quants to scribble their equations.

Eyeing Simons across a long, narrow wooden table, Sussman couldn't help smiling. His guest was bearded, balding, and graying, bearing little resemblance to most of the investors who made regular pilgrimages to his office asking for money. Simons's tie was slightly askew, and his jacket tweed, a rarity on Wall Street. He came alone, without the usual entourage of handlers and advisors. Simons was just the kind of brainy investor Sussman enjoyed helping.

"He looked like an academic," Sussman recalls.

Simons began his pitch, relaying how his Medallion hedge fund had refined its approach. Assured and plainspoken, Simons spent more than an hour outlining his firm's performance, risks, and volatility, and he broadly described his new short-term model.

"Now I really have it," Simons enthused. "We've had a breakthrough."

He asked Sussman for a $10 million investment in his hedge fund, expressing certainty he could generate big gains and grow Renaissance into a major investment firm.

"I've had a revelation," Simons said. "I can do it in size."

Sussman listened patiently. He was impressed. There was no way he was giving Simons any money, though. Privately, Sussman worried about potential conflicts of interest, since he was the sole source of capital for Shaw's hedge fund. He was even helping Shaw's firm hire academics and traders to extend its lead over Simons and other fledgling quantitative traders. If Sussman had cash to spare, he figured, he probably should put it in D. E. Shaw. Besides, Shaw was scoring annual gains of 40 percent. Renaissance didn't seem to have a shot at matching those gains.

"Why would I give money to a theoretical competitor?" Sussman asked Simons. "I'm sorry, but I already have David."

They stood up, shook hands, and promised to stay in touch. As Simons turned to leave, Sussman noticed a fleeting look of disappointment on his face.

Simons didn't have much more luck with other potential backers. Investors wouldn't say it to his face, but most deemed it absurd to rely on trading models generated by computers. Just as preposterous were Simons's fees, especially his requirement that investors hand over 5 percent of the money he managed for them each year, well above the 2 percent levied by most hedge funds.

"I pay the fees, too," Simons told one potential investor, noting that he also was an investor in Medallion. "Why shouldn't you?"

Simons didn't get very far with that logic; the fees he paid went right back to his own firm, rendering his argument unconvincing. Simons was especially hamstrung by the fact that his fund had fewer than two years of impressive returns.

When a Wall Street veteran named Anita Rival met with Simons in his Manhattan office to discuss an investment from the firm she represented, she became the latest to snub him.

"He wouldn't explain how the computer models worked," she recalls. "You couldn't understand what he was doing."

Within Renaissance, word circulated that Commodities Corporation—a firm credited with launching dominant hedge funds run by commodity-focused traders including Paul Tudor Jones, Louis Bacon, and Bruce Kovner—also passed on backing Simons's fund.

"The view from the industry was—'It's a bunch of mathematicians using computers. . . . What do *they* know about the business?'" says a friend of Simons. "They had no track record . . . the risk was they were going to put themselves out of business."

Simons still had his trading system, now managing a bit more than $70 million after a gain of 39 percent in 1991. If Simons could figure out a way to extend his winning streak, or even improve Medallion's returns, he was sure investors would eventually come around. Berlekamp, Ax, and Baum were long gone, though. Straus was in charge of the firm's trading, data collection, and more, but he wasn't a researcher capable of uncovering hidden trading signals. With competition growing, Medallion would have to discover new ways to profit. Seeking help, Simons turned to Henry Laufer, a mathematician who already had demonstrated a flair for creative solutions.

=

Laufer never claimed any of the prestigious mathematics awards given to Simons and Ax, nor did he have a popular algorithm named after him, like Lenny Baum or Elwyn Berlekamp. Nonetheless, Laufer had scaled his own heights of accomplishment and recognition, and he would prove Simons's best partner yet.

Laufer had finished his undergraduate work at the City College of New York and graduate school at Princeton University in two years each, earning acclaim for progress he'd made on a stubborn problem in a field of mathematics dealing with functions of complex variables and for discovering new examples of *embeddings*, or structures within other math structures.

Joining Stony Brook's math department in 1971, Laufer focused on complex variables and algebraic geometry, veering away from classical areas of complex analysis to develop insights into more contemporary problems. Laufer came alive in the classroom and was popular with students, but he was more timid in his personal life. High school friends remember a bookish introvert who carried a slide rule. Early on at Stony Brook, Laufer told colleagues he wanted to get married and was eager to put himself in the best position to find the right woman. Once, on a ski trip with fellow mathematician Leonard Charlap, Laufer suggested they go down to the hotel's bar "to meet some girls."

Charlap looked at his friend and just laughed.

"Henry, you're not that kind of guy," Charlap said, knowing Laufer would be too shy to hit on women in a hotel bar.

"He was a nice Jewish boy," Charlap recalls.

Laufer eventually met and married Marsha Zlatin, a speech-language pathology professor at Stony Brook who shared Laufer's liberal politics. Marsha had a more upbeat personality, often using the word "swell" to describe her mood, no matter the challenge. After suffering a series of miscarriages, Marsha amazed friends with her buoyancy, eventually giving birth to healthy children. Later, she earned a PhD in speech-language pathology.

Marsha's outlook on life seemed to influence Laufer. Among colleagues, he was known as a willing collaborator. They noticed Laufer had a special interest in investing, and they were disappointed, but not shocked, when he rejoined Simons as a full-time employee in 1992.

Academics who shift to trading often turn nervous and edgy, worried about each move in the market, concerns that hounded Baum when he joined Simons. Laufer, then forty-six, had a different reaction—his improved pay relieved stress he had felt about the cost of his daughters' college education, friends say, and Laufer seemed to relish the intellectual challenge of crafting profitable trading formulas.

For Simons, Laufer's geniality was a welcome relief after years of dealing with the complicated personalities of Baum, Ax, and Berlekamp. Simons became Renaissance's big-picture guy, wooing investors, attracting talent, planning for emergencies, and mapping a strategy for how his team—with Laufer leading research in a new Stony Brook office, and Straus running trading in Berkeley—might build on the recent strong returns.

Laufer made an early decision that would prove extraordinarily valuable: Medallion would employ a single trading model rather than maintain various models for different investments and market conditions, a style most quantitative firms would embrace. A collection of trading models was simpler and easier to pull off, Laufer acknowledged. But, he argued, a single model could draw on Straus's vast trove of pricing data, detecting correlations, opportunities, and other signals across various asset classes. Narrow, individual models, by contrast, can suffer from too little data.

Just as important, Laufer understood that a single, stable model based on some core assumptions about how prices and markets behave would make it easier to add new investments later on. They could even toss investments with relatively little trading data into the mix if they were deemed similar to other investments Medallion traded with lots of data. Yes, Laufer acknowledged, it's a challenge to combine various investments, say a currency-futures contract and a US commodity contract. But, he argued, once they figured out ways to "smooth" out those wrinkles, the single model would lead to better trading results.

Laufer spent long hours at his desk refining the model. At lunchtime, the team usually piled into Laufer's aging Lincoln Town Car and headed to a local joint, where the deliberations continued. It didn't take long to come up with a new way to look at the market.

Straus and others had compiled reams of files tracking decades of prices of dozens of commodities, bonds, and currencies. To make it all easier to digest, they had broken the trading week into ten segments—five overnight sessions, when stocks traded in overseas markets, and five day sessions. In effect, they sliced the day in half, enabling the team to search for repeating patterns and sequences in the various segments. Then, they entered trades in the morning, at noon, and at the end of the day.

Simons wondered if there might be a better way to parse their data trove. Perhaps breaking the day up into finer segments might enable the team to dissect intraday pricing information and unearth new, undetected patterns. Laufer began splitting the day in half, then into quarters, eventually deciding five-minute *bars* were the ideal way to carve things up. Crucially, Straus now had access to improved computer-processing power, making it easier for Laufer to compare small slices of historic data. Did the 188th five-minute bar in the cocoa-futures market regularly fall on days investors got nervous, while bar 199 usually rebounded? Perhaps bar 50 in the gold market saw strong buying on days investors worried about inflation but bar 63 often showed weakness?

Laufer's five-minute bars gave the team the ability to identify new trends, oddities, and other phenomena, or, in their parlance, *nonrandom trading effects*. Straus and others conducted tests to ensure they hadn't mined so deeply into their data that they had arrived at bogus trading strategies, but many of the new signals seemed to hold up.

It was as if the Medallion team had donned glasses for the first time, seeing the market anew. One early discovery: Certain trading bands from Friday morning's action had the uncanny ability to predict bands later that same afternoon, nearer to the close of trading. Laufer's work also showed that, if markets moved higher late in a day, it often paid to buy futures contracts just before the close of trading and dump them at the market's opening the next day.

The team uncovered predictive effects related to volatility, as well as a series of *combination effects*, such as the propensity of pairs of investments—such as gold and silver, or heating oil and crude oil—to move in the same direction at certain times in the trading day compared with others. It wasn't immediately obvious why some of the new trading signals worked, but as long as they had *p-values*, or probability values, under 0.01—meaning they appeared statistically significant, with a low probability of being statistical mirages—they were added to the system.

Wielding an array of profitable investing ideas wasn't nearly enough, Simons soon realized.

"How do we pull the trigger?" he asked Laufer and the rest of the team.

Simons was challenging them to solve yet another vexing problem: Given the range of possible trades they had developed and the limited amount of money that Medallion managed, how much should they bet on each trade? And which moves should they pursue and prioritize? Laufer began developing a computer program to identify optimal trades throughout the day, something Simons began calling his *betting algorithm*. Laufer decided it would be "dynamic," adapting on its own along the way and relying on real-time analysis to adjust the fund's mix of holdings given the probabilities of future market moves—an early form of machine learning.

Driving to Stony Brook with a friend and Medallion investor, Simons could hardly contain his excitement.

"Our system is a living thing; it's always modifying," he said. "We really should be able to grow it."

With only a dozen or so employees, Simons had to build a full staff if he wanted to catch up to D. E. Shaw and take on the industry's trading powers. One day, a Stony Brook PhD student named Kresimir Penavic drove over for a job interview. As he waited to speak with Laufer, Simons, wearing torn pants and penny loafers, a cigarette dangling between two fingers, wandered over to assess his new recruit.

"You're at Stony Brook?" he asked Penavic, who nodded. "What have you done?"

Unsure who the guy with all the questions was, Penavic, who stood six-foot-six, began describing his undergraduate work in applied mathematics.

Simons was unimpressed.

"That's trivial stuff," he sniffed. It was the most devastating put-down a mathematician could deliver.

Undeterred, Penavic told Simons about another paper he'd written focused on an unsolved algebraic problem.

"That problem is *not* trivial," Penavic insisted.

"That's *still* trivial," Simons said with a wave of his hand, cigarette fumes wafting past Penavic's face.

As the young recruit burned, Simons started grinning, as if he had been playing a practical joke on Penavic.

"I like you, though," Simons said.

A bit later, Penavic was hired.

Around the same time, a researcher named Nick Patterson was added to the staff—though he didn't exactly celebrate his job offer. Patterson couldn't shake his suspicion that Simons was running some kind of scam. It wasn't just that, in 1992, Medallion was enjoying a third straight year of annual returns topping 33 percent, as Laufer's short-term tactics paid off. Nor was it the enormous fees the fund charged clients or the $100 million it supposedly managed. It was the *way* Simons was racking up the alleged profits, relying on a computer model that he and his employees themselves didn't fully understand.

Even the office itself didn't seem entirely legitimate to Patterson. Simons had moved Renaissance's research operation into the top floor of a nineteenth-century home on tree-lined North Country Road in a residential area of Stony Brook. There were nine people crammed into the house, all working on various businesses backed by Simons, including some venture-capital investments and a couple of guys downstairs trading stocks. No one knew much about what anyone else was doing, and Simons didn't even come in every day.

The space was so tight, Patterson didn't have a proper place to sit. Eventually, he pushed a chair and desk into an empty corner of Simons's own office. Simons spent half the week in a New York City office and told Patterson he didn't mind sharing.

Patterson was well aware of Simons's accomplishments in mathematics and code-breaking, but they did little to allay his suspicions.

"Mathematicians can be crooks, too," Patterson says. "It's quite easy to launder money in hedge funds."

For a full month, Patterson surreptitiously jotted down the closing prices that Medallion used for various investments in its portfolio, carefully checking them against pages of the *Wall Street Journal*, line by line, to see if they matched.*

Only after Simons's numbers checked out did a relieved Patterson turn his full attention to using his mathematical skills to help the effort. It had

*Patterson had more reason for paranoia than even he realized; around the same time, another investor from Long Island, Bernard Madoff, was crafting history's largest Ponzi scheme.

taken Patterson years to realize that he actually enjoyed math. Early in his life, math was just a tool for Patterson, one he used for protection. Patterson suffered from facial dysplasia, a rare congenital disorder that distorted the left side of his face and rendered his left eye blind.[1] An only child who grew up in the Bayswater section of central London, Patterson was sent to Catholic boarding school and bullied unmercifully. Unable to speak with his parents more than once a week, and determined to maintain a stiff British upper lip, Patterson turned his prowess in the classroom into an advantage.

"I evolved into the school brain, a British stock character," Patterson recalls. "I was seen as odd but useful, so they left me alone."

Patterson was mostly attracted to mathematics because he was über-competitive, and it was gratifying to discover a field he could dominate. Only at the age of sixteen did Patterson notice he actually enjoyed the subject. A few years later, after graduating from the University of Cambridge, Patterson took a job that required him to write commercial code. He proved a natural, gaining an advantage over fellow mathematicians, few of whom knew how to program computers.

A strong chess player, Patterson spent much of his free time at a London coffee shop that rented chess boards and hosted intense matches between customers. Patterson regularly trounced players many years his senior. After a while, he deduced the shop was no more than a front—there was a secret staircase leading to an illegal, high-stakes poker game run by a local thug. Patterson gained entrance to the game and it quickly became clear he was a stud at poker as well, pocketing fistfuls of cash. The tough guy took notice of Patterson's abilities, making him an offer he figured Patterson couldn't refuse: If you hustle chess downstairs for me, I'll share your winnings and handle all your losses.

There was no risk to Patterson, but he rejected the offer, nonetheless. The brute told him he was making a big mistake.

"Are you nuts? You can't make any money in *mathematics*," he sneered.

The experience taught Patterson to distrust most moneymaking operations, even those that appeared legitimate—one reason why he was so skeptical of Simons years later.

After graduate school, Patterson thrived as a cryptologist for the British government, building statistical models to unscramble intercepted messages and encrypt secret messages in a unit made famous during World War II when Alan Turing famously broke Germany's encryption codes. Patterson harnessed the simple-yet-profound Bayes' theorem of probability, which argues that, by updating one's initial beliefs with new, objective information, one can arrive at improved understandings.

Patterson solved a long-standing problem in the field, deciphering a pattern in the data others had missed, becoming so valuable to the government that some top-secret documents shared with allies were labeled "For US Eyes Only and for Nick Patterson."

"It was James Bond stuff," he says.

Several years later, when a new pay scale was instituted that elevated the group's administrators above the cryptologists, Patterson became livid.

"It was the insult, not the money," says Patterson, who told his wife he'd rather drive a bus than remain in the group. "I had to get out of there."

Patterson moved to the Institute for Defense Analyses, where he met Simons and Baum, but he turned nervous as he approached his fiftieth birthday.

"My father had a hard time in his late fifties, and that worried me," recalls Patterson, who had two children at the time who were preparing to go to college. "I didn't have enough money, and I didn't want to go down that road."

When a senior colleague received permission to travel to Russia for an amateur-radio conference, Patterson realized the Cold War was ending, and he had to act fast.

I'm going to lose my job!

Fortuitously, Simons soon called, out of the blue, sounding urgent.

"We need to talk," Simons said. "Will you work for me?"

A move to Renaissance made sense to Patterson. Simons's group was analyzing large amounts of messy, complicated pricing data to predict future prices. Patterson thought his natural skepticism could prove valuable discerning true signals from random market fluctuations. He also knew his programming skills would come in handy. And, unlike many of Renaissance's dozen or so employees, Patterson actually read the business pages, at least occasionally, and knew a bit about finance.

"I thought I was pretty cutting-edge because I owned an index fund," he says.

Patterson saw the world "becoming extremely mathematical" and knew computer firepower was expanding exponentially. He sensed Simons had an opportunity to revolutionize investing by applying high-level math and statistics.

"Fifty years earlier, we couldn't have done anything, but this was the perfect time," he says.

After lugging a computer into the corner of Simons's office and concluding that Renaissance likely wasn't a fraud, Patterson began helping Laufer with a stubborn problem. Profitable trade ideas are only half the game; the act of buying and selling investments can itself affect prices to such a degree that gains can be whittled away. It's meaningless to know that copper prices will rise from $3.00 a contract to $3.10, for example, if your buying pushes the price up to $3.05 before you even have a chance to complete your transaction—perhaps as dealers hike the price or as rivals do their own buying—slashing potential profits by half.

From the earliest days of the fund, Simons's team had been wary of these transaction costs, which they called *slippage*. They regularly compared their trades against a model that tracked how much the firm *would* have profited or lost were it not for those bothersome trading costs. The group coined a name for the difference between the prices they were getting and the theoretical trades their model made without the pesky costs. They called it *The Devil.*

For a while, the actual size of The Devil was something of a guess. But, as Straus collected more data and his computers became more powerful, Laufer and Patterson began writing a computer program to track how far their trades strayed from the ideal state, in which trading costs barely weighed on the fund's performance. By the time Patterson got to Renaissance, the firm could run a simulator that subtracted these trading costs from the prices they had received, instantly isolating how much they were missing out.

To narrow the gap, Laufer and Patterson began developing sophisticated approaches to direct trades to various futures exchanges to reduce the market impact of each trade. Now Medallion could better determine which investments to pursue, a huge advantage as it began trading new markets and investments. They added German, British, and Italian bonds, then interest-rate contracts in London, and, later, futures on Nikkei Stock Average, Japanese government bonds, and more.

The fund began trading more frequently. Having first sent orders to a team of traders five times a day, it eventually increased to sixteen times a day, reducing the impact on prices by focusing on the periods when there was the most volume. Medallion's traders still had to pick up the phone to transact, but the fund was on its way toward faster trading.

=

Until then, Simons and his colleagues hadn't spent too much time wondering *why* their growing collection of algorithms predicted prices so presciently. They were scientists and mathematicians, not analysts or economists. If certain signals produced results that were statistically significant, that was enough to include them in the trading model.

"I don't know why planets orbit the sun," Simons told a colleague, suggesting one needn't spend too much time figuring out why the market's patterns existed. "That doesn't mean I can't predict them."

Still, the returns were piling up so fast, it was getting a bit absurd. Medallion soared over 25 percent just in June 1994, on its way to a 71 percent surge that year, results that even Simons described as "simply remarkable." Even more impressive: The gains came in a year the Federal Reserve surprised investors by hiking interest rates repeatedly, leading to deep losses for many investors.

The Renaissance team was curious by nature, as were many of its investors. They couldn't help wonder what the heck was going on. If Medallion was emerging as a big winner in most of its trades, who was on the other side suffering steady losses?

Over time, Simons came to the conclusion that the losers probably weren't those who trade infrequently, such as buy-and-hold individual investors, or even the "treasurer of a multinational corporation," who adjusts her portfolio of foreign currencies every once in a while to suit her company's needs, as Simons told his investors.

Instead, it seemed Renaissance was exploiting the foibles and faults of fellow speculators, both big and small.

"The manager of a global hedge fund who is guessing on a frequent basis the direction of the French bond market may be a more exploitable participant," Simons said.

Laufer had a slightly different explanation for their heady returns. When Patterson came to him, curious about the source of the money they were raking in, Laufer pointed to a different set of traders infamous for both their excessive trading and overconfidence when it came to predicting the direction of the market.

"It's a lot of dentists," Laufer said.

Laufer's explanation sounds glib, but his perspective, as well as Simons's viewpoint, can be seen as profound, even radical. At the time, most academics were convinced markets were inherently efficient, suggesting that there were no predictable ways to beat the market's return, and that the financial decision-making of individuals was largely rational. Simons and his colleagues sensed the professors were wrong. They believed investors are prone to cognitive biases, the kinds that lead to panics, bubbles, booms, and busts.

Simons didn't realize it, but a new strain of economics was emerging that would validate his instincts. In the 1970s, Israeli psychologists Amos Tversky and Daniel Kahneman had explored how individuals make decisions, demonstrating how prone most are to act irrationally. Later, economist Richard Thaler used psychological insights to explain anomalies in investor behavior, spurring the growth of the field of *behavioral economics*, which explored the cognitive biases of individuals and investors. Among those identified: *loss aversion*, or how investors generally feel the pain from losses twice as much as the pleasure from gains; *anchoring*, the way judgment is skewed by an initial piece of information or experience; and the *endowment effect*, how investors assign excessive value to what they already own in their portfolios.

Kahneman and Thaler would win Nobel Prizes for their work. A consensus would emerge that investors act more irrationally than assumed, repeatedly making similar mistakes. Investors overreact to stress and make emotional decisions. Indeed, it's likely no coincidence that Medallion found itself making its largest profits during times of extreme turbulence in financial markets, a phenomenon that would continue for decades to come.

Like most investors, Simons, too, became nervous when his fund went through rocky times. In a few rare circumstances, he reacted by paring the firm's overall positions. On the whole, though, Simons maintained faith in his trading model, recalling how difficult it had been for him to invest using his instincts. He made a commitment to refrain from overriding the model, hoping to ensure that neither Medallion's returns, nor the emotions of his employees at Renaissance, influenced the fund's moves.

"Our P&L isn't an input," Patterson says, using trading lingo for profits and losses. "We're mediocre traders, but our system never has rows with its girlfriends—that's the kind of thing that causes patterns in markets."

Simons hadn't embraced a statistics-based approach because of the work of any economists or psychologists, nor had he set out to program algorithms to avoid, or take advantage of, investors' biases. Over time, though, Simons and his team came to believe that these errors and overreactions were at least partially responsible for their profits, and that their developing system seemed uniquely capable of taking advantage of the common mistakes of fellow traders.

"What you're really modeling is human behavior," explains Penavic, the researcher. "Humans are most predictable in times of high stress—they act instinctively and panic. Our entire premise was that human actors will react the way humans did in the past . . . we learned to take advantage."

=

Investors finally began taking note of Medallion's gains. A year earlier, in 1993, GAM Holding—a London-based investment firm managing money for wealthy clients that was one of the first institutions to invest in hedge funds—had given Renaissance about $25 million. By then, Simons and his team had turned wary of sharing much of anything about how their fund operated, lest rivals catch on. That put GAM executives, accustomed to fully understanding details of how funds operated, in a difficult position. They'd confirm that Renaissance had proper audits, and that their investors' money was secure, but GAM couldn't fully understand how Medallion was making so much money. The GAM brass were thrilled with the results of Simons's fund, but, like other clients, perpetually anxious about their investment.

"I always lived scared, worried something would go wrong," says David McCarthy, who was in charge of monitoring GAM's investment in Medallion.

Soon, Simons's challenges would become apparent.

═

Simons did an about-face. By the end of 1993, Medallion managed $280 million, and Simons worried profits might suffer if the fund got too big and its trades started pushing prices higher when it bought, or lower when it sold. Simons decided not to let any more clients into the fund.

Simons's team turned more secretive, telling clients to dial a Manhattan phone number for a recording of recent results and to speak with Renaissance's lawyers if they needed detailed updates. The additional steps were to keep rivals from learning about the fund's activities.

"Our very good results have made us well known, and this may be our most serious challenge," Simons wrote in a letter to clients. "Visibility invites competition, and, with all due respect to the principles of free enterprise—the less the better."

Simons pressured his investors not to share any details of the operation. "Our only defense is to keep a low profile," he told them.

The secretive approach sometimes hurt the firm. In the winter of 1995, a scientist at Brookhaven National Laboratory's Relativistic Heavy Ion Collider named Michael Botlo received a call from a Renaissance executive asking if he'd be interested in a job.

Fighting a snowstorm, Botlo drove his dented Mazda hatchback to Renaissance's new offices located in a high-tech incubator close to a hospital and a dive bar near Stony Brook's campus. Botlo entered the office, brushed off the snow, and was immediately underwhelmed by the small, tacky, beige-and-teal offices. When Botlo sat down to speak with Patterson and other staff members, they wouldn't share even bare details of their trading approach, focusing instead on the inclement weather, frustrating Botlo.

Enough of the chitchat, he thought.

Botlo was told Renaissance used a decade-old computer-programming language called Perl, rather than languages like C++ that big Wall Street trading firms relied upon, making him even more skeptical. (In reality, Renaissance employed Perl for bookkeeping and other operations, not its trading, but no one wanted to share that information with a visitor.)

"It looked like four guys in a garage. They didn't seem that skilled at computer science, and a lot of what they were doing seemed by the seat of their pants, a few guys dabbling at computing," Botlo says. "It wasn't very appealing."

Days later, Botlo wrote Patterson a note: "I've chosen to learn the business properly by joining Morgan Stanley."

Ouch.

In 1995, Simons received a call from a representative of PaineWebber, a major brokerage firm, expressing interest in an acquisition of Renaissance. Finally, after years of hard work and outsize gains, Wall Street's big boys had taken notice of Simons's pioneering methods. A huge payday surely was in the offing.

Simons appointed Patterson to meet with a few PaineWebber executives, but it didn't take him long to realize the brokerage firm wasn't convinced of Simons's revolutionary strategies or interested in his acclaimed staffers. The PaineWebber executives were simply after the hedge fund's client list, astonished by the enormous fees they were paying to invest with Simons. After getting their hands on Renaissance's customers, PaineWebber would likely gut the firm and try to sell its own products to Renaissance's well-heeled clientele.

The talks went nowhere, disappointing some at Renaissance. The mainstream still didn't trust computer trading; it just felt wrong and risky.

"They assumed the algorithms were basically nonsense," Patterson says.

═

Medallion was still on a winning streak. It was scoring big profits trading futures contracts and managed $600 million, but Simons was convinced the hedge fund was in a serious bind. Laufer's models, which measured the fund's impact on the market with surprising precision, concluded that Medallion's returns would wane if it managed much more money. Some commodity markets, such as grains, were just too small to handle additional buying and selling by the fund without pushing prices around. There were also limitations to how much more Medallion could do in bigger bond and currency markets.

Word had spread that Medallion had a knack for profitable bets, and shady traders were taking advantage. On a visit to Chicago, a staffer caught someone standing above the Eurodollar-futures pits watching Medallion's trades. The spy would send hand signals whenever Medallion bought or sold, enabling a confederate to get in just before Simons's fund took any actions, reducing Medallion's profits. Others seemed to have index cards listing the times of day Medallion usually transacted. Some on the floor had even coined a nickname for Simons's team: "the Sheiks," a reflection of their prominence in some commodity markets. Renaissance adjusted its activity to make it more secretive and unpredictable, but it was one more indication the firm was outgrowing various financial markets.

Simons worried his signals were getting weaker as rivals adopted similar strategies.

"The system is always leaking," Simons acknowledged in his first interview with a reporter. "We keep having to keep it ahead of the game."[2]

Some at the firm didn't see the big deal. Okay, the capital constraints meant Medallion never could become the world's largest or greatest hedge fund—so what? If they kept the fund around its current size, they'd all become fabulously wealthy and successful, anyway.

"Why don't we keep it at $600 million?" Straus asked Simons. That way, Medallion could rack up $200 million or so in annual profits, more than enough to make its employees happy.

"No," Simons responded. "We can do better."

Simons insisted on finding a way to grow the fund, frustrating some staffers.

"Emperors want empires," one griped to a colleague.

Robert Frey, the former Morgan Stanley quant who was working at Kepler, the separate stock-trading venture backed by Simons, had a kinder interpretation of Simons's stubborn push to grow Medallion. Simons was determined to accomplish something special, says Frey, maybe even pioneer a new approach to trading.

"What Jim wants to do is matter," Frey says. "He wanted a life that meant something. . . . If he was going to do a fund, he wanted to be the best."

Frey has an additional theory about why Simons was so intent on expanding the fund.

"Jim saw his chance to be a billionaire," Frey says.

Simons had long been driven by two ever-present motivations: proving he could solve big problems, and making lots and lots of money. Friends never fully understood his need to accumulate more wealth, but it was ceaseless and ever-present.

There was only one way Simons could grow Medallion without crippling its returns: expand into stock investing. Because equity markets are deep and easy to trade, even huge size wouldn't impede profits. The catch was that making money in equity markets had long confounded Simons and his team. Frey was still working on his trading strategies at Kepler, but the results were lackluster, adding to Simons's pressures.

Hoping to keep the fund's performance afloat and improve the operation's efficiency, Simons moved to consolidate all his operations on Long Island, uprooting ten longtime employees in Northern California, including Sandor Straus, who had a son in high school and protested the move. Straus said he was unwilling to leave for Long Island and was unhappy Simons was forcing his California-based colleagues to transplant their lives. Straus ran the trading operation, was the last remaining member of the original firm, and was a key reason for its success. Straus owned a piece of Renaissance, and he demanded a vote of fellow shareholders on the cross-country relocation. Straus lost, leading to more frustration.

In 1996, Straus sold his Renaissance shares and quit, a fresh blow for Simons. Later, Simons would force Straus and other nonemployees to pull their money out of Medallion. Straus could have insisted on special treatment that might have allowed him to invest in the fund indefinitely, but he figured he'd just invest with funds that enjoyed similar prospects.

"I thought we were one of many," Straus says. "If I thought there was some secret sauce, I would have made sure I could stay invested in Medallion."

=

As Simons and his team struggled to find a new direction and deal with Straus's departure, he didn't get much sympathy from his old friends in mathematics. They still didn't get why he was devoting so much time and energy to financial markets; all they saw was a generational talent wasting his time on frivolity. One weekend afternoon after Simons left Stony Brook, Dennis Sullivan, a well-known topologist at Stony Brook, visited Simons at home, watching as he organized a birthday party for his son, Nathaniel, Simons's third child with Barbara. As Simons handed out water guns and participated in the ensuing high jinks, Sullivan rolled his eyes.

"It annoyed me," Sullivan says. "Math is sacred, and Jim was a serious mathematician who could solve the hardest problems. . . . I was disappointed in his choices."

Other times, Simons was seen joking around with Nicholas, his first child with Marilyn, who was outgoing like his father and shared his sometimes-mischievous sense of humor.

Sullivan's perspective slowly changed as he grew closer with Simons, spending time at his home and witnessing Simons's devotion to his aging parents, who frequently visited from Boston. Sullivan gained an appreciation for the attention Simons gave to his children, especially Paul, who continued to battle his birth disorder. At seventeen, Paul had suffered an epileptic seizure, and he subsequently began taking medication that eliminated future attacks.

Jim and Barbara saw signs of emerging self-confidence in their son. All his life, Paul worked to strengthen his body, doing a series of pull-ups and push-ups almost every day, while also becoming an accomplished skier and endurance bicycle rider. A free spirit, Paul demonstrated little interest in mathematics or trading. As an adult, he hiked, skied, played with his dog, Avalon, and developed a close relationship with a local young woman. Paul especially enjoyed cycling through tranquil, dormant land near Mill Pond in Stony Brook, spending hours at a time on his favorite bike route.

In September 1996, after turning thirty-four years old, Paul donned a jersey and shorts, hopped on his world-class bicycle, and set off on a fast ride through Old Field Road in Setauket, near his boyhood home. Out of nowhere, an elderly woman backed her car out of the driveway, unaware the young man was riding past. She hit Paul, crushing and killing him instantly, a random and tragic accident. Several days later, the woman, traumatized by the experience, had a heart attack and died.

Jim and Barbara were devastated. For weeks afterward, Simons was a shell of himself.

Simons leaned on his family for support, withdrawing from work and other activities. Colleagues didn't know how Simons would cope with his pain, or how long it would last.

"You never get over it," Barbara says. "You just learn to deal with it."

When Simons eventually returned to work, his friends sensed he needed a distraction. Simons refocused on his team's disappointing efforts to master stock trading, his last chance to build his firm into a power.

For a while, it seemed Simons was wasting his time.

CHAPTER NINE

No one ever made a decision because of a number.
They need a story.

Daniel Kahneman, economist

Jim Simons seemed to have discovered the perfect way to trade commodities, currencies, and bonds: predictive mathematical models. Yet, Simons knew, if he wanted Renaissance Technologies to amount to much of anything, he'd have to get his computers to make money in stocks.

It wasn't clear why Simons thought he had a chance of success. The early 1990s was a golden age for *fundamental* investors, those who generally chat up companies and digest annual reports, financial filings and statements à la Warren Buffett. These investors tap instinct, cunning, and experience. It was all about brainpower, not computing power. When it came to stocks, Simons seemed well out of his depth.

Peter Lynch was a paragon of the fundamental approach. From 1977 to 1990, Lynch's prescient stock picks helped Fidelity Investments' Magellan mutual fund grow from a $100 million pip-squeak into a $16 billion power, averaging annual gains of 29 percent, beating the market in eleven of those years. Ignoring historic and overlooked pricing patterns—the stuff Simons obsessed over—Lynch said investors could trounce the market simply by sticking with companies they understood best. "Know what you own" was Lynch's mantra.

Searching for *story* stocks that he believed would experience surging earnings, Lynch made a killing on Dunkin' Donuts, the doughnut retailer beloved in Fidelity's home state of Massachusetts, purchasing shares partly because the company "didn't have to worry about low-priced Korean imports." Another time, Lynch's wife, Carolyn, brought home a pair of L'eggs, a brand of pantyhose that was stuffed into distinctive, egg-shaped plastic containers and sold in supermarket and drugstore checkout aisles. Carolyn loved L'eggs, so her husband did, too, backing up the truck to buy shares of its manufacturer, Hanes, even though most hosiery products at the time were sold in department stores and women's clothing stores, not in drugstores.

"I did a little bit of research," Lynch later explained. "I found out the average woman goes to the supermarket or a drugstore once a week, and they go to a woman's specialty store or department store once every six weeks. And all the good hosiery, all the good pantyhose, is being sold in department stores. They were selling junk in the supermarkets."

When a rival brand of pantyhose was introduced, Lynch bought forty-eight pairs and asked employees to test them out, determining they couldn't match the quality of his L'eggs. Over time, Lynch rode Hanes to a gain of ten times his fund's initial investment.

Lynch's most important tool was his telephone, not his computer. He'd regularly call, or sometimes visit, a network of well-placed executives, asking for updates on their businesses, competitors, suppliers, customers, and more. These were legal tactics at the time, even though smaller investors couldn't access the same information.

"The computer won't tell you [if a business trend] is going to last a month or a year," Lynch said.[1]

By 1990, one out of every one hundred Americans was invested in Magellan, and Lynch's book, *One Up on Wall Street*, sold more than a million copies, inspiring investors to search for stocks "from the supermarket to the workplace." As Fidelity came to dominate mutual funds, it began sending young analysts to call on hundreds of companies each year. Lynch's successors, including Jeffrey Vinik, used the trips to gain their own, entirely legal, information advantage over rivals.

"Vinik would ask us to have conversations with cabdrivers on our way from and to the airport to get a sense of the local economy or the particular company we were visiting," recalls J. Dennis Jean-Jacques, who was a Fidelity analyst at the time. "We would also eat in the company cafeteria . . . or at a nearby restaurant, so we could ask the waiter questions about the company across the street."

As Lynch and Vinik racked up big gains in Boston, Bill Gross was on the other side of the country, on the shores of Newport Beach, California, building a bond empire at a company called Pacific Investment Management Company, or PIMCO. Gross, who paid his way through business school with blackjack winnings after reading Ed Thorp's book on gambling, was especially adept at predicting the direction of global interest rates. He became well known in the financial world for thoughtful, colorful market observations, as well as a unique look. Each day, Gross wore open-collared, custom-made dress shirts with a tie draped loosely around his neck, a style adopted after vigorous exercise and yoga sessions left him overheated and unwilling to knot his tie once in the office.

Like Simons, Gross used a mathematical approach to dissect his investments, though Gross melded his formulas with a heavy dose of intuition and intelligence. Gross emerged as a true market savant in 1995, after a huge wager on falling interest rates generated gains of 20 percent for his bond mutual fund, which became the largest ever of its kind. Investors crowned him "the Bond King," a name that would stick as Gross began an extended reign atop debt markets.

Around the same time, so-called macro investors grabbed headlines and instilled fear in global political leaders with their own distinct style. Instead of placing thousands of bets, like Simons, these traders made the bulk of their profits from a limited number of gutsy moves aimed at anticipating global political and economic shifts.

Stanley Druckenmiller was one of the traders on the ascent. A shaggy-haired Pittsburgh native who had dropped out of a PhD program in economics, Druckenmiller was a top-performing mutual-fund manager before taking over George Soros's billion-dollar hedge fund, the Quantum Fund. Thirty-five years old at the time, Druckenmiller arrived at his investment decisions after scrutinizing news and studying economic statistics and other information, aiming to place his trades well ahead of big global events.

It only took six months for Soros to regret hiring Druckenmiller. As Druckenmiller flew to Pittsburgh, Soros dumped his bond positions without even a warning, worried they were losers. Apprised of the move after landing, Druckenmiller found a nearby pay phone and called in his resignation.[2]

A bit later, back in the office, nerves calmed and apologies issued, Soros said he was departing for a six-month trip to Europe, a separation period to see if Druckenmiller's early losing streak was due to "us having too many cooks in the kitchen, or whether you're just inept."

Months later, the Berlin Wall dividing West Germany and East Germany was opened and eventually toppled. The world cheered, but investors worried the West German economy and its currency, the deutsche mark, would be crippled by a merger with much-poorer East Germany. That view didn't make much sense to Druckenmiller; an influx of cheap labor seemed likely to bolster the German economy, not hurt it, and the German central bank could be expected to bolster its currency to keep inflation at bay.

"I had a very strong belief that the Germans were obsessed with inflation," Druckenmiller recalls, noting that surging inflation after World War I had paved the way for the rise of Adolf Hitler. "There was no way they would let the currency go down."

With Soros out of the way, Druckenmiller placed a huge bet on deutsche marks, resulting in a gain of nearly 30 percent for the Quantum Fund in 1990. Two years later, with Soros back in New York and relations improved between the two men, Druckenmiller walked into Soros's expansive midtown office to share his next big move: slowly expanding an existing wager against the British pound. Druckenmiller told Soros authorities in the country were bound to break from the European Exchange Rate Mechanism and allow the pound to fall in value, helping Britain emerge from recession. His stance was unpopular, Druckenmiller acknowledged, but he professed confidence the scenario would unfold.

Complete silence from Soros. Then, an expression of bewilderment.

Soros gave a look "like I was a moron," Druckenmiller recalls.

"That doesn't make sense," Soros told him.

Before Druckenmiller had a chance to defend his thesis, Soros cut him off.

"Trades like this only happen every twenty years or so," Soros said.

He was imploring Druckenmiller to expand his bet.

The Quantum Fund sold short about $10 billion of the British currency. Rivals, learning what was happening or arriving at similar conclusions, were soon doing the same, pushing the pound lower while exerting pressure on British authorities. On September 16, 1992, the government abandoned its efforts to prop up the pound, devaluing the currency by 20 percent, earning Druckenmiller and Soros more than $1 billion in just twenty-four hours. The fund gained over 60 percent in 1993 and soon controlled over $8 billion of cash from investors, dwarfing anything Simons dreamed of managing. For more than a decade, the trade would be considered the greatest ever, a testament to how much can be made with heavy doses of savvy and moxie.

It was self-evident that the surest way to score huge sums in the market was by unearthing corporate information and analyzing economic trends. The idea that someone could use computers to beat these seasoned pros seemed far-fetched.

Jim Simons, still struggling to make money trading stocks, didn't need any reminder. Kepler Financial, the company launched by former Morgan Stanley math and computer specialist Robert Frey that Simons had backed, was just plodding along. The firm was improving on the statistical-arbitrage strategies Frey and others had employed at Morgan Stanley by identifying a small set of market-wide factors that best explained stock moves. The trajectory of United Airlines shares, for example, is determined by the stock's sensitivity to the returns of the overall market, changes in the price of oil, the movement of interest rates, and other factors. The direction of another stock, like Walmart, is influenced by the same explanatory factors, though the retail giant likely has a very different sensitivity to each of them.

Kepler's twist was to apply this approach to statistical arbitrage, buying stocks that didn't rise as much as expected based on the historic returns of these various underlying factors, while simultaneously selling short, or wagering against, shares that underperformed. If shares of Apple Computer and Starbucks each rose 10 percent amid a market rally, but Apple historically did much better than Starbucks during bullish periods, Kepler might buy Apple and short Starbucks. Using time-series analysis and other statistical techniques, Frey and a colleague searched for *trading errors*, behavior not fully explained by historic data tracking the key factors, on the assumption that these deviations likely would disappear over time.

Betting on relationships and relative differences between groups of stocks, rather than an outright rise or fall of shares, meant Frey didn't need to predict where shares were headed, a difficult task for anyone. He and his colleagues also didn't really care where the overall market was going. As a result, Kepler's portfolio was *market neutral*, or reasonably immune to the stock market's moves. Frey's models usually just focused on whether relationships between clusters of stocks returned to their historic norms—a reversion-to-the-mean strategy. Constructing a portfolio of these investments figured to dampen the fund's volatility, giving it a high Sharpe ratio. Named after economist William F. Sharpe, the Sharpe ratio is a commonly used measure of returns that incorporates a portfolio's risk. A high Sharpe suggests a strong and stable historic performance.

Kepler's hedge fund, eventually renamed Nova, generated middling results that frustrated clients, a few of whom bolted. The fund was subsumed into Medallion while Frey continued his efforts, usually without tremendous success.

The problem wasn't that Frey's system couldn't discover profitable strategies. It was unusually good at identifying profitable trades and forecasting the movement of groups of shares. It was that, too often, the team's profits paled in comparison to those predicted by their model. Frey was like a chef with a delicious recipe who cooked a series of memorable meals but dropped most of them on the way to the dinner table.

Watching Frey and his colleagues flail, some Renaissance staffers began to lose patience. Laufer, Patterson, and the others had developed a sophisticated system to buy and sell various commodities and other investments, featuring a betting algorithm that adjusted its holdings given the range of probabilities of future market moves. Frey's team had nothing of the sort for stocks. Staffers carped that his trading model seemed much too sensitive to tiny market fluctuations. It sometimes bought shares and sold them before they had a chance to rise, spooked by a sudden move in price. There was too much noise in the market for Frey's system to hear any of its signals.

It would take two oddballs to help solve the problem for Simons. One rarely talked. The other could barely sit still.

=

As Nick Patterson worked with Henry Laufer in the early 1990s to improve Medallion's predictive models, he began a side job he seemed to relish as much as discovering overlooked price trends: recruiting talent for Renaissance's growing staff. To upgrade the firm's computer systems, for example, Patterson helped hire Jacqueline Rosinsky as the first systems administrator. Rosinsky, whose husband ditched an accounting career to become a captain in the New York City Fire Department, would eventually head information technology and other areas. (Later, women would manage legal and other departments, but it would be a while before they'd play significant roles on the research, data, or trading sides of the operation.*) Patterson required a few things from his hires. They needed to be supersmart, of course, with identifiable accomplishments, such as academic papers or awards, ideally in fields lending themselves to the work Renaissance was doing. Patterson steered clear of Wall Street types. He didn't have anything against them, per se; he just was convinced he could find more impressive talent elsewhere.

"We can teach you about money," Patterson explains. "We can't teach you about smart."

Besides, Patterson argued to a colleague, if someone left a bank or hedge fund to join Renaissance, they'd be more inclined to bolt at some point for a rival, if the opportunity ever arose, than someone without a familiarity with the investment community. That was crucial, because Simons insisted that everyone at the firm actively share their work with each other. Simons needed to trust that his staffers weren't going to take that information and run off to a competitor.

One last thing got Patterson especially excited: if a potential recruit was miserable in their current job.

---

*It wasn't that the company had a problem hiring women. Like other trading firms, Renaissance didn't receive many resumes from female scientists or mathematicians. It's also the case that Simons and others didn't go out of their way to recruit women or minorities.

"I liked smart people who were probably unhappy," Patterson says.

One day, after reading in the morning paper that IBM was slashing costs, Patterson became intrigued. He was aware of the accomplishments of the computer giant's speech-recognition group and thought their work bore similarity to what Renaissance was doing. In early 1993, Patterson sent separate letters to Peter Brown and Robert Mercer, deputies of the group, inviting them to visit Renaissance's offices to discuss potential positions.

Brown and Mercer both reacted the exact same way—depositing Patterson's letter in the closest trash receptacle. They'd reconsider after experiencing family upheaval, laying the groundwork for dramatic change at Jim Simons's company, and the world as a whole.

=

Robert Mercer's lifelong passion had been sparked by his father.

A brilliant scientist with a dry wit, Thomas Mercer was born in Victoria, British Columbia, later becoming a world expert on aerosols, the tiny particles suspended in the atmosphere that both contribute to air pollution and cool the earth by blocking the sun. Thomas spent more than a decade as a professor of radiation biology and biophysics at the University of Rochester before becoming department head of a foundation devoted to curing respiratory disease in Albuquerque, New Mexico. It was there that Robert, the eldest of Thomas's three children, was born in 1946.

His mother, Virginia Mercer, was passionate about the theater and arts, but Robert was riveted by computers. It began the very moment Thomas showed Robert the magnetic drum and punch cards of an IBM 650, one of the earliest mass-produced computers. After Thomas explained the computer's inner workings to his son, the ten-year-old began creating his own programs, filling up an oversize notebook. Bob carried that notebook around for years before he ever had access to an actual computer.

At Sandia High School and the University of New Mexico, Mercer was a bespectacled, lanky, and low-key member of the school's chess, auto, and Russian clubs. He came alive for math, though, sharing a proud, handsome smile in a photo appearing in the *Albuquerque Journal* after he and two classmates won top honors in a national mathematics contest in 1964.[3]

After high school graduation, Mercer spent three weeks at the National Youth Science Camp in the mountains of West Virginia. There, Mercer discovered a single computer, a donated IBM 1620, that could do fifty ten-digit multiplications a second but was neglected by most campers. Apparently, sitting indoors all day in the summer wasn't as enticing to them as it was to Mercer, so he got to play with the computer as much as he wanted, learning to program in Fortran, a language developed mainly for scientists. That summer, Neil Armstrong paid a visit to the camp, five years prior to becoming the first man to set foot on the moon. He told the campers that astronauts were using the latest computer technology, some of it the size of a match. Mercer sat listening, mouth agape.

"I couldn't see how that would even be possible," he later recalled.

While studying physics, chemistry, and mathematics at the University of New Mexico, Mercer got a job at a weapons laboratory at the Kirtland Air Force Base eight miles away, just so he could help program the base's supercomputer. Much as baseball players appreciate the smell of fresh-cut outfield grass or the site of a well-groomed pitcher's mound, Mercer came to delight in the sights and smells of Kirtland's computer lab.

"I loved everything about computers," Mercer later explained. "I loved the solitude of the computer lab late at night. I loved the air-conditioned smell of the place. I loved the sound of the discs whirring, and the printers clacking."

It might seem a bit unusual, even odd, for a young man to be so enthralled by a computer laboratory, but, in the mid-1960s, these machines came to represent unexplored terrain and fresh possibility. A subculture developed of young computer specialists, academics and hobbyists who stayed up late into the night *coding*, or writing instructions so computers could solve problems or execute specified, automated tasks. The instructions were given using algorithms, which entailed a series of logical, step-by-step procedures.

Bright young men and women, the programmers were counterculture rebels, boldly exploring the future, even as their peers chased the fleeting pleasures of the day, forging a spirit and energy that would change the world for decades to come.

"We suffered socially and psychologically for being right," says Aaron Brown, a member of the emerging coder crew who became a senior executive of the quant-trading world.

As an inductee into the cult, Mercer spent the summer on the lab's mainframe computer rewriting a program that calculated electromagnetic fields generated by nuclear fusion bombs. In time, Mercer found ways to make the program one hundred times faster, a real coup. Mercer was energized and enthused, but his bosses didn't seem to care about his accomplishment. Instead of running the old computations at the new, faster speed, they instructed Mercer to run computations that were one hundred times the size. It seemed Mercer's revved-up speed made little difference to them, an attitude that helped mold the young man's worldview.

"I took this as an indication that one of the most important goals of government-financed research is not so much to get answers as it is to consume the computer budget," Mercer later said.

He turned cynical, viewing government as arrogant and inefficient. Years later, Mercer would embrace the view that individuals need to be self-sufficient and avoid state aid.

The summer experience "left me, ever since, with a jaundiced view of government-financed research," Mercer explained.[4]

After earning his PhD in computer science at the University of Illinois, Mercer joined IBM in 1972, even though he was dismissive of the quality of the company's computers. It was a different part of the company that had impressed him. Mercer had agreed to visit the Thomas J. Watson Research Center in the New York City suburb of Yorktown Heights and was struck by hard-charging IBM staffers pushing to discover innovations that could power the company's future.

Mercer joined the team and began working in the company's newly formed speech-recognition group. Eventually, he was joined by a young and outgoing mathematician in a hurry to accomplish something big.

═

As a teenager, Peter Brown watched his father deal with a series of daunting business challenges. In 1972, when Peter was seventeen, Henry Brown and a partner came up with the idea of cobbling together investments from individual investors to buy relatively safe, yet higher-yielding debt, introducing the world's first money-market mutual fund. Henry's fund offered higher rates than those available in bank savings accounts, but few investors had even a passing interest. Peter would help his father stuff envelopes and mail letters to hundreds of potential customers, hoping to elicit interest in the new fund. Henry worked every day that year except Christmas, resorting to eating peanut-butter sandwiches and taking out a second mortgage to fund his business, as his wife, Betsey, worked as a family therapist.

"A combination of starvation and pure greed drove us," Henry explained to the *Wall Street Journal*.[5]

His lucky break came the next year in the form of a *New York Times* article about the fledgling fund. Clients began calling, and soon Henry and his partner were managing $100 million in their Reserve Primary Fund. The fund grew, reaching billions of dollars, but Henry resigned, in 1985, to move with Betsey to the Brown family's farm in a Virginia hamlet, where he raised cattle on five hundred acres. Henry also competed in trebuchet, a kind of mechanical catapult, winning competitions with a contraption that sent an

Simons as a student.

Simons (left) setting out for Buenos Aires with his friends.

Simons (left) with Lee Neuwirth and Jack Ferguson, co-workers at the IDA.

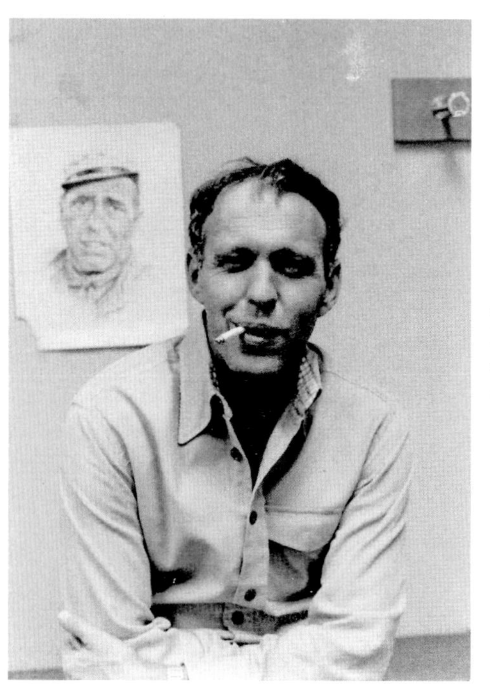

Simons was known among his friends for his humor—and a passing resemblance to Humphrey Bogart.

Renaissance's original offices, near a women's clothing boutique, a pizza restaurant, and the Stony Brook train station.

Lenny Baum became a devoted Go player despite his deteriorating eyesight.

James Ax was brilliant, handsome—
and frequently angry.

Later in life, Ax moved to San Diego.

Elwyn Berlekamp helped Simons during a crucial period.

Bob Mercer (left) and Peter Brown were responsible for Renaissance's key breakthroughs. COURTESY OF *WALL STREET JOURNAL* AND JENNY STRASBURG

Bob and Rebekah Mercer played active roles in aiding Donald Trump's presidential quest.

Simons and his wife, Marilyn, with acclaimed academics Shiing-Shen Chern (seated) and Chen Ning Yang.

Simons lecturing about mathematics.

Simons with his favorite lemur at a Stony Brook event.

Jim and Marilyn Simons.

eight-pound pumpkin over one thousand feet. In their new neighborhood, Betsey became a civic activist and local Democratic politician.

Henry's business still dominated his thoughts, though. For more than a decade, he squabbled with his former partner, Bruce Bent, whom Henry accused of reneging on an agreement to buy his half-interest in the company. Henry eventually filed a lawsuit, claiming Bent was rewarding himself excessively while running the fund, before the men finally worked out a deal for Brown to sell his half-ownership to Brent in 1999. (In 2008, the fund would lose so much money from the debt of investment bank Lehman Brothers, among other things, that its troubles would sow fear throughout the financial system.)

While his family had wealth, friends say Peter sometimes expressed anxiety about his finances, perhaps due to his father's early challenges or his extended battle with his partner. Peter reserved his own ambitions for science and math. After graduating from Harvard University with an undergraduate degree in mathematics, Brown joined a unit of Exxon that was developing ways to translate spoken language into computer text, an early form of speech-recognition technology. Later, he'd earn a PhD in computer science from Carnegie Mellon University in Pittsburgh.

In 1984, at the age of twenty-nine, Brown joined IBM's speech group, where Mercer and others had been working to develop computer software to transcribe spoken text. Conventional wisdom in the decades-old field was that only linguists and phoneticians, teaching computers rules of syntax and grammar, had a chance at getting computers to recognize language.

Brown, Mercer, and their fellow mathematicians and scientists, including the group's hard-driving leader, Fred Jelinek, viewed language very differently from the traditionalists. To them, language could be modeled like a game of chance. At any point in a sentence, there exists a certain probability of what might come next, which can be estimated based on past, common usage. "Pie" is more likely to follow the word "apple" in a sentence than words like "him" or "the," for example. Similar probabilities also exist for pronunciation, the IBM crew argued.

Their goal was to feed their computers with enough data of recorded speech and written text to develop a probabilistic, statistical model capable of predicting likely word sequences based on sequences of sounds. Their computer code wouldn't necessarily *understand* what it was transcribing, but it would learn to transcribe language, nonetheless.

In mathematical terms, Brown, Mercer, and the rest of Jelinek's team viewed sounds as the output of a sequence in which each step along the way is random, yet dependent on the previous step—a hidden Markov model. A speech-recognition system's job was to take a set of observed sounds, crunch the probabilities, and make the best possible guess about the "hidden" sequences of words that could have generated those sounds. To do that, the IBM researchers employed the Baum-Welch algorithm—codeveloped by Jim Simons's early trading partner Lenny Baum—to zero in on the various language probabilities. Rather than manually programming in static knowledge about how language worked, they created a program that *learned* from data.

Brown, Mercer, and the others relied upon Bayesian mathematics, which had emerged from the statistical rule proposed by Reverend Thomas Bayes in the eighteenth-century. Bayesians will attach a degree of probability to every guess and update their best estimates as they receive new information. The genius of Bayesian statistics is that it continuously narrows a range of possibilities. Think, for example, of a spam filter, which doesn't know with certainty if an email is malicious, but can be effective by assigning odds to each one received by constantly learning from emails previously classified as "junk." (This approach wasn't as strange as it might seem. According to linguists, people in conversation unconsciously guess the next words that will be spoken, updating their expectations along the way.)

The IBM team was as unique in personality as in method, especially Mercer. Tall and fit, Mercer jumped rope to stay in shape. As a younger man, he had displayed a passing resemblance to the actor Ryan Reynolds, but that was about all Mercer had in common with Hollywood flash. He developed a laconic, efficient style of interaction, wasting few words and avoiding speaking unless he deemed it necessary, a quirk some fellow scientists appreciated. Mercer sometimes let out an "I cracked it!" after solving a difficult computation, but he generally was content humming or whistling to himself all day long, usually classical music. Mercer didn't drink coffee, tea, or alcohol; he mostly stuck with Coca-Cola. On the rare occasions that he became frustrated, Mercer would yell out "bull-twaddle," which colleagues understood to be an amalgam of "bullshit" and "twaddle," or idle talk.

Mercer had such long arms that his wife sewed him dress shirts with extended sleeves, as well as odd colors and patterns. At a Halloween party one year, Jelinek, who had a mean streak, came dressed as Mercer, wearing a shirt with impossibly long sleeves. Mercer laughed along with his colleagues.

Mercer got to the office at six o'clock in the morning and met Brown and other colleagues for lunch at 11:15 a.m. Mercer consumed the same thing almost every day: a peanut-butter-and-jelly or tuna sandwich packed in a reusable Tupperware container or a used, folded brown paper bag, which fellow researchers interpreted as a sign of frugality. After his sandwich, Mercer would open a bag of potato chips, lay them out on a table in order of size, eat the broken ones first, and then the rest, smallest to largest.

On Friday afternoons, the team met for soda, tea, cookies, and coffee cake. As they chatted, the researchers sometimes complained about IBM's substandard pay. Other times, Mercer shared sections from an etymological dictionary he found especially amusing. Once in a while, he'd issue statements that seemed aimed at getting a rise out of his lunch-mates, such as the time he declared that he thought he would live forever.

Brown was more animated, approachable, and energetic, with thick, curly brown hair and an infectious charm. Unlike Mercer, Brown forged friendships within the group, several members of which appreciated his sneaky sense of humor.

As the group struggled to make progress in natural-language processing, though, Brown showed impatience, directing special ire at an intern named Phil Resnik. A graduate student at the University of Pennsylvania who had earned a bachelor of arts in computer science at Harvard University and would later become a respected academic, Resnik hoped to combine mathematical tactics with linguistic principles. Brown had little patience for Resnik's approach, mocking his younger colleague and jumping on his mistakes.

One day, as a dozen IBM staffers watched Resnik work through an issue on an office whiteboard, Brown ran up to him, grabbed the marker out of Resnik's hand, and sneered, "This is kindergarten computer science!"

Resnik sat back down, embarrassed.

Another time, Brown called Resnik "worthless" and "a complete idiot."

Brown developed insulting nicknames for many of his junior colleagues, members of the group recall. He called Meredith Goldsmith, the only woman in the group, "Merry Death," for example, or referred to her as "Jennifer," the name of a previous member of the group. Most frequently, Brown called Goldsmith "little Miss Meredith," a name the recent Yale University graduate viewed as particularly belittling.

Mercer and Brown helped mentor Goldsmith, which she appreciated. But Mercer also shared his opinion with her that women belonged at home, taking care of children, not in the working world.

Brown, whose wife had been appointed head of public health for New York City, viewed himself a progressive. He valued Goldsmith's contributions and told her she was like a daughter to him. Yet, that didn't stop Brown from allowing inappropriate jokes to flow amid the group's locker-room environment.

"They told dirty jokes all the time; it was a sport," she recalls.

Goldsmith eventually quit, partly due to the uncomfortable environment in the group.

"In a sense they were both nice and sexist to me," Goldsmith says. "I definitely felt objectified and not taken seriously."

Brown didn't mean anything personal by the insults, or at least that's what members of the group told themselves. And he wasn't the only one who enjoyed chewing out or mocking others. A fierce and ruthless culture existed within the group, inspired by Jelinek's ornery personality. Researchers would posit ideas and colleagues would do everything they could to eviscerate them, throwing personal jabs along the way. They'd fight it out until reaching a consensus on the merits of the suggestion. Twin brothers in the group, Stephen and Vincent Della Pietra, each of whom had undergraduate degrees in physics from Princeton and doctorates in physics from Harvard, leveled some of the most vicious assaults, racing to a whiteboard to prove how foolish each other's arguments had been. It was no-holds-barred intellectual combat. Outside of a research lab, such behavior might be considered rude and offensive, but many of Jelinek's staffers usually didn't take it personally.

"We ripped each other to shreds," recalls David Magerman, an intern on the IBM speech team. "And then we played tennis together."

Beyond a talent for cruel and colorful nicknames, Brown stood out for having unusual commercial instincts, perhaps the result of his father's influence. Brown urged IBM to use the team's advances to sell new products to customers, such as a credit-evaluation service, and even tried to get management to let them manage a few billion dollars of IBM's pension-fund investments with their statistical approach, but failed to garner much support.

"What kind of investing experience do you have?" a colleague recalls an IBM executive asking Brown.

"None," Brown replied.

At one point, Brown learned of a team of computer scientists, led by a former Carnegie Mellon classmate, that was programming a computer to play chess. He set out to convince IBM to hire the team. One winter day, while Brown was in an IBM men's room, he got to talking with Abe Peled, a senior IBM research executive, about the exorbitant cost of the upcoming Super Bowl's television commercials. Brown said he had a way to get the company exposure at a much lower cost—hire the Carnegie Mellon team and reap the resulting publicity when their machine beat a world champion in chess. The team members also might be able to assist IBM's research, Brown argued.

The IBM brass loved the idea and hired the team, which brought its Deep Thought program along. As the machine won matches and attracted attention, though, complaints emerged. It turned out that the chess machine's name made people think of something else—famed 1972 pornographic film *Deep Throat*, a movie at the forefront of what is known as the Golden Age of Porn (details to follow in my next book). IBM knew it faced a real problem the day the wife of a member of the chess team, who taught at a Catholic college, spoke with the college's president, an elderly nun, and the sister kept referring to IBM's amazing "Deep Throat" program.

IBM ran a contest to rename the chess machine, choosing Brown's own submission, Deep Blue, a nod to IBM's longtime nickname, Big Blue. A few years later, in 1997, millions would watch on television as Deep Blue defeated Garry Kasparov, the chess world champion, a signal that the computing age had truly arrived.[6]

Brown, Mercer, and the rest of the team made progress enabling computers to transcribe speech. Later, Brown realized probabilistic mathematical models also could be used for translation. Using data that included thousands of pages of Canadian parliamentary proceedings featuring paired passages in French and English, the IBM team made headway toward translating text between languages. Their advances partly laid the groundwork for a revolution in computational linguistics and speech processing, playing a role in future speech-recognition advances, such as Amazon's Alexa, Apple's Siri, Google Translate, text-to-speech synthesizers, and more.

Despite that progress, the researchers were frustrated by IBM's lack of a clear plan to let the group commercialize its advances. Weeks after throwing Patterson's letter in the garbage, Brown and Mercer were forced to reexamine the direction of their lives.

On a late-winter day in southeastern Pennsylvania in 1993, Mercer's mother was killed and his sister injured when another driver skidded on ice and crashed into their car. That Easter, twenty days later, Mercer's father succumbed to a progressive illness. A few months later, when Patterson called to ask why he hadn't received a response to his previous letter, Mercer began to consider a move. Mercer's third daughter had begun college, and his family lived in a modest split-level home near ugly electrical power lines. Eating lunch out of used brown paper bags had begun to lose its charm.

"Just come and talk to me," Patterson said. "What have you got to lose?"

Mercer told a colleague he was skeptical that hedge funds added anything to society. Another IBM staffer said any effort to profit from trading was "hopeless" because markets are so efficient. But Mercer came back from the visit impressed. Renaissance's offices, in a high-tech incubator on Stony Brook campus, were quite bland. But they had been designed originally as a chemistry lab, with tiny windows high up on the walls, a layout that suggested science, not finance, was the focus of Simons's firm, something that appealed to Mercer.

As for Brown, he had heard of Simons, but his accomplishments meant little to him. Simons was a geometer, after all, a member of a very different field. But when Brown learned Simons's original partner was Lenny Baum, coinventor of the Baum-Welch algorithm the IBM speech team relied upon, Brown became more enthused. By then, his wife, Margaret, had given birth to their first child, and he faced his own financial concerns.

"I looked at our newborn daughter, and thought about Bob struggling with college bills, and began to think that it might actually make some sense to work in the investment area for a few years," Brown later told a group of scientists.

Simons offered to double Brown's and Mercer's salaries and they eventually came on board in 1993—just as tension was building over the firm's continued inability to master stock trading. Some researchers and others urged Simons to terminate the effort. Frey and his team had spent enough time and still didn't have much to show for themselves, these critics said.

"We're wasting our time," one told Frey one day in the Renaissance lunchroom. "Do we really need to do this?"

"We're making progress," Frey insisted.

Some on the futures team said Frey should give up on his stock research and work on projects with them. Publicly and privately, Simons came to Frey's defense. Simons said he was sure the team would discover ways to make huge profits in stock trading, just as Laufer, Patterson, and others had on their thriving futures-trading side business.

"Let's just wait a little longer," Simons told a skeptic.

Others times, he tried bolstering Frey's confidence.

"That's good work," Simons told Frey. "Never give up."

Brown and Mercer watched the equity team's struggles with particular interest. Shortly after arriving from IBM, they were split up. Mercer was sent to work in the futures group, while Brown helped Frey with the stock picks. Simons was hoping to better integrate them into the firm, like kids being separated in a classroom out of fear they'd only talk to each other. In their spare time, though, Brown and Mercer met, searching for ways to solve Simons's dilemma. They thought they might have a solution. For a true breakthrough, however, they'd need help from another unusual IBM staffer.

CHAPTER TEN

David Magerman shut the door of his Boston apartment well before dawn on a cool morning in the fall of 1994. He jumped into a silver Toyota Corolla, adjusted the car's manual windows, and headed south. The twenty-six-year-old drove more than three hours on Interstate 95 before catching a ferry to the tip of Long Island, arriving for a job interview at Renaissance Technologies' offices in Stony Brook before ten a.m.

Magerman seemed a shoo-in for the position. Jim Simons, Henry Laufer, Nick Patterson, and other staffers were acclaimed mathematicians and theoreticians, but Renaissance was starting to develop more-complex computer-trading models, and few employees could program very well. That was Magerman's specialty. He'd completed a productive stint at IBM, getting to know Peter Brown and Bob Mercer, and it was Brown who had invited him for the morning visit, giving Magerman reason to expect things to go well.

They didn't. Magerman arrived exhausted from his morning journey, regretting his penny-pinching decision not to fly from Boston. Almost immediately, Renaissance staffers got under Magerman's skin, presenting a series of difficult questions and tasks to test his competence in mathematics and other areas. Simons was low-key in a brief sit-down, but one of his researchers grilled Magerman on an obscure academic paper, making him work out a vexing problem at a tall whiteboard. It didn't seem fair; the paper was the staffer's own overlooked PhD dissertation, yet he expected Magerman to somehow demonstrate a mastery of the topic.

Magerman took the challenges a bit too personally, unsure why he was being asked to prove himself, and he overcompensated for his nervousness by acting cockier than he actually felt. By the day's end, Simons's team had decided Magerman was too immature for the job. His appearance added to the juvenile image. Sandy-haired and husky, with a baby face and rosy-pink cheeks, Magerman looked very much like an overgrown boy.

Brown stood up for Magerman, vouching for his programming skills, while Mercer also lent support. They both saw Medallion's computer code growing in size and complexity and concluded that the hedge fund desperately needed additional firepower.

"You're sure about him?" someone asked Brown. "You're sure he's good?"

"Trust us," Brown responded.

Later, when Magerman expressed interest in the job, Brown toyed with him, pretending that Renaissance had lost its interest, a prank that left Magerman anxious for days. Finally, Brown extended a formal offer. Magerman joined the firm in the summer of 1995, determined to do everything possible to win over his doubters. Until then, Magerman had spent much of his life trying to please authority figures, usually with mixed results.

Growing up, Magerman had a strained relationship with his father, Melvin, a Brooklyn cabbie plagued with awful luck. Unable to afford a taxi medallion in New York, Melvin moved his family to Kendall, Florida, fourteen miles southwest of Miami, ignoring David's heated protests. (On the eve of their departure, the eight-year-old ran away from home in a fit of anger, getting as far as a neighbor's house across the street, where he spent the afternoon until his parents retrieved him.)

For several years, Melvin drove a taxi, stuffing cash into Maxwell House coffee tins hidden around the home as he and his brother-in-law, with help from a wealthy patron, crafted a plan to buy a local cab company. On the eve of the deal, the patron suffered a fatal heart attack, scuttling Melvin's big plans. Plagued by depression throughout his life, Melvin found his mood turning still darker, and he was unable to drive a cab. Melvin collected rent at his brother-in-law's trailer park as his mental health deteriorated further. He grew aloof with David and his sister, both of whom had close relationships with their mother, Sheila, an office manager at an accounting firm.

The Magerman family lived in a lower-middle-class neighborhood populated by a mix of young families, criminals, and oddballs—including drug dealers across the street who entertained visitors at all hours, and a gun nut who liked to shoot at birds, which landed with some regularity in the Magerman backyard.

For most of his youth, David skirted serious trouble. To raise spending cash, he hawked flowers on the side of a road and sold candy in school. He'd buy candy bars and other merchandise with his father at a local drugstore and sell it out of a duffel bag to classmates at slightly higher prices. The unsanctioned business thrived until the school's rival candy man, a muscular Russian kid, was busted and pointed to David as his operation's ringleader. The school's principal, who already had labeled David a troublemaker, suspended him. While serving time in a library room with other miscreants, as in *The Breakfast Club*, an attractive female classmate asked David to join her cocaine-delivery operation in Miami. (It wasn't clear if she realized David had been busted for distributing Snickers and 3 Musketeers bars, experience that wouldn't have been of much use when selling cocaine.) David politely declined, noting that he had only a bicycle for transportation.

David placed most of his focus on his studies, relishing the unequivocal praise he received from teachers, parents, and others, especially after winning trophies at academic competitions. David participated in a local program for gifted students, learned to program computers at a community college, and won a scholarship after seventh grade to attend a private middle school a forty-five-minute bus ride away. There he learned Latin and jumped two grades in math.

Outside the classroom, David felt ostracized. He was insecure about his family's economic position, especially compared with those of his new schoolmates, and vowed to enjoy his own wealth one day. David ended up spending large chunks of the day in the school's computer lab.

"That's where we nerds hid from the football players," he says.

At home, Melvin, a math whiz who never had the opportunity to fully employ his talents, took his frustrations out on his son. After Melvin criticized David for being overweight, the young man became a long-distance runner, starving himself one summer until he showed signs of anorexia, hoping for some kind of praise from his father. Later, David entered long-distance races, emulating his track coach, though his body usually broke down by the thirteenth mile of their training sessions.

"I was easily motivated by coaches," Magerman recalls.

He continued to seek the approval of those in positions of power and seek new father figures, even as he developed a mystifying need to pick fights, even unnecessary ones.

"I needed to right wrongs and fight for justice, even if I was turning molehills into mountains," Magerman acknowledges. "I clearly had a messiah complex."

One year in high school, when he learned a track meet was scheduled for the second night of Passover, Magerman rallied local rabbis to his cause to have the meet canceled. His disappointed teammates didn't understand why Magerman cared so much; even he wasn't entirely sure.

"I was a mediocre runner and wasn't even religious. I don't think we even had a second seder," Magerman recalls. "It was a schmucky thing to do."

During his senior year, Magerman and a couple of friends announced they were leaving to spend the second semester studying at a school in Israel, partly because the principal of their high school had warned him against the idea. Magerman seemed to be searching for structure in his life. In Jerusalem, the young man began memorizing religious books, studying history, and adopting religious practices, drinking in the praise from teachers and the school's headmaster.

Before leaving for Israel, Magerman left his college essays and applications with his mother in Florida, so she could mail them to the various schools. That spring, Magerman was accepted by the University of Pennsylvania but was rejected by every other Ivy League school, surprising and disappointing him. Years later, while clearing out his mother's home, Magerman stumbled upon a copy of his Harvard University application. He discovered that she had reworked his essay, as she had for almost every other school, excising all references to Israel and Judaism, worried that anti-Semitism might deter schools from accepting him. For whatever reason, she thought Penn was a Jewish university, so she left that one untouched.

Magerman thrived at Penn, partly because he had embraced a new cause—proving the other schools had made a mistake turning him down. He excelled in his majors, computer science and mathematics. Chosen to be a teaching assistant in a computational-linguistics course, he lapped up the resulting attention and respect of his fellow students, especially the coeds. His senior-year thesis also gained some recognition. Magerman, an adorable, if insecure, teddy bear of a kid, was finally in his element.

At Stanford University, Magerman's doctoral thesis tackled the exact topic Brown, Mercer, and other IBM researchers were struggling with: how computers could analyze and translate language using statistics and probability. In 1992, IBM offered Magerman an internship. By then, he had adopted a somewhat thicker exterior and flourished in the group's sharp-elbowed culture. Magerman eventually received a full-time position at IBM, though he saw less success in other areas of his life. After spotting a young woman named Jennifer in his group, Magerman hit on her, suffering almost immediate rejection.

"She wanted nothing to do with me," he says.

It probably was for the best—it turned out that Jennifer, who went by Jenji, was the eldest daughter of Bob Mercer.

When Magerman joined Renaissance in 1995, Simons's firm didn't seem close to becoming an investing power. Its headquarters had been built to house a cutting-edge startup, but the dreary space, close to a hospital, looked more appropriate for a fading insurance company. Simons's thirty or so employees sat in drab cubicles and nondescript offices. The walls were a bare, ugly off-white, and the furniture resembled Rent-A-Center rejects. On warm days, Simons meandered around in Bermuda shorts and open-toed sandals, underscoring the hedge fund's not-ready-for-prime-time feel.

Yet there also was something vaguely intimidating about the place, at least to Magerman. Part of it was simply the stature of his new colleagues—figuratively and physically. Almost everyone was well over six feet tall, towering over the five-foot-five Magerman, breeding new insecurities in the bachelor. Magerman didn't have friends or family in the area, either. He was thrilled when Mercer's wife, Diana, invited him to a family movie outing, capped by dessert at a Friendly's restaurant. Magerman gratefully joined the Mercers on subsequent evenings, easing his transition.

It didn't take long for Magerman to realize Renaissance had a serious problem on its hands. Frey's stock-trading system had proved a dud, losing nearly 5 percent of its money in 1994. There was a certain genius to Frey's model—its statistical-arbitrage trades looked great on paper and *should* have made a lot of money. They never did, though, at least not nearly as much as the model's simulations suggested they should. It was like detecting obvious signs of gold buried deep in a mountain without having a reliable way to get it out.

In meetings, Simons sometimes shook his head, appearing to grow disappointed with the system, which they called "Nova," taking the name of Frey's firm, which had been subsumed into Renaissance.

"It's just limping along," Simons said one day.

Mercer, who continued to work with Brown on the side, tweaking their own version of a stock-trading model, diagnosed the key problem. With a look of delight on his face, Mercer roamed the halls quoting a proverb: "There's many a slip 'twixt the cup and the lip."

In those few words, Mercer was acknowledging that Frey's trading system was churning out brilliant trade ideas. But something was going wrong as it tried to implement the trades, preventing the system from making much money. Eventually, Simons and Frey decided it was best for Frey to shift to a different company project.

"I wasn't the best person to get the trains running on time," he acknowledges.

Around the same time, Mercer won approval from Simons to join Brown in the stock-research area. It was a last chance for Simons to create something special and grow his firm.

"Guys, let's make some money," Simons said in a weekly meeting, his patience appearing to grow thin.

The Brown-Mercer reunion represented a new chapter in an unusual partnership between two scientists with distinct personalities who worked remarkably well together. Brown was blunt, argumentative, persistent, loud, and full of energy. Mercer conserved his words and rarely betrayed emotion, as if he was playing a never-ending game of poker. The pairing worked, though, yin with yang.

Years earlier, as Brown was completing his doctoral thesis, he shed some light on how much he leaned on his cryptic colleague.

"Time and time again, I would come up with some idea and then realize that it was just something that Bob had urged me to try months before," Brown wrote in his introduction. "It was as if, step by step, I was uncovering some master plan."

At industry conferences during their tenure at IBM, Brown and Mercer sometimes sat together, rows from the stage, consumed by their intense chess matches while ignoring the ongoing lectures until it was time for their own presentation. They developed a certain work style—Brown would quickly write drafts of their research and then pass them to Mercer, a much better writer, who would begin slow and deliberate rewrites.

Brown and Mercer threw themselves into their new assignment to revamp Frey's model. They worked late into the evening and even went home together; during the week they shared a living space in the attic of a local elderly woman's home, returning to their families on weekends. Over time, Brown and Mercer discovered methods to improve Simons's stock-trading system. It turned out that Frey's model made suggestions that were impractical, or even impossible. For example, the Nova fund faced broker-imposed limits to the amount of *leverage*, or borrowed money, it could use. So, when Nova's leverage crossed a certain threshold, Frey and staffers manually shrank the portfolio to remain within the necessary limits, overriding their model's recommendations.

Other times, Frey's model picked trades that seemed attractive but couldn't actually be completed. For instance, it told Nova to short, or bet against, certain stocks that weren't actually available to be sold, so Frey had to ignore the recommendations.

Not completing desired trades resulted in more than just poor performance. The factor-trading system generated a series of complicated and intertwined trades, each necessary to score profits while also keeping risk at reasonable levels. By contrast, futures trading was simple stuff; if a trade didn't happen, there were few consequences. With Frey's stock-trading system, failing to get just a few moves done threatened to make the entire portfolio more sensitive to market shifts, jeopardizing its overall health. And missed trades sometimes cascaded into bigger, systemic problems that compromised the accuracy of the entire model. Getting it even a little wrong caused big problems that Frey and his team, using mid-1990s' technology and their own subpar software engineering skills, couldn't address.

"It was like finding a common solution to hundreds of equations simultaneously," Frey says.

Brown and Mercer seized on a different approach. They decided to program the necessary limitations and qualifications into a single trading system that could automatically handle all potential complications. Since Brown and Mercer were computer scientists, and they had spent years developing large-scale software projects at IBM and elsewhere, they had the coding chops to build a single automated system for trading stocks. By contrast, the coding of Frey's previous system had been done piecemeal, making it hard to unify the entire portfolio in a way that allowed it to meet all of the trading requirements.

"The people at Renaissance . . . didn't really know how to make big systems," Mercer later explained.[1]

Brown and Mercer treated their challenge as a math problem, just as they had with language recognition at IBM. Their inputs were the fund's trading costs, its various leverages, risk parameters, and assorted other limitations and requirements. Given all of those factors, they built the system to solve and construct an ideal portfolio, making optimal decisions, all day long, to maximize returns.

The beauty of the approach was that, by combining all their trading signals and portfolio requirements into a single, monolithic model, Renaissance could easily test and add new signals, instantly knowing if the gains from a potential new strategy were likely to top its costs. They also made their system *adaptive*, or capable of learning and adjusting on its own, much like Henry Laufer's trading system for futures. If the model's recommended trades weren't executed, for whatever reason, it self-corrected, automatically searching for buy-or-sell orders to nudge the portfolio back where it needed to be, a way of solving the issue that had hamstrung Frey's model. The system repeated on a loop several times an hour, conducting an optimization process that weighed thousands of potential trades before issuing electronic trade instructions. Rivals didn't have self-improving models; Renaissance now had a secret weapon, one that would prove crucial to the fund's future success.

Eventually, Brown and Mercer developed an elaborate stock-trading system that featured a half million lines of code, compared to tens of thousands of lines in Frey's old system. The new system incorporated all necessary restrictions and requirements; in many ways, it was just the kind of automated trading system Simons had dreamed of years earlier. Because the Nova fund's stock trades were now less sensitive to the market's fluctuations, it began holding on to shares a bit longer, two days or so, on average.

Crucially, Brown and Mercer retained the prediction model Frey had developed from his Morgan Stanley experience. It continued to identify enough winning trades to make serious money, usually by wagering on reversions after stocks got out of whack. Over the years, Renaissance would add twists to this bedrock strategy, but, for more than a decade, those would just be *second order* complements to the firm's core reversion-to-the-mean predictive signals.

An employee boils it down succinctly: "We make money from the reactions people have to price moves."

Brown and Mercer's new and improved trading system was implemented in 1995, a welcome relief for Simons and others. Soon, Simons made Brown and Mercer partners in Renaissance, and they were elevated to managers, receiving *points*, or a percentage of the firm's profits, like other senior members of the team.

Simons acted too quickly, it turned out. It soon became clear that the new stock-trading system couldn't handle much money, undermining Simons's original purpose in pushing into equities. Renaissance placed a puny $35 million in stocks; when more money was traded, the gains dissipated, much like

Frey's system a couple years earlier. Even worse, Brown and Mercer couldn't figure out why their system was running into so many problems.

Looking for help, they began to reassemble their team from IBM, recruiting new talent, including the Della Pietra twins, and then Magerman, who hoped to be the one to save the system.

=

As soon as he joined Renaissance, Magerman focused on solving problems and gaining the appreciation of his new colleagues. At one point, Magerman convinced staffers that they needed to learn C++, a general-purpose computer language that he insisted was much better than C and other languages the hedge fund used.

"C is *so* 1980," Magerman told a colleague.

It was true that C++ was a better language, though the shift wasn't quite as necessary as he suggested, especially at that juncture. Magerman, an expert in C++, had an ulterior motive—he wanted to become indispensable to his officemates. His stratagem worked. The company converted to C++ and, before long, mathematicians and others were begging Magerman for help, day and night.

"I became their pet," he recalls.

Magerman spent all of his free time learning the firm's stock-trading tactics, devouring each morsel of information. Brown, who had a natural ability to understand the needs of underlings, acted impressed, sensing he could motivate Magerman to work even harder by lobbing some accolades his way.

"I really thought it would take you more time" to develop such deep knowledge of the stock-trading system, Brown told him one day, as Magerman beamed with pride.

Magerman understood Brown was manipulating him, but he soaked the compliments up, nonetheless, eager to find additional ways to help. Back at IBM, Magerman had developed a *script*, or a short list of instructions, to monitor the memory and resources of the company's computers so he and others could commandeer the top brass's powerful and underutilized machines to enter outside coding competitions and engage in other unauthorized activity. Magerman, who had found an ingenious way to erase traces of his activity, called his program Joshua, after the computer gifted with artificial intelligence in the 1983 hacker film *WarGames.*

Eventually, Magerman was caught by a furious IBM executive who said his machine had been purchased under a top-secret government contract and could contain classified material. He threatened to report Magerman for committing a federal crime.

"How was I supposed to know?" Magerman responded, referring to the company's secret relationship with the government.

Magerman's hacking continued, of course, but he and his colleagues made sure to sidestep the angry executive's computer and tap into others' machines instead when they needed extra computing power.

At Renaissance, Magerman rewrote the same monitoring tool. True, there weren't any underused computers at the hedge fund like there were at IBM, but Magerman thought his program could be useful, at least down the line. Mostly, he just couldn't help himself.

"I wanted to be the most indispensable person in the company," he explains.

Magerman tricked Renaissance's systems administrator and created a backdoor way to launch his monitoring system. Then, he sat back in his chair, proudly, waiting for the accolades to roll in. Magerman's high lasted a fleeting moment or two. Suddenly, he heard shouts from alarmed colleagues. As Magerman stared at his computer screen, his jaw dropped—his unauthorized monitoring program had unleashed a computer virus that was infecting Renaissance's computers, smack in the middle of the trading day, jeopardizing all kinds of research. As staffers raced to deal with the crisis, an abashed Magerman admitted he was responsible for the chaos.

Staffers were furious—the equities team wasn't making any money, and now the stupid group was crashing the network!

Brown, red with rage, hustled over to Magerman and got in his face.

"This isn't *IBM*!" Brown screamed. "We're trading real money here! If you get in the way with your stupid stunts, you're going to ruin things for us!"

Weeks into his tenure, Magerman was a sudden outcast. He fretted about his job and wondered if he had any future at Renaissance.

"It was a huge blunder, socially," he says.

The gaffe couldn't have come at a worse time. Brown and Mercer's new stock-trading system was struggling with a painful and inexplicable losing streak. Something was awry and no one could figure out what it was. Members of the futures team, which continued to rack up profits, whispered that the problems stemmed from the new hires, who were "just computer guys." Even at Renaissance, that could be a dis, it turned out.

In public, Simons professed confidence, encouraging his team to keep at it.

"We have to keep trying," he said in a group meeting in the summer of 1995, still an intimidating presence despite his shorts and sandals.

Privately, though, Simons wondered if he was wasting his time. Maybe the team would never figure out equities, and Renaissance was destined to remain a relatively small futures-trading firm. It was a conclusion Laufer, Patterson, and others in the futures group already had reached.

"We had given it years already," Patterson says. "If I was calling the shots, I might very well have pulled the plug."

Simons remained a stubborn optimist. But even he decided enough was enough. Simons gave Brown and Mercer an ultimatum: Get your system to work in the next six months, or I'm pulling the plug. Brown stayed up nights searching for a solution, sleeping on a Murphy bed built into his office. Mercer's hours weren't quite as long, but they were equally intense. They still couldn't find the problem. The trading system scored sizable gains when it managed tiny amounts of money, but when Simons fed it leverage and the trades got bigger, profits evaporated. Brown and Mercer's simulations kept saying they should be making money with the larger sums, but the system's actual moves were losers, not unlike Frey's own trades years earlier.

Mercer seemed calm and unperturbed, but Brown's nerves were on edge, as others turned anxious around him.

"Every two- or three-day losing streak felt like the beginning of the end," says a team member.

Magerman watched the mounting frustrations and ached to aid the effort. If he could save the day, maybe he'd win his bosses over despite his earlier, costly flub. Magerman knew enough at that point not to volunteer his assistance. On his own, though, he pored over code, day and night. At the time, Magerman lived in an apartment that was an absolute mess—it lacked a working stove and there was usually close to nothing in the refrigerator—so he effectively lived in the office, searching for a way to help.

Early one evening, his eyes blurry from staring at his computer screen for hours on end, Magerman spotted something odd: A line of simulation code used for Brown and Mercer's trading system showed the Standard & Poor's 500 at an unusually low level. This test code appeared to use a figure from back in 1991 that was roughly half the current number. Mercer had written it as a static figure, rather than as a variable that updated with each move in the market.

When Magerman fixed the bug and updated the number, a second problem—an algebraic error—appeared elsewhere in the code. Magerman spent most of the night on it but he thought he solved that one, too. Now the simulator's algorithms could finally recommend an ideal portfolio for the Nova system to execute, including how much borrowed money should be employed to expand its stock holdings. The resulting portfolio seemed to generate big profits, at least according to Magerman's calculations.

Overcome with excitement, he raced to tell Brown what he had discovered.

Brown flashed his breathless colleague a look of deep skepticism but agreed to hear Magerman out. Afterward, Brown still showed little enthusiasm. Mercer had done the coding for the system, after all. Everyone knew Mercer rarely made errors, especially mathematical ones. Crestfallen, Magerman slunk away. His screwup had branded him a nuisance, not any kind of potential savior.

Without much to lose, Magerman brought his work to Mercer, who also agreed to take a look. Sitting at his desk, hunched over his computer, Mercer patiently examined the old code, line by line, comparing it to Magerman's new code. Slowly, a smile formed on his face. Mercer reached for some paper and a pencil from his desk and began working on a formula. He was checking Magerman's work. After about fifteen minutes of scribbling, Mercer put his pencil down and looked up.

"You're right," Mercer told Magerman.

Later, Mercer convinced Brown that Magerman was on to something. But when Brown and Mercer told other staffers about the problem that had been uncovered, as well as the fix, they were met with incredulity, even laughter. A junior programmer fixed the problem? The same guy who had crashed the system a few weeks after being hired?

Brown and Mercer ignored the doubts and restarted the system, with Simons's backing, incorporating the improvements and corrections. Instant gains resulted, defying the skeptics. The long losing streak was over. Magerman finally received the appreciation he longed for, receiving a cherished pat on the back from Brown.

"This is great," Simons boomed at a weekly meeting. "Let's keep it going."

A new era for both Magerman and the firm seemed within reach.

CHAPTER ELEVEN

Jim Simons walked the halls, full of nervous energy.

It was the summer of 1997, and Simons sensed he might be close to something special. His Medallion hedge fund now managed over $900 million, mostly in futures contracts tracking commodities, currencies, bonds, and stock indexes. Henry Laufer's group, which traded all these investments, was on a roll. Laufer's key strategies—including buying on the most propitious days of the week, as well as at the ideal moments of the day—remained winners. Simons's team also had perfected the skill of mapping the two-day trajectories of various investments.

Now Simons was becoming convinced Peter Brown and Bob Mercer's ten-person team had turned a corner with its statistical-arbitrage strategy, providing Simons with a welcome distraction as he dealt with enduring grief from his son's death a year earlier. Though the stock-trading profits were a puny few million dollars a month, they were enough to spur Simons to merge the Nova fund into Medallion, creating a single hedge fund trading almost every investment.

Simons and his team had yet to solve the market, however. Medallion gained 21 percent in 1997, a bit lower from the 32 percent results a year earlier, the over 38 percent gain in 1995, and the 71 percent jump in 1994. Its trading system still ran into serious issues. One day, a data-entry error caused the fund to purchase five times as many wheat-futures contracts as it intended, pushing prices higher. Picking up the next day's *Wall Street Journal*, sheepish staffers read that analysts were attributing the price surge to fears of a poor wheat harvest, rather than Renaissance's miscue.

A bit later, Patterson helped roll out a new model to trade equity options, but it generated only modest profits, frustrating Simons.

"Nick, your options system needs help," Simons told him in a meeting. "It needs to be better."

Simons pointed to the huge, steady gains that another investor was making trading equity options at his growing firm, Bernard L. Madoff Investment Securities.

"Look at what Madoff is doing," Simons told Patterson.

The criticism grated on Patterson, who gave Simons a tart retort: "Maybe you should hire Bernie." (A few years later, Simons would become suspicious of Madoff's extraordinary results and pull money he had invested in Madoff's fund. In 2008, Madoff would acknowledge running history's largest Ponzi scheme.)

Nervous about the slipping returns, Simons proposed a new idea. Each year, tens of thousands of peer-reviewed research papers are published in disciplines including economics, finance, and psychology. Many delve into the inner workings of financial markets and demonstrate methods of scoring outsize returns, yet are left in history's dustpan. Each week, Simons decided, Brown, Mercer, and other senior executives would be assigned three papers to read, digest, and present—a book club for quants with a passion for money rather than sex or murder.

After reading several hundred papers, Simons and his colleagues gave up. The tactics sounded tantalizing, but when Medallion's researchers tested the efficacy of the strategies proposed by the academics, the trade recommendations usually failed to pan out. Reading so many disappointing papers reinforced a certain cynicism within the firm about the ability to predict financial moves.

"Any time you hear financial experts talking about how the market went up because of such and such—remember it's all nonsense," Brown later would say.

=

As he led weekly meetings, chatted with employees, and huddled with Laufer, Brown, and Mercer in their cramped offices in Stony Brook's high-tech incubator, Simons emphasized several long-held principles, many of which he had developed earlier in his career breaking code at the IDA and in his years working with talented mathematicians at Stony Brook University. Now he was fully applying them at Renaissance.

A key one: Scientists and mathematicians need to interact, debate, and share ideas to generate ideal results. Simons's precept might seem self-evident, but, in some ways, it was radical. Many of Renaissance's smartest staffers had enjoyed achievement and recognition earlier in their careers toiling away on individual research, rather than teaming with others. Indeed, talented quants can be among the least comfortable working with others. (A classic industry joke: Extroverted mathematicians are the ones who stare at *your* shoes during a conversation, not their own.)

Rival trading firms often dealt with the issue by allowing researchers and others to work in silos, sometimes even competing with each other. Simons insisted on a different approach—Medallion would have a single, monolithic trading system. All staffers enjoyed full access to each line of the source code underpinning their moneymaking algorithms, all of it readable in cleartext on the firm's internal network. There would be no corners of the code accessible only to top executives; anyone could make experimental modifications to improve the trading system. Simons hoped his researchers would swap ideas, rather than embrace private projects. (For a while, even the firm's secretaries had access to the source code, though that ultimately proved unwieldy.)

Simons created a culture of unusual openness. Staffers wandered into colleagues' offices offering suggestions and initiating collaborations. When they ran into frustrations, the scientists tended to share their work and ask for help, rather than move on to new projects, ensuring that promising ideas weren't "wasted," as Simons put it. Groups met regularly, discussing intimate details of their progress and fielding probing questions from Simons. Most staffers ate lunch together, ordering from local restaurants and then squeezing into a tiny lunchroom. Once a year, Simons paid to bring employees and their spouses to exotic vacation locales, strengthening the camaraderie.

Peer pressure became a crucial motivational tool. Researchers, programmers, and others spent much of their time working on presentations. They burned to impress each other—or, at least, not embarrass themselves in front of colleagues—spurring them to plug away at challenging problems and develop ingenious approaches.

"If you didn't make much progress, you'd feel pressure," Frey says. "That was how your self-worth was determined."

Simons used compensation to get staffers focused on the firm's overall success. Every six months, employees received a bonus, but only if Medallion surpassed a certain profit level. The firm paid some of the money over several years, helping to keep the talent around. It didn't matter if staffers uncovered new signals, cleaned data, or did other lower-profile tasks; if they distinguished themselves, and Medallion thrived, they were rewarded with bonus points, each of which represented a percentage of Renaissance's profit pool and was based on clear, understood formulas.

"You know your formula from the beginning of the year. It's the same as everyone else's with just a couple of different coefficients, depending on your position," says Glen Whitney, who was a top manager of Renaissance's infrastructure. "You want a bigger bonus? Help the fund get higher returns in whatever way you can: discover a predictive source, fix a bug, make the code run faster, get coffee for the woman down the hall with a great idea, whatever . . . bonuses depend on how well the fund performs, not if your boss liked your tie."

Simons began sharing equity, handing a 10 percent stake in the firm to Laufer and, later, giving sizable slices to Brown, Mercer, and Mark Silber, who now was the firm's chief financial officer, and others, steps that reduced Simons's ownership to just over 50 percent. Other top-performing employees could buy shares, which represented equity in the firm. Staffers also could invest in Medallion, perhaps the biggest perk of them all.

Simons was embracing immense risk. Hotshot researchers and others were liable to become frustrated working in a flat organization that spread its largesse around and made it harder to stand out. Full access to the system's code enabled staffers to walk out the door, join a rival, and tap Renaissance's secrets. But, since so many of them were PhDs from the world of academia with limited familiarity with Wall Street, Simons believed the chance of defection was relatively small. Unusually onerous lifetime nondisclosure agreements, as well as noncompete contracts, also reduced the danger. (Later, they'd learn the agreements couldn't eliminate the risk of employees defecting with the firm's intellectual property.)

Other than a few old-school traders who completed transactions, many at Renaissance didn't seem to prioritize wealth. When celebrated computer scientist Peter Weinberger interviewed for a job in 1996, he stood in the parking lot, sizing up the researchers he was about to meet. He couldn't help chuckling.

"It was a lot of old, crappy cars," he recalls. "Saturns, Corollas, and Camrys."

Some employees didn't know if the fund was making or losing money each day; a few had no idea how to even locate monthly performance figures on Renaissance's web page. During the few losing streaks Medallion encountered in the period, these oblivious staffers walked around happy-go-lucky, annoying employees more conscious of the troubles.

Some employees seemed embarrassed by their swelling wealth. As a group of researchers chatted in the lunchroom in 1997, one asked if any of his colleagues flew first-class. The table turned silent. Not a single one did, it seemed. Finally, an embarrassed mathematician spoke up.

"I do," he admitted, feeling the need to offer an explanation. "My wife insists on it."

Despite the Medallion fund's impressive gains, hiring could present a challenge. Few recruits had heard of Renaissance, and joining the firm meant sacrificing individual recognition to work on projects that never would garner publicity or acclaim, a foreign concept to most academics. To woo talent, Simons, Nick Patterson, and others emphasized the positive aspects of their jobs. Many scientists and mathematicians are born puzzle-solvers, for example, so the Renaissance executives spoke of the rewards that come with solving difficult trading problems. Others were attracted to the camaraderie and fast pace of a hedge fund. Academics can slog along for years on academic papers; by contrast, Simons pushed for results within weeks, if not days, an urgency that held appeal. The atmosphere was informal and academic, yet intense; one visitor likened it to a "perpetual exam week."[1]

At IBM, Mercer had become frustrated with the speech-recognition world, where scientists could pretend to make progress, relying on what he called "parlor tricks." At Renaissance, he and his colleagues couldn't fool anyone.

"You have money in the bank or not, at the end of the day," Mercer told science writer Sharon McGrayne. "You don't have to wonder if you succeeded . . . it's just a very satisfying thing."[2]

The interview process was somewhat ad hoc—discuss your achievements, tackle some challenging problems involving probability theory and other areas, and see if there might be a fit at the firm. Candidates usually were grilled by a half dozen staffers for forty-five minutes each and then were asked to present lectures about their scientific research to the entire firm. Simons and Patterson generally focused on hiring seasoned academics who boasted a series of accomplishments, or new PhDs with dissertations they deemed strong. Even big-name recruits had to pass a coding test, a requirement that sent a message that everyone was expected to program computers and do tasks deemed menial at other firms. They'd also have to get along with each other.

"The chemistry is important," says a current executive. "It's like joining a family."

═

By 1997, Medallion's staffers had settled on a three-step process to discover statistically significant moneymaking strategies, or what they called their trading *signals*. Identify anomalous patterns in historic pricing data; make sure the anomalies were statistically significant, consistent over time, and nonrandom; and see if the identified pricing behavior could be explained in a reasonable way.

For a while, the patterns they wagered on were primarily those Renaissance researchers could understand. Most resulted from relationships between price, volume, and other market data and were based on the historic behavior of investors or other factors. One strategy with enduring success: betting on retracements. About 60 percent of investments that experienced big, sudden price rises or drops would snap back, at least partially, it turned out. Profits from these retracements helped Medallion do especially well in volatile markets when prices lurched, before retracing some of that ground.

By 1997, though, more than half of the trading signals Simons's team was discovering were *nonintuitive*, or those they couldn't fully understand. Most quant firms ignore signals if they can't develop a reasonable hypothesis to explain them, but Simons and his colleagues never liked spending too much time searching for the causes of market phenomena. If their signals met various measures of statistical strength, they were comfortable wagering on them. They only steered clear of the most preposterous ideas.

"Volume divided by price change three days earlier, yes, we'd include that," says a Renaissance executive. "But not something nonsensical, like the outperformance of stock tickers starting with the letter *A*."

It's not that they *wanted* trades that didn't make any sense; it's just that these were the statistically valid strategies they were finding. Recurring patterns without apparent logic to explain them had an added bonus: They were less likely to be discovered and adopted by rivals, most of whom wouldn't touch these kind of trades.

"If there were signals that made a lot of sense that were very strong, they would have long-ago been traded out," Brown explained. "There are signals that you can't understand, but they're there, and they can be relatively strong."[3]

The obvious danger with embracing strategies that don't make sense: The patterns behind them could result from meaningless coincidences. If one spends enough time sorting data, it's not hard to identify trades that seem to generate stellar returns but are produced by happenstance. Quants call this flawed approach *data overfitting*. To highlight the folly of relying on signals with little logic behind them, quant investor David Leinweber later would determine that US stock returns can be predicted with 99 percent accuracy by combining data for the annual butter production in Bangladesh, US cheese production, and the population of sheep in Bangladesh and the US.[4]

Often, the Renaissance researchers' solution was to place such head-scratching signals in their trading system, but to limit the money allocated to them, at least at first, as they worked to develop an understanding of why the anomalies appeared. Over time, they frequently discovered reasonable explanations, giving Medallion a leg up on firms that had dismissed the phenomena. They ultimately settled on a mix of sensible signals, surprising trades with strong statistical results, and a few bizarre signals so reliable they couldn't be ignored.

"We ask, 'Does this correspond to some aspect of behavior that seems reasonable?'" Simons explained a few years later.[5]

Just as astronomers set up powerful machines to continuously scan the galaxy for unusual phenomena, Renaissance's scientists programmed their computers to monitor financial markets, grinding away until they discovered overlooked patterns and anomalies. Once they were determined to be valid, and the firm determined how much money to place in the trades, the signals were placed into the system and left to do their thing, without any interference. By then, Medallion increasingly was relying on strategies that its system taught itself, a form of machine learning. The computers, fed with enough data, were trained to spit out their own answers. A consistent winner, for example, might automatically receive more cash, without anyone approving the shift or even being aware of it.

═

Simons became more enthused about the prospects of his stat-arb team, though it still managed a small amount of money. His growing confidence about Renaissance's future spurred him to move the firm into a nearby one-story, wood-and-glass compound, where each office enjoyed a relaxing, bucolic view of the nearby woods. The headquarters featured a gym, lighted tennis courts, a library with a fireplace, and a large auditorium with exposed beams where Simons hosted biweekly seminars from visiting scholars, usually having little to do with finance. The trading room, staffed with twenty or so people, was no bigger than a conference room, but the cafeteria and common areas were expansive, allowing staffers to meet, discuss, and debate, filling whiteboards with formulas and diagrams.

As the stat-arb stock-trading results improved, Brown and Mercer exhibited a new assertiveness around the office, and they began wooing former

IBM colleagues to the team. "How would you like to sell out and join our technical trading firm?" Brown wrote in an email to one IBM staffer.

Soon, a half dozen IBM alumni were contributing to the firm, including the Della Pietra twins. The brothers—known for their massive collection of nutcracker figurines and Stephen's insistence that colleagues place his name before his brother's on group emails—managed to speed up parts of a stock-trading system that relied on multiple programs, a network of computers, and hundreds of thousands of lines of code.

Intense and energetic, Brown hustled from meeting to meeting, riding a unicycle through the halls and almost running over colleagues. Brown worked much of the night on a computer near the Murphy bed in his office, grabbing a nap when he tired. Once, as he worked on a complicated project late in the evening, full of manic energy despite the hour, Brown picked up the phone to call a junior associate at home with a pressing question. A colleague stopped Brown before he could dial.

"Peter, you can't call him," he said. "It's *two a.m.*"

Brown looked confused, forcing the colleague to explain himself.

"He doesn't get paid enough to answer questions at two a.m."

"Fine, let's give him a raise, then," Brown replied. "But we *have* to call him!"

Brown's wife, Margaret Hamburg, had spent six years as New York City's health commissioner, instituting a needle-exchange program to combat HIV transmission, among other initiatives. In 1997, Hamburg and their children moved to Washington, DC, where she took a senior job in the US Department of Health and Human Services and later would become the commissioner of the US Food and Drug Administration. Brown flew to Washington to be with his family on weekends, but he now seemed to spend even more time at work, creating pressure for other members of his group to match his focus.

"When I'm away from my family, I just like to work," he explained to a friend after dragging his feet for weeks about meeting for dinner.

Analytical and unemotional, Mercer was a natural sedative for his jittery partner. Mercer worked hard, but he liked to go home around six p.m. He became involved with more drama away from the office. Several years earlier, Mercer's youngest daughter, Heather Sue, had persuaded her father to accompany her to a football field near their home and hold a toy football on the ground so she could practice placekicking.

"I thought she'd get this kicking out of her system," he told a reporter.[6]

Heather Sue blasted the ball through the uprights, astonishing her father. She became her high school's starting kicker and then enrolled at Duke University, winning a spot on the varsity football team, the first woman on a Division I football roster. The following year, Heather Sue was pushed off the team by her coach, who later admitted to feeling embarrassed that rival coaches were mocking him for having a female kicker. After graduating in 1998, Heather Sue sued Duke for discrimination, winning $2 million in punitive damages.

Back at the office, Mercer began to show a new side to his personality. When staffers lunched together, they mostly steered clear of controversial topics. Not Mercer. He hardly spoke during many work meetings, but Mercer turned oddly loquacious over these meals. Some of his comments—such as his support for the gold standard and affection for *More Guns, Less Crime*, the John R. Lott Jr. book arguing that crime falls when gun ownership rises—reflected conservative beliefs. Others were more iconoclastic.

"Gas prices are up . . . we really should fix that," Mercer said one day.

Mercer enjoyed goading his colleagues, many of whom were liberal or libertarian, surprising them with views that were becoming increasingly radical.

"Clinton should be in jail," Mercer said over lunch one day, referring to

President Bill Clinton, who was accused of perjury and obstruction of justice in 1998 related to his relationship with White House intern Monica Lewinsky. Mercer called Clinton a "rapist" and a "murderer," repeating a conspiracy theory that the president had been involved in a secret drug-running scheme with the CIA.

Most of Mercer's colleagues inched away, unwilling to get into a heated debate. Others, like Patterson, a fellow political junkie, remained at the lunch table, debating Mercer. He was stunned a smart scientist could hold opinions with such flimsy support.

Over time, Mercer's colleagues would have more reason for surprise.

=

By the mid-1990s, the internet era was in full swing and activity was heating up in Silicon Valley. On Wall Street, investment banks and trading firms were hiring their own computer pros, high-IQ scientists, and mathematics PhDs, finally convinced that quantitative strategies could help them score gains. Simons and his team remained mere blips on the industry's radar screen, though. That was partly by design: Simons instructed his troops to keep their tactics to themselves, fretting competitors might adopt their most successful methods.

"At the NSA, the penalty for leaking is twenty-five years in prison," Simons liked to tell employees, somewhat ominously. "Unfortunately, all we can do is fire you."

Brown became borderline maniacal about silencing staffers and investors. Once, when a representative of a large Japanese insurance company paid a visit, the visitor placed a tape recorder on a conference room table, so he could play the conversation back later and be sure nothing had been lost in the translation. Walking into the room, Brown saw the machine and nearly had a nervous breakdown.

"There's a recorder on the table!" he said, startling the guest and a Renaissance client representative.

Almost convulsing, Brown pulled his colleague out of the room.

"I don't want anyone recording us!" he screamed, appearing a bit frightened.

The embarrassed representative had to ask the visitor to kindly turn off his machine.

They were going a bit overboard. At that point, no one really cared what Simons and his team were up to. His two largest rivals, Long-Term Capital Management and D. E. Shaw, were commanding the full attention of investors.

Founded by John Meriwether—himself a former mathematics instructor—Long-Term Capital Management also filled its ranks with professors, including Eric Rosenfeld, an MIT-trained finance PhD and computer devotee, and Harvard's Robert C. Merton and Myron Scholes, who would become Nobel laureates. The team—mostly introverts, all intellectuals—downloaded historic bond prices, distilled overlooked relationships, and built computer models predicting future behavior.

Like Renaissance, Meriwether's group didn't care where the overall market or even individual investments were headed. LTCM's models identified pricing anomalies, often between similar investments, then the Greenwich, Connecticut, hedge fund wagered that the irregularities would converge and dissipate. Some of LTCM's favorite trades entailed buying bonds that had fallen below historic levels, while selling short, or betting against, similar bonds that seemed overpriced. LTCM then waited for a convergence of the bond prices, profiting as it happened. LTCM grew its positions with a lot of leverage, or borrowed money, to amplify the gains. Banks were eager lenders, partly because the hedge fund eschewed big, risky trades, placing a thousand or so small, seemingly safe bets.

Mesmerized by LTCM's all-star team of brainiacs, investors poured money into the fund. After launching in 1994, LTCM gained an average of nearly 50 percent in its first three years, managing close to $7 billion in the summer of 1997, making Simons's Medallion fund look like a pip-squeak. After rivals expanded their own arbitrage trades, Meriwether's team shifted to newer strategies, even those the team had little experience with, such as merger-stock trading and Danish mortgages.

After an annual golf outing in the summer of 1997, LTCM's partners announced that investors would have to withdraw about half their cash as a result of what executives saw as diminishing opportunities in the market. Clients lost their minds, pleading with Meriwether and his colleagues—please, keep our money!

LTCM's models weren't prepared for several shocking events in the summer of 1998, however, including Russia's effective default on its debt and a resulting panic in global markets. As investors fled investments with risk attached to them, prices of all kinds of assets reacted in unexpected ways. LTCM calculated it was unlikely to lose more than $35 million in a day, but it somehow dropped $553 million on *one* Friday in August of that year. Billions evaporated in a matter of weeks.

Meriwether and his colleagues dialed investors, trying to raise cash, confident prices would revert to historic norms, as their models predicted. Reality sunk in when Meriwether visited a friend, Vinny Mattone, a veteran trader who favored black silk shirts, weighed about three hundred pounds, and wore a gold chain and pinkie ring.

"Where are you?" Mattone asked, bluntly.

"We're down by half," Meriwether said.

"You're finished," Mattone replied, shocking Meriwether.

"When you're down by half, people figure you can go down all the way," Mattone explained. "They're going to push the market against you. . . . You're *finished*."[7]

So it was. As LTCM's equity dropped under $1 billion, and its leverage skyrocketed, the Federal Reserve stepped in, scared the fund's collapse would take the financial system along with it. Prodded by the Fed, a consortium of banks took control of the fund. In a matter of months, Meriwether and his colleagues had lost nearly $2 billion of personal wealth, marks on their careers they would never erase.

The fiasco soured investors on the whole idea of using computer models to trade in a systematic way.

"The reputation of quantitative investing itself has been dealt long-term damage," *BusinessWeek* magazine judged a month later. "Even if these quants do spring back this autumn, it will be impossible for many of them to claim that they can reliably produce low-volatility profits."[8]

D. E. Shaw didn't seem likely to feel much impact from the troubles. By 1998, the hedge fund started by former Columbia University computer-science professor David Shaw with backing from investor Donald Sussman had grown to several hundred employees. Building on the statistical-arbitrage stock strategies Shaw had developed at Morgan Stanley, his company claimed annual returns of 18 percent on average since launching. On some days, it was responsible for about 5 percent of all trading on the New York Stock Exchange. The fund's portfolio was market neutral, impervious to the overall stock market's ups and downs.

D. E. Shaw embraced a different hiring style than Renaissance. In addition to asking specific, technical questions about an applicant's field of expertise, the firm challenged recruits with brainteasers, situational mathematical challenges, and probability puzzles, including the famed Monty Hall problem, a brain teaser based on the old television show *Let's Make a Deal*. Employees, many of whom were fans of the British science-fiction television show *Doctor Who*, dressed informally, breaking Wall Street's stiff mold.

A 1996 cover story in *Fortune* magazine declared D. E. Shaw "the most intriguing and mysterious force on Wall Street . . . the ultimate quant shop, a nest of mathematicians, computer scientists, and other devotees of quantitative analysis." As Shaw and other quant firms expanded, the New York Stock Exchange was forced to automate, an electronic stock exchange evolved, and eventually stocks were traded in penny increments, reducing trading costs for all investors.

Shaw began spending time away from the office, advising Vice President Al Gore and President Bill Clinton on technology policy. His firm also embraced new endeavors: launching Juno, the first free email service; and forming a joint venture with BankAmerica Corporation to borrow $1.4 billion. D. E Shaw's hedge fund leveraged some of that money into a bond portfolio worth $20 billion while pushing into still more new businesses, such as an internet bank.[9] Flush with cash, Shaw hired over six hundred employees, housing them in cutting-edge offices in New York, Tokyo, London, San Francisco, Boston, and a spot in Hyderabad, India, featuring a sculpture-filled atrium.

Then came the market turmoil of the fall of 1998. Within months, D. E. Shaw had suffered over $200 million in losses in its bond portfolio, forcing it to fire 25 percent of its employees and retrench its operations. D. E. Shaw would recover and reemerge as a trading power, but its troubles, along with LTCM's huge losses, provided lasting lessons for Simons and Renaissance.

=

Patterson and others dissected their rivals' sudden setbacks. Medallion gained 42 percent in 1998, and the fund benefited as other investors panicked in the fall, but Patterson had to make sure his firm wasn't making the same mistakes as LTCM. Patterson knew Renaissance didn't borrow as much money as Meriwether's firm, and LTCM's trades needed to work within a certain time frame, unlike those favored by Simons. Renaissance hired mathematicians and computer scientists, not economists, another factor that distinguished it from LTCM.

Still, there were enough similarities to warrant a search for deeper lessons. For Patterson and his colleagues, the LTCM collapse reinforced an existing mantra at Renaissance: Never place too much trust in trading models. Yes, the firm's system seemed to work, but all formulas are fallible. This conclusion reinforced the fund's approach to managing risk. If a strategy wasn't working, or when market volatility surged, Renaissance's system tended to automatically reduce positions and risk. For example, Medallion cut its futures trading by 25 percent in the fall of 1998. By contrast, when LTCM's strategies floundered, the firm often grew their size, rather than pull back.

"LTCM's basic error was believing its models were truth," Patterson says. "We never believed our models reflected reality—just some aspects of reality."

D. E. Shaw and LTCM also had drifted into markets the firms didn't fully understand or had little experience in—Danish mortgages! Online banking! It was a reminder for Simons's team of the need to hone their approach, not enter new businesses.

═

For all of the work Brown, Mercer, and others had put into their system, stock trading still contributed only about 10 percent of the firm's profits in 1998. It was Henry Laufer's futures trades that powered Renaissance, even as Simons pushed the equities team to improve their performance. As usual, David Magerman wanted to be the hero who would change all that.

Magerman had been the one who managed to locate and fix the computer bug that had prevented Brown and Mercer's stock-trading system from profiting. Subsequently, Magerman was given more responsibility, emerging as the architect of the software Medallion used for its *production*, or its actual stock trades. Now he was the watchdog of all changes to the system, a crucial player in all its improvements, and the boss of a dozen PhDs.

Magerman was on a clear roll. He was well paid. Even better, his work garnered treasured praise from Brown, Mercer, and Simons. Magerman used his swelling pay to upgrade his wardrobe and even began wearing suspenders, trying to look like Mercer. Winning approval from dominant male figures had long motivated Magerman, and the appreciation he was receiving thrilled him.

Despite his growing success, Magerman detected a certain iciness from Mercer's family, especially Mercer's middle daughter Rebekah, who had joined Renaissance and worked for Magerman. There were no more outings to restaurants or invitations to the Mercer home, perplexing Magerman. At one point, he wrote a five-page letter, hoping to renew the friendship, but he got no reply. He couldn't figure out what had happened. He examined the possibilities. Perhaps it was the time he publicly berated Rebekah—his boss's daughter, mind you—over her work in the trading group, embarrassing Rebekah in front of her new colleagues.

"I thought it was well deserved," Magerman says.

The rift also could have resulted from the firm's summer outing, when Magerman took Heather Sue out for a romantic canoe ride, a move he was sure had left Bekah jealous. For whatever reason, Mercer's daughters and his wife, Diana, now wouldn't speak to him.

"I was persona non grata in their house and at family-hosted events," he says.

To stay in Robert Mercer's good graces, Magerman decided to focus on his work. In 1999, Magerman developed a way to tweak the computer code governing the firm's stock trading, making it more efficient. Almost immediately, however, Medallion's futures trades went from winners to losers. Staffers scrambled to understand what had happened, but Magerman knew—he had made a careless mistake and unleashed a powerful bug that was infecting the firm, once again.

I caused this!

For weeks, Magerman beat himself up, wondering how he could have committed such a dumb error. True, Magerman's stock-trading group didn't share much computer code with Henry Laufer's futures staffers, but Magerman was sure he somehow was the culprit. Unwilling to acknowledge his mistake this time, Magerman worked through the night, but failed to find his bug.

As the quarter ended, Medallion told clients it had suffered a slight but surprising loss, its first quarterly downturn in a decade. Racked with worry and waiting to be fired, Magerman could hardly sleep.

"I was losing my mind," he says.

Magerman met with a therapist who diagnosed generalized anxiety disorder, starting him on weekly sessions to calm his nerves. Slowly, Medallion's returns rebounded and Magerman allowed himself to relax, concluding that he probably hadn't been responsible for the losses, after all.

In January 2000, Medallion surged 10.5 percent, the hedge fund's best one-month return in years. By early March, the fund was sitting on over $700 million of profits as the Nasdaq Composite index reached a record amid a wave of enthusiasm for technology stocks, especially internet-related companies.

Then came true trouble for Magerman and his colleagues. The tech bubble burst on March 10, sending shares plummeting, with little news to account for the shift in sentiment. A month later, the Nasdaq would be down 25 percent, on its way to a full 78 percent drop from its peak. Medallion faced inexplicable losses. It lost about $90 million in a single day in March; the next day it was $80 million more. Nerves began to fray—until then, Medallion had never lost more than $5 million in a day.

It wasn't just the mounting losses that had everyone concerned—it was the uncertainty over *why* things were so bad. The Medallion portfolio held commodities, currencies, and bond futures, and its stock portfolio was largely composed of offsetting positions aimed at sidestepping broad market moves. The losses *shouldn't be happening*. But because so many of the system's trading signals had developed on their own through a form of machine learning, it was hard to pinpoint the exact cause of the problems or when they might ebb; the machines seemed out of control.

Amid the sell-off, a recruit visited the Long Island office to interview with Patterson and several colleagues. When they met to discuss the candidacy the next morning, not a single person remembered even meeting the recruit. The losses had left the researchers in an utter daze.

Mercer remained stoic, interacting with colleagues as if nothing unusual was happening. Not Brown. He had never experienced deep, sudden losses, and it showed. High-strung and emotional, Brown couldn't hide his building fears. Unable to sleep, Brown spent the night checking his computer to get updates on the troubles. Around the office, Brown looked pale, his lack of sleep showing, shocking colleagues. Friends said he felt responsible for the losses since they emanated from his stock-trading system.

On the third day of the meltdown, Magerman drove to work, checked the level of stock futures on his computer, and received a fresh jolt—another absolutely awful day was ahead. Magerman turned slightly nauseous. Brown and Mercer were already in an emergency meeting with Simons and other top executives, but Magerman felt the need to alert them to the escalating problems. He slowly opened a heavy door to a small, cramped conference room packed with a dozen executives, a videoconference screen showing the faces of others around the globe. At the head of a long table sat Simons, grim and focused. Magerman bent low, whispering into Brown's ear: "We're down another ninety million."

Brown froze. Medallion's losses now approached $300 million. Brown was distraught, even fearful. He looked at Simons, desperate for help.

"Jim, what should we do?"

Simons tried to reassure Brown and the other executives, expressing confidence their fortunes would improve.

"Trust the model," Simons told them. "We have to let it ride; we can't panic."

Later, Simons reminded staffers that their trading system was prepared for trying times. Besides, there was little they could do; Medallion trades about eight thousand stocks. There was no way they could quickly revamp the portfolio.

After several more all-nighters, a couple of researchers developed a theory about what was causing the problems: A once-trusted strategy was bleeding money. It was a rather simple strategy—if certain stocks rallied in previous weeks, Medallion's system had taught itself to buy more of those shares, under the assumption the surge would continue. For several years, this trending signal had worked, as the fund automatically bought Nasdaq shares that were racing still higher. Now the system's algorithms were instructing Medallion to buy *more* shares, even though a vicious bear market had begun.

Simons often emphasized the importance of not overriding their trading system, but, in a market crisis, he tended to pull back on the reliance on certain signals, to the chagrin of researchers who didn't believe in ever adjusting their computer programs. Now even those staffers were fine dumping their faulty signal, especially since their system did a better job predicting short-term moves, not the longer-term ones on which the defective signal focused. They quickly ditched the momentum strategy, stemming the losses. Soon, gains were piling up once again.

Brown remained shaken, though. He offered to resign, feeling responsible for the deep pain. Simons rejected the offer, telling Brown he was even more valuable now that he had learned "never to put your full faith in a model."[10]

=

By the fall of 2000, word of Medallion's success was starting to leak out. That year, Medallion soared 99 percent, even after it charged clients 20 percent of their gains and 5 percent of the money invested with Simons. The firm now managed nearly $4 billion. Over the previous decade, Medallion and its 140 employees had enjoyed a better performance than funds managed by George Soros, Julian Robertson, Paul Tudor Jones, and other investing giants.

Just as impressive, Medallion had recorded a Sharpe ratio of 2.5 in its most recent five-year period, suggesting the fund's gains came with low volatility and risk compared with those of many competitors.

Letting his guard down, Simons consented to an interview with Hal Lux, a writer at *Institutional Investor* magazine. Over coffee in his New York office, and later while sipping gin and tonics at Renaissance's Long Island headquarters, Simons expressed confidence his gains would continue.

"The things we are doing will not go away," Simons told Lux. "We may have bad years, we may have a terrible year sometimes, but the principles we've discovered are valid."

Brown, Mercer, and Laufer were just as confident that a rare, even historic, opportunity was at hand. They pushed to hire new employees to take advantage.

"The markets are dripping with inefficiencies," a senior staffer told a colleague. "We're leaving money on the table."

The new hires would transform the firm in ways Simons and his colleagues never could have anticipated.

PART TWO

Money Changes Everything

CHAPTER TWELVE

Something unusual was going on at Jim Simons's hedge fund in 2001. Profits were piling up as Renaissance began digesting new kinds of information. The team collected every trade order, including those that hadn't been completed, along with annual and quarterly earnings reports, records of stock trades by corporate executives, government reports, and economic predictions and papers.

Simons wanted more. "Can we do anything with news flashes?" he asked in a group meeting.

Soon, researchers were tracking newspaper and newswire stories, internet posts, and more obscure data—such as offshore insurance claims—racing to get their hands on pretty much any information that could be quantified and scrutinized for its predictive value. The Medallion fund became something of a data sponge, soaking up a terabyte, or one trillion bytes, of information annually, buying expensive disk drives and processors to digest, store, and analyze it all, looking for reliable patterns.

"There's no data like more data," Mercer told a colleague, an expression that became the firm's hokey mantra.

Renaissance's goal was to predict the price of a stock or other investment "at every point in the future," Mercer later explained. "We want to know in three seconds, three days, three weeks, and three months."

If there was a newspaper article about a shortage of bread in Serbia, for example, Renaissance's computers would sift through past examples of bread shortages and rising wheat prices to see how various investments reacted, Mercer said.[1]

Some of the new information, such as quarterly corporate earnings reports, didn't provide much of an advantage. But data on the earnings predictions of stock analysts and their changing views on companies sometimes helped. Watching for patterns in how stocks traded following earnings announcements, and tracking corporate cash flows, research-and-development spending, share issuance, and other factors, also proved to be useful activities. The team improved its predictive algorithms by developing a rather simple measure of how many times a company was mentioned in a news feed—no matter if the mentions were positive, negative, or even pure rumors.

It became clear to Mercer and others that trading stocks bore similarities to speech recognition, which was part of why Renaissance continued to raid IBM's computational linguistics team. In both endeavors, the goal was to create a model capable of digesting uncertain jumbles of information and generating reliable guesses about what might come next—while ignoring traditionalists who employed analysis that wasn't nearly as data driven.

As more trading became electronic, with human market-makers and middlemen elbowed out of the business, Medallion spread its moves among an expanding number of electronic networks, making it easier and more efficient to buy and sell. Finally, Simons was close to his original goal of building a fully automated system with little human interface.

Staffers became excited about developing super-short-term signals to trade in a matter of seconds, or even less, a method that would become known as *high-frequency trading*. Renaissance's computers proved too slow to beat others to the market, however. Medallion made between 150,000 and 300,000 trades a day, but much of that activity entailed buying or selling in small chunks to avoid impacting the market prices, rather than profiting by stepping in front of other investors. What Simons and his team were doing wasn't quite investing, but they also weren't flash boys.

Whatever you wanted to call it, the results were extraordinary. After soaring 98.5 percent in 2000, the Medallion fund rose 33 percent in 2001. By comparison, the S&P 500, the commonly used barometer of the stock market, managed a measly average gain of 0.2 percent over those two years, while rival hedge funds gained 7.3 percent.

Simons's team was still flying under the radar of most in the investing world. As the *Institutional Investor* article in 2000 said, "Chances are you haven't heard of Jim Simons, which is fine by him. Nor are you alone."[2]

Still, Brown and Mercer's system worked so well that researchers could test and develop new algorithms and plop them into their existing, single trading system. New employees began identifying predictive signals in markets in Canada, Japan, the United Kingdom, France, Germany, and Hong Kong, as well as in smaller locales, including Finland, the Netherlands, and Switzerland. Foreign markets usually follow the US, but they don't move in lockstep. By combining signals from these new markets with Medallion's existing predictive algorithms in one main trading system, something remarkable seemed to happen. The correlations of Medallion's trades to the overall market dropped, smoothing out returns and making them less connected to key financial markets.

Investment professionals generally judge a portfolio's risk by its Sharpe ratio, which measures returns in relation to volatility; the higher one's Sharpe, the better. For most of the 1990s, Medallion had a strong Sharpe ratio of about 2.0, double the level of the S&P 500. But adding foreign-market algorithms and improving Medallion's trading techniques sent its Sharpe soaring to about

6.0 in early 2003, about twice the ratio of the largest quant firms and a figure suggesting there was nearly no risk of the fund losing money over a whole year.

Simons's team appeared to have discovered something of a holy grail in investing: enormous returns from a diversified portfolio generating relatively little volatility and correlation to the overall market. In the past, a few others had developed investment vehicles with similar characteristics. They usually had puny portfolios, however. No one had achieved what Simons and his team had—a portfolio as big as $5 billion delivering this kind of astonishing performance.

The accomplishment opened the door to new possibilities.

=

Peter Brown paced his office, determined to find a way to expand the hedge fund's equity bets. Brown remained haunted by the painful losses of early 2000, however, and how flummoxed he had been about how to react. He wanted a way to protect the firm in case of an even greater market catastrophe.

Brown was in luck—banks were warming to Renaissance, sensing opportunity. In many ways, Simons's firm was a dream borrower, with returns that were huge, placid, and uncorrelated to the broader market. Simons had okayed Brown's plan to use more leverage to amplify its profits, making Renaissance an eager borrower. (Just as homeowners take out mortgages to buy homes that are more expensive than they can afford with the money they have in the bank, so too do hedge funds like Medallion, as a way to boost profits, borrow money to accumulate larger investment portfolios than their capital would allow.)

Banks were loosening purse strings and lending standards. Global interest rates were falling, the housing market was revving up, and lenders were offering an array of aggressive loans, even for borrowers with scuffed or no credit history. By comparison, Renaissance seemed a safe bet, especially since it generally held an equal number of long and short trades, reducing potential risk in a market tumble. That's part of why Deutsche Bank and Barclays Bank began selling the hedge fund a new product called *basket* options that seemed a perfect solution to Brown's problems.

Basket options are financial instruments whose values are pegged to the performance of a specific basket of stocks. While most options are valued based on an individual stock or financial instrument, basket options are linked to a group of shares. If these underlying stocks rise, the value of the option goes up—it's like owning the shares without actually doing so. Indeed, the banks were legal owners of shares in the basket, but, for all intents and purposes, they were Medallion's property. The fund's computers told the banks which stocks to place in the basket and how they should be traded. Brown himself helped create the code to make it all happen. All day, Medallion's computers sent automated instructions to the banks, sometimes an order a minute or even a second. After a year or so, Medallion exercised its options, claiming whatever returns the shares generated, less some related costs.[3]

The basket options were a crafty way to supercharge Medallion's returns. Brokerage and other restrictions place limits on how much a hedge fund can borrow through more traditional loans, but the options gave Medallion the ability to borrow significantly more than it otherwise was allowed to. Competitors generally had about seven dollars of financial instruments for each dollar of cash. By contrast, Medallion's options strategy allowed it to have $12.50 worth of financial instruments for every dollar of cash, making it easier to trounce the rivals, assuming it could keep finding profitable trades. When Medallion spied especially juicy opportunities, such as during a 2002 market downturn, the fund could boost its leverage, holding close to $20 of assets for each dollar of cash, effectively placing the portfolio on steroids. In 2002, Medallion managed over $5 billion, but it controlled more than $60 billion of investment positions, thanks in part to the options helping the fund score a gain of 25.8 percent despite a tough year for the broader market. (The S&P 500 lost 22.1 percent in 2002, a year marked by the bankruptcies of internet companies and reverberations from the collapse of the trading and energy company Enron and the telecommunications giant WorldCom.)

The options also were a way of shifting enormous risk from Renaissance to the banks. Because the lenders technically owned the underlying securities in the basket-options transactions, the most Medallion could lose in the event of a sudden collapse was the premium it had paid for the options and the collateral held by the banks. That amounted to several hundred million dollars. By contrast, the banks faced billions of dollars of potential losses if Medallion were to experience deep troubles. In the words of a banker involved in the lending arrangement, the options allowed Medallion to "ring-fence" its stock portfolios, protecting other parts of the firm, including Laufer's still-thriving futures trading, and ensuring Renaissance's survival in the event something unforeseen took place. One staffer was so shocked by the terms of the financing that he shifted most of his life savings into Medallion, realizing the most he could lose was about 20 percent of his money.

The banks embraced the serious risk despite having ample reason to be wary. For one thing, they had no clue why Medallion's strategies worked. And the fund only had a decade of impressive returns. In addition, Long-Term Capital Management had imploded just a few years earlier, providing a stark lesson regarding the dangers of relying on murky models.

Brown realized there was another huge benefit to the basket options: They enabled Medallion's trades to become eligible for the more favorable long-term capital gains tax, even though many of them lasted for just days or even hours. That's because the options were exercised after a year, allowing Renaissance to argue they were long-term in nature. (Short-term gains are taxed at a rate of 39.5 percent while long-term gains face a 20 percent tax.)

Some staffers were uncomfortable with the stratagem, calling it "legal but wrong," but Brown and others relied on the thumbs-up they received from legal advisors. Several years later, the Internal Revenue Service would rule that Medallion had improperly claimed profits from the basket options as long-term gains. Simons, who had approved the transactions, along with other Renaissance executives, paid a whopping $6.8 billion *less* in taxes than they should have, the IRS said. In 2014, a Senate subcommittee said Renaissance had "misused" the complex structures "to claim billions of dollars in unjustified tax savings." Renaissance challenged the IRS's finding and the dispute was still ongoing as of the summer of 2019.

Other hedge funds crafted their own ways to reduce taxes, some using versions of the basket-options agreements. No one relied on them like Renaissance, though. By the early 2000s, the options had emerged as the firm's secret weapon, so important that Renaissance dedicated several computer programmers and about fifty staff members to ensuring a seamless coordination with the banks.

=

Money is seductive, even to scientists and mathematicians. Slowly, Renaissance staffers, even those who once had been abashed about making so much cash, began to enjoy their winnings. A staffer developed a widget so they could see a running tally of their profits (and, once in a while, losses) in the corner of their computer screens. Moods began to shift with the changing figures.

"It was a rush," an employee says. "But it also was distracting."

Their spending picked up along with the returns. So many scientists bought mansions in a nearby area called Old Field that it became known as the Renaissance Riviera. Simons had his fourteen-acre estate in East Setauket overlooking Long Island Sound, his picture windows providing a spectacular view of the herons on Conscious Bay. Henry Laufer paid nearly $2 million for a nearby five-bedroom, six-and-a-half-bathroom, Mediterranean-style estate on almost ten acres, with more than four hundred feet of his own frontage on the Sound. Laufer spent another $800,000 to buy an adjacent 2.6-acre parcel, combining them into a mega-property. In the same area, Simons's cousin, Robert Lourie, who had left academia for a senior position at the hedge fund, built an equestrian arena for his daughter, with arches so large a bridge into New York City had to be shut down to facilitate their journey to Long Island.[4]

Mercer's mansion was down a long dirt road with sand on all sides, overlooking Stony Brook Harbor. He and Diana decorated their living room with full-length portraits of their daughters, Heather Sue, Rebekah, and Jenji.[5] When the family hosted Heather Sue's blowout wedding, guests gawked at the colossal water fountain and gorgeous rose garden, while stepping around thousands of dead bugs killed for their comfort on the eve of the event. (There were so many pictures and videos of Bob and Heather Sue some guests joked they weren't sure who the groom was.)

Porsches, Mercedes, and other upscale cars took up more space in Renaissance's parking lot, though Tauruses and Camrys still abounded. Some executives even took helicopters to dinner in New York City.[6] In the lunchroom, someone affixed a number to an office refrigerator—the percentage of his compensation's most recent annual gain. When it fell, he told friends, he was going to quit.

One day, as a few researchers sat around complaining about all the taxes they were paying, Simons walked past, a frown quickly forming on his face.

"If you didn't make so much money, you wouldn't pay so much in taxes," Simons said, before wandering away.

They were getting so wealthy—researchers and others were paid millions or even tens of millions of dollars each year, and they were making just as much from their investments in Medallion—that some felt a need to justify the gains. The Renaissance staff was largely former academics, after all, and some couldn't help question the outsize compensation.

Do I deserve all this money?

Most employees concluded that their heavy trading was adding to the market's *liquidity*, or the ability of investors to get in and out of positions easily, helping the financial system, though that argument was a bit of a stretch since it wasn't clear how much overall impact Renaissance was having. Others committed to giving their money away after they had built a sufficient treasure chest, while trying not to focus on how their expanding profits necessarily meant dentists and other investors were losing from their trades.

"There was internal struggle," says Glen Whitney, the senior executive who helped facilitate the firm's research.

Brown had mixed feelings about his own accumulating riches. He had long battled anxieties about money, colleagues said, so he relished the big bucks. But Brown tried to shield his children from the magnitude of his wealth, driving a Prius and sometimes wearing clothing with holes. His wife, who had taken a job as a scientist at a foundation dedicated to reducing the threat from nuclear weapons, rarely spent money on herself. Still, it became hard to mask the money. Colleagues shared a story that once, when the Brown family visited Mercer's mansion, Brown's son, then in grade school, got a look at the scale of the Mercer home and turned to his father, a look of confusion on his face.

"Dad, don't you and Bob do the same thing?"

=

As their stock-trading business thrived, Brown and Mercer assumed greater influence at the firm, while Laufer's power waned. The two groups seemed to operate at entirely different levels of urgency, just like their leaders. Laufer remained calm and measured, no matter the market. Members of his team came in, drank a cup of coffee or two, perused the *Financial Times*, and got to work. Their software was a bit clunky at times, unable to quickly test and implement trade ideas or discover lots of new relationships and patterns, but the returns remained strong, even if they were stagnating. Laufer's gang never fully understood why Simons needed to grow the fund, anyway. They all were making millions of dollars each year, so what was the big problem?

Brown and Mercer's staffers often spent the night programming their computers, competing to see who could stay in the office longest, then rushing back in the morning to see how effective their changes had been. If Brown was going to push himself all day and sleep by his computer keyboard at night, his underlings felt the need to keep up. Brown disparaged his researchers, developing demeaning nicknames for everyone in the group (other than Mercer) and prodded each for even greater effort. But his staffers developed a certain pride in knowing they could handle his insults, and they assumed he mostly used them as motivational tools. Brown himself often looked pained, as if he wore the weight of the world on his shoulders, suggesting he cared as much as anyone about the work. He also could be exuberant and entertaining. A huge fan of *Candide*, Brown liked to sprinkle references to the French satire in his presentations, making staffers chuckle.

Quietly, the team worked on a souped-up trading model capable of replacing the one used by the futures team. When they presented it to Simons, he was unhappy they had built their model in secret, but he agreed it should replace the one Laufer's team was using.

By 2003, the profits of Brown and Mercer's stock-trading group were twice those of Laufer's futures team, a remarkable shift in just a few years. Rewarding his ascending stars, Simons announced that Brown and Mercer would become executive vice presidents of the entire firm, co-managing all of Renaissance's trading, research, and technical activities. Once, Laufer had seemed Simons's obvious heir apparent. Now he was given the title of chief scientist and tasked with dealing with the firm's problem areas, among other things. Brown and Mercer were the firm's future. Laufer was its past.

Over a lunch of cheeseburgers at Billie's 1890, a wood-paneled saloon in nearby Port Jefferson, Simons told Brown and Mercer he was thinking about retiring.

"You'll take over," Simons told them, saying he wanted them to become co-CEOs.[7]

As word leaked out, some employees began to panic. Brown's team could handle his invective, but others couldn't stand the guy. Once, on the phone with an employee in the New York office where Renaissance handled its accounting and investors relations duties, Brown lashed out in irritation.

"You're just stupid!"

As for Mercer, while he continued to have regular conversations with Brown, he rarely said anything in group settings. When he did, it often was to inflame. Mercer had long enjoyed debating underlings. Now he appeared to be outright provoking them, usually while in the Renaissance lunchroom. Often, Mercer zeroed in on left-leaning colleagues, chiefly Nick Patterson, a habit staffers began to refer to as "Nick-baiting."

Patterson generally enjoyed the back-and-forth. Sometimes it went a bit overboard, though. One day, Mercer insisted to Patterson that climate-change worries were overblown, handing him a research paper written by a biochemist named Arthur Robinson and some others. Patterson took the paper home and studied it; it turned out Robinson was also a sheep rancher who cofounded a project to stockpile and then analyze thousands of vials of urine, "to improve our health, our happiness and prosperity, and even the academic performance of our children in school."[8] After reading the paper, Patterson sent Mercer a note that it was "probably false and certainly politically illiterate." Mercer never responded.

Mercer especially liked quantifying things, as if the only way to measure accomplishments, costs, and much else in society was through numbers, usually dollars and cents.

"Why do we need more than fines to punish people?" he asked Whitney, the senior computer executive, whom Mercer also enjoyed baiting.

"What are you talking about?" Whitney responded.

Some of Mercer's comments were downright abhorrent. Once, Magerman recalls, Mercer tried to quantify how much money the government spent on African Americans in criminal prosecution, schooling, welfare payments, and more, and whether the money could be used, instead, to encourage a return to Africa. (Mercer later denied making the comment.)

Oddly, Mercer was a scientist who demanded robust arguments and definitive proof at the office, but he relied on flimsy data when it came to his personal views. One day, Mercer brought in research that purported to show that exposure to radiation had extended the lives of those living outside Hiroshima and Nagasaki in the years after the US dropped atomic bombs on the cities, suggesting to him that nuclear war wasn't nearly as worrisome as widely assumed. The paper struck the researchers as unconvincing pseudoscience.

Mercer was the most senior person in the lunchroom, so some staffers bit their tongues, unwilling to challenge the boss. Once, Mercer told a young researcher and avowed atheist he didn't believe in evolution, handing him a book that argued for creationism, though Mercer himself wasn't a believer in the divine.

"There isn't enough time" to judge evolution's accuracy, Mercer told the employee.

To most of the staff, even the targets of his baiting, Mercer was a provocateur. Occasionally amusing, often annoying, but generally harmless. Their perspective would change.

=

Simons wasn't ready to pass the baton to Brown and Mercer, but he assigned them more responsibilities, sometimes pulling the pair away from day-to-day trading. A new set of employees began to assert themselves, changing the company in fundamental ways.

Eager to expand in the late 1990s and early 2000s, Renaissance sometimes deviated from its usual practice by hiring employees who had been at rival firms, many of whom were scientists with roots in Russia and Eastern Europe. Among them was Alexander Belopolsky, who had spent time at a unit of D. E. Shaw, the quant hedge fund. It was a hiring decision that Nick Patterson had protested. It wasn't just that Belopolsky had worked on Wall Street. He fielded tough questions in his interview at Renaissance a bit too smoothly, Patterson felt, as if he had been coached.

Other foreign-born scientists also demonstrated an uncanny ability to ace the kinds of challenging questions that usually stumped interviewees. After Whitney posed his favorite problem to a job candidate, he began receiving the same response: a dramatic pause, apparent confusion, then, suddenly, a stroke of brilliance and an absolutely beautiful solution.

"Oh, I have it!"

Later, Whitney realized someone had been feeding answers to the foreign-born recruits.

"They were real actors," Whitney says. "I felt like a stooge."

Medallion employees made an absolute fortune, but because the fund's size was capped at about $5 billion in 2003, staffers sometimes found it challenging to grow their compensation, leading to some tension. On Wall Street, traders often are most miserable after terrific years, not terrible ones, as resentments emerge—yes, I made a ton, but someone wholly undeserving got *more*!

At Renaissance, some of the newcomers launched whisper campaigns against well-paid colleagues, including Peter Weinberger, a legendary computer scientist. In 1996, Simons had hired Weinberger to work with Laufer in futures trading. A former head of computer-science research at Bell Labs, Weinberger was famous for helping to develop the programming language called AWK (the W represented his last name). Behind his back, newcomers questioned Weinberger, saying his technique was antiquated and that he wasn't contributing.

"Yeah, he's famous, but what does he *do*?" one sniffed. (Weinberger left the firm in 2003.)

Some veterans had sympathy for the new staffers despite their rough edges. Many had spent formative years living under communist rule, so it was understandable they'd be less open and trusting, the defenders argued. Sometimes, the foreign-born scientists shared tales about enduring hardship in their youth. And it wasn't like *every* member of the new breed was dissing older colleagues.

The tenor of the firm was changing, though, and nervousness grew.

=

David Magerman was unhappy, once again. Never one to keep his opinions to himself, he wasn't going to start now.

First there was Simons's smoking. Yes, Simons was the pioneer of quantitative investing, a billionaire, and the founder and majority owner of his firm. But *come on*, enough with the smoking! Magerman felt it was exacerbating his asthma, leaving him coughing after meetings. He was determined to do something about it.

This is too much!

"Jim, I called human resources to file an OSHA complaint," Magerman told Simons one day, referring to the federal agency governing workplace violations. "This is *illegal*."

Magerman said he'd no longer attend meetings if Simons kept smoking. Simons got the message and purchased a machine that sucked cigarette smoke from the air, which was enough to get Magerman to end his mini-boycott.

Simons still employed a few old-school traders, something else that bothered Magerman. Simons believed in computer trading, but he didn't entirely trust an automated system in unstable markets, a stance Magerman couldn't understand. Sometimes, Magerman threw things to express his irritation—usually cans of Diet Coke, once a computer monitor. Eventually, Brown convinced Magerman the issue wasn't worth fighting over.

Others at the firm became animated over more trivial issues. A few miles from Renaissance's East Setauket headquarters, close by West Meadow Beach, the longest public beach north of Florida, stood a row of ninety cottages. Renaissance employees owned some of the ramshackle wooden bungalows, which enjoyed views of Stony Brook Harbor. The firm also owned a cottage. They'd been built on illegally acquired public land, though, and the city made plans to demolish them. When a group emerged, backed by Renaissance staffers, to keep the cottages in private hands, Whitney, a former math professor who joined the company in 1997, became outraged. He started a website to support the city's demolition, while Magerman printed and handed out bumper stickers that said—"Dump the Shacks!"

"It's just wrong," Whitney insisted in the lunchroom. "It's a public park!"

Mercer took an opposing stance, of course.

"What's the big deal?" Mercer asked, needling Whitney and others.

Tensions grew; at one point, some Renaissance employees wouldn't let their kids play with Whitney's children. More than flimsy cottages seemed at stake—Whitney and others sensed Renaissance was shifting amid the influx of new staffers, becoming a less caring and collegial place. The shacks came down, but the anger lingered.

In 2002, Simons increased Medallion's investor fees to 36 percent of each year's profits, raising hackles among some clients. A bit later, the firm boosted the fees to 44 percent. Then, in early 2003, Simons began kicking all his investors out of the fund. Simons had worried that performance would ebb if Medallion grew too big, and he preferred that he and his employees kept all the gains. But some investors had stuck with Medallion through difficult periods and were crushed.

Whitney, Magerman, and others argued against the move. To them, it was one more indication that the firm's priorities were changing.

=

Among the most ambitious of the new employees was a mathematician and Ukraine native named Alexey Kononenko. At the age of sixteen, Kononenko earned a spot at Moscow State University, moving to Moscow to study pure mathematics at the famed university. In 1991, before he could complete his studies, Kononenko and his family fled the USSR, joining a wave of emigrants impacted by the nation's rampant anti-Semitism.

In 1996, Kononenko received his PhD from Penn State, where he studied with respected geometer and fellow Russian immigrant Anatole Katok. Later, Kononenko did postdoc work at the University of Pennsylvania. With colleagues, he wrote a dozen research papers, some of which proved influential, including one addressing the trajectory of billiard balls.

Confident and outgoing, Kononenko was offered a coveted postdoc position at the Mathematical Sciences Research Institute, the renowned institution in Berkeley, California. When a colleague wished Kononenko congratulations, however, the young man appeared disappointed with his new position, rather than delighted.

"Alex was hoping to get a tenure track offer from Princeton, Harvard, or the University of Chicago, which wasn't realistic at that point," recalls a fellow academic. "He had achieved an awful lot, but he could have had more perspective and patience."

Kononenko seemed to place a greater priority on money than his peers did, perhaps because he was focused on achieving financial security after dealing with challenging circumstances in the Soviet Union. They weren't shocked when Kononenko quit academia to join Renaissance. There, Kononenko quickly rose through the ranks, playing a key role in various breakthroughs in foreign-stock trading. By 2002, Kononenko—who was thin, clean-shaven, and good-looking, with hair that showed signs of gray at the temples—was pocketing well over $40 million a year, colleagues estimated, about half from his pay and half from investing in Medallion. He used some of his winnings to build an impressive art collection.

Despite their mounting wealth, Kononenko and some of his newer colleagues grew unhappy. They complained that there were too many "deadwood" employees who weren't pulling their weight and were being paid way too much.

"What do they even contribute?" a newcomer was overheard asking about some of Renaissance's senior executives.

Some even viewed Brown and Mercer as expendable. By then, Brown's intense pace and nonstop typing had caught up with him—he suffered from carpal tunnel syndrome and sometimes seemed discouraged, likely due to his inability to put in the same hours on his computer. Mercer suffered from joint pain and sometimes missed work. Kononenko was heard bad-mouthing Brown and Mercer, one veteran recalls. After he discovered an error in the construction of the stock portfolio, Kononenko raised questions about whether Brown and Mercer should be running the company, Brown told at least one person. Simons defended the executives but word spread of Kononenko's boldness.

Complaints even emerged about Simons, who was spending less time around the office, yet still received about half the firm's profits.

"He doesn't do anything anymore," a staffer griped to Magerman one day in a hallway. "He's *screwing* us."

Magerman couldn't believe what he was hearing.

"He's *earned* the right" to his enormous pay, Magerman responded.

Soon, Kononenko was pushing a plan to shift points from Simons and members of the old guard to deserving newcomers and others. The idea divided the firm but Simons agreed to implement a reallocation. Even that didn't quell the grumbling, however.

The firm was changing, partly because some longtime staffers were leaving. After nearly a decade scrutinizing market patterns, Nick Patterson quit to join an institute in Cambridge, Massachusetts, and analyze another kind of complicated data—the human genome—to gain a better understanding of human biology.

Soon, there was a *Lord of the Flies* feel to the place. Veterans worried that newcomers were targeting those at the firm with a lot of points, or equity, in the firm to free up money for themselves. Some of the Eastern Europeans liked to stay late at the office, charging the company for dinner while discussing why Simons and others were paid too much, employees say. The next day, they'd gang up to mock the work done by others in the equities group.

Quietly, two senior scientists on Brown and Mercer's stock team—Belopolsky, the former D. E. Shaw executive, and a colleague named Pavel Volfbeyn—began clandestine discussions to quit. Earlier, Renaissance's human-resources staff had made a crucial mistake. When Belopolsky and Volfbeyn became principals of the firm, they had been given nondisclosure and noncompete agreements. The pair hadn't signed the noncompete agreements, though, and no one had noticed. It gave them an opening.

In July 2003, Belopolsky and Volfbeyn delivered a bombshell: They were joining Millennium Management, a rival firm run by billionaire hedge-fund manager Israel Englander, who had promised them the chance to make an even larger fortune.

Simons was gripped with fear, worried that Belopolsky and Volfbeyn had millions of lines of Medallion's source code. Simons was sure his secrets were about to get out, crippling the hedge fund.

"They stole from us!" he told a colleague in anger.

Simons hardly had a chance to digest the departures before he was confronted with true tragedy.

=

Nicholas Simons inherited his father's love of adventure. In 2002, a year after graduating from college, the young man, Simons's third-eldest son, took a job in Kathmandu, Nepal's capital, working with hydroelectric power for the Nepalese government as a contractor for a US consulting company. Nick fell in love with the city, renowned as a gateway to the spectacular Himalayas and a paradise for mountain trekkers.

Back on Long Island, Nick, who bore a resemblance to his father and shared his passion for hiking, told his parents he wanted to work in a Third World country, perhaps opening a medical clinic in Nepal to help its poorest residents. Nick would go on an around-the-world adventure with a friend and then return to learn organic chemistry and apply to medical school.

A week before he was scheduled to come home, Nick stopped in Amed, a long, coastal strip of fishing villages in eastern Bali and a hub for freediving, an exhilarating underwater sport in which divers hold their breath until resurfacing, eschewing scuba gear. One warm July day, Nick and his friend took turns diving one hundred feet down, enjoying the sea's clear, currentless conditions. The friends spotted each other, one up, one down, a freediving protocol meant to minimize the danger of the pressure changes and other serious threats far below the surface.

At one point, Nick's partner's mask fogged up, so he swam ashore to adjust his gear. Gone for just five minutes, he returned but couldn't locate Nick. He was found on the bottom of the sea. When Nick's body was brought to the surface, he couldn't be resuscitated. In the middle of the night, Jim and Marilyn were awoken by a call from their son's friend.

"Nick drowned," he said.

At the funeral, Jim and Marilyn were inconsolable, appearing pale and hollowed-out. The mourners' darkness was amplified by a hard rainstorm that evening and the kind of thunder and lightning a friend described as "apocalyptic."

Simons had an unswerving belief in logic, rationality, and science. He had played the odds in his trading, fighting a daily battle with chance, usually emerging victorious. Now Simons had suffered two tragic, unpredictable accidents. The events had been outliers, unexpected and almost inconceivable. Simons had been felled by randomness.

Simons struggled to comprehend how he could have so much good fortune in his professional life, yet be so ill-fated personally. As he sat shiva in his New York City home, Robert Frey, the Renaissance executive, drew Simons close, giving him a hug.

"Robert, my life is either aces or deuces," Simons told him. "I don't understand."

Seven years earlier, Paul's sudden death had been a crushing blow. Nick's passing was just as painful. Now, though, Simons's grief was mixed with anger, friends say, an emotion they rarely had seen in Simons. He turned crusty, even ornery, with colleagues and others.

"He saw the death as a betrayal," a friend says.

Dealing with intense pain, Jim and Marilyn spoke about purchasing a large part of St. John, moving to the island, and disappearing. Fitfully, they exited their tailspin. In September, Jim, Marilyn, and other family members traveled to Nepal for the first time, joining some of Nick's friends in searching for a way to continue Nick's legacy. Nick had been drawn to Kathmandu and had an interest in medicine, so they funded a maternity ward at a hospital in the city. Later, Jim and Marilyn would start the Nick Simons Institute, which offers health care assistance to those living in Nepal's rural areas, most of whom don't have basic emergency services.

At the office, Simons remained checked-out. For a while, he contemplated retirement and spent time working on mathematics problems with his friend Dennis Sullivan, looking for an escape.

"It was a refuge. A quiet place in my head," Simons said.[9]

Renaissance executives couldn't gain his attention, creating a leadership void as the firm's rifts grew. Long-simmering tensions were about to burst to the surface.

═

Brown and Mercer walked through the front door of Simons's home, claiming seats on one side of a long, formal dining room table. Magerman, Whitney, and others joined a bit later, grabbing spots around the table, with Simons pulling up a chair at the head.

It was the spring of 2004, and thirteen of Renaissance's top executives were meeting for dinner at Simons's twenty-two-acre estate in East Setauket, Long Island. None of the group really wanted to be there that evening, but they had to decide what to do about Alexey Kononenko.

By then, Kononenko's behavior had become a true distraction. He regularly ignored assignments from Brown and Mercer. When they scheduled a meeting to discuss his uncooperative behavior, Kononenko didn't show up.

(Someone close to Kononenko disputes how he and his actions have been portrayed by others who worked with him.)

Simons and the others were in a difficult bind, though. If they fired or reprimanded Kononenko and the half dozen colleagues he directed, the group was liable to bolt, just like Belopolsky and Volfbeyn. Their nondisclosure agreements were difficult to enforce, and while their noncompete contracts might prevent them from trading in the US, Kononenko and the others could return home to Eastern Europe, far from the reach of US law.

Wielding polished silverware, the executives dug into juicy steaks while sipping delicious red wine. The small talk died down as Simons turned serious.

"We have a decision to make," he said, which his tablemates understood to refer to Kononenko's "noncollaborative" conduct.

Brown was energized and adamant, arguing that they needed to retain Kononenko and his group. They represented about a third of the researchers who analyzed stocks and were too important to lose. Besides, they had spent so much time training the group that it would be a shame to see them leave.

"He adds value," Brown said with confidence. "The group is productive."

Brown's view reflected the sentiments of some at Renaissance who felt that while Kononenko ruffled feathers and could be unusually blunt, his behavior likely reflected the culture he had become accustomed to in Russia.

Mercer said hardly anything, of course, but he seemed to agree with Brown and others at the table voting to ignore Kononenko's infractions. Simons also seemed in favor of keeping the team.

"We can fire these guys," Simons said. "But if they leave, they'll compete with us and make our lives harder."

Simons didn't approve of Kononenko's behavior, but he thought Kononenko could be groomed into a team player, and even emerge as an effective manager.

"He was a pain in the ass, and it was a difficult decision," Simons later told a friend. "But he didn't steal from us," alluding to the alleged actions of Belopolsky and Volfbeyn.

As Magerman listened to the arguments, he tensed up. He couldn't believe what he was hearing. Kononenko's team had tried to get Brown and Mercer fired. They had forced Simons to take a pay cut and gave everyone a hard time, upending the collaborative, collegial culture that helped Renaissance thrive. Simons saw potential in Kononenko? Magerman wasn't standing for it.

"This is disgusting!" he said, looking at Simons and then at Brown. "If we don't shut them down or fire them, I'm quitting."

Magerman looked over at Whitney, hoping for some support. He didn't hear anything. Whitney knew they were outnumbered. Privately, Whitney had told Simons he was leaving the firm if Alexey wasn't fired. Simons and the others were sure Magerman and Whitney were bluffing; they weren't going anywhere. A consensus was reached: Kononenko and his gang would stay. Soon, he'd even get a promotion.

"Give us time, David, we'll manage it," Brown said.

"We have a plan," Simons added, also trying to reassure Magerman.

Magerman and Whitney filed out of the room, solemn and distressed. Soon, they'd form their own plans.

=

Close to midnight, after his staffers left, Simons returned to the quiet of his home. His firm was torn in two. Senior staffers were about to spill Medallion's most treasured secrets. Nicholas's death still haunted him. Simons had to find a way to deal with it all.

CHAPTER THIRTEEN

All models are wrong, but some are useful.

George Box, statistician

Jim Simons faced a growing list of problems.

He had one possible solution.

Staffers were squabbling, and two key scientists had bolted, possibly taking Medallion's secrets with them. Simons had concerns about his remaining employees, as well. Yes, the hedge fund, which managed over $5 billion, continued to score strong annual gains of about 25 percent after fees. In 2004, Medallion's Sharpe ratio even hit 7.5, a jaw-dropping figure that dwarfed that of its rivals. But Simons worried about his employees slacking. Renaissance had hired dozens of mathematicians and scientists over the course of several years, and Simons felt pressure to keep them busy and productive. He needed to find them a new challenge.

"All these scientists are wealthier than they ever imagined," Simons told a colleague. "How do I motivate them?"

Simons had another, more personal reason to seek a new project. He continued to struggle with intense, enduring emotional pain from the sudden death of his son, Nicholas. A few years earlier, Simons had seemed eager to retire from the trading business; now he was desperate for distractions.

Simons had no interest in shaking up Medallion's operations. Once a year, the fund returned its gains to its investors—mostly the firm's own employees—ensuring that it didn't get too big. If Medallion managed much more money, Simons, Henry Laufer, and others were convinced that its performance—still tied to various short-term price fluctuations—would suffer.

The size limit meant Medallion sometimes identified more market aberrations and phenomena than it could put to use. The discarded trading signals usually involved longer-term opportunities. Simons's scientists were more confident about short-term signals, partly because more data was available to help confirm them. A one-day trading signal can incorporate data points for every trading day of the year, for instance, while a one-year signal depends on just one annual data point. Nonetheless, the researchers were pretty sure they could make solid money if they ever had a chance to develop algorithms focused on a longer holding period.

That gave Simons an idea—why not start a new hedge fund to take advantage of these extraneous, longer-term predictive signals? The returns likely wouldn't be as good as Medallion's, Simons realized, given that a new fund wouldn't be able to take advantage of the firm's more-dependable short-term trades, but such a fund likely could manage a lot more money than Medallion. A mega-fund holding investments for long periods wouldn't incur the trading costs that a similarly sized fast-trading fund would, for example. Relying on longer-term trades would also prevent the new fund from cannibalizing Medallion's returns.

Researching and then rolling out a new hedge fund would represent a fresh challenge to galvanize the firm, Simons concluded. There was an added bonus to the idea, too. Simons was thinking about finding a buyer for Renaissance. Maybe not for the entire firm, but for a piece of it. Simons was approaching seventy years of age and he thought it wouldn't be a bad idea to sell some of his equity in the firm, though he wasn't willing to tell anyone. A giant new hedge fund generating dependable, recurring income from its fees and returns would carry special appeal for potential buyers.

Some at Renaissance didn't see the point of such a venture. It likely would disrupt their work and lead to an influx of nosy investors traipsing through the hallways. But Simons had the last word, and he wanted the fund. His researchers settled on one that would trade with little human intervention, like Medallion, yet would hold investments a month or even longer. It would incorporate some of Renaissance's usual tactics, such as finding correlations and patterns in prices, but would add other, more fundamental strategies, including buying inexpensive shares based on price-earnings ratios, balance-sheet data, and other information.

After thorough testing, the scientists determined the new hedge fund could beat the stock market by a few percentage points each year, while generating lower volatility than the overall market. It would produce the kinds of steady returns that hold special appeal for pension funds and other large institutions. Even better, the prospective fund could score those returns even if it managed as much as $100 billion, they calculated, an amount that would make it history's largest hedge fund.

As a newly hired sales team began pitching the fund, named the Renaissance Institutional Equities Fund, or RIEF, they made it clear the fund wouldn't resemble Medallion. Some investors ignored the disclaimer, considering it a mere formality. Same firm, same researchers, same risk and trading models, same returns, they figured. By 2005, Medallion sported annualized returns of 38.4 percent over the previous fifteen years (after those enormous fees), a performance that RIEF's sales documents made sure to note. The new fund's returns would have to be *somewhat* close to Medallion's results, the investors figured. Plus, RIEF was only charging a 1 percent management fee and 10 percent of all performance of any gains, a bargain compared to Medallion.

RIEF opened its doors in the summer of 2005. A year later, with the new fund already a few percentage points ahead of the broader stock market, investors started lining up to hand their money over. Soon, they had plowed $14 billion into RIEF.

Some prospective investors seemed most excited by the prospect of meeting Simons, the celebrity investor, or his secretive staffers, who seemed blessed with magical trading abilities. When David Dwyer, a senior sales executive, led tours of Renaissance's campus for potential clients, he'd stop and point out scientists and mathematicians as they went about their daily routines, as if they were exotic, rarely seen creatures in their natural habitat.

"In that conference room, our scientists review their latest predictive signals."

Ooh.

"That's where the crucial peer-review process happens."

Aah.

"Over there, Jim Simons meets with his top executives to map strategy."

Wow!

As the visitors passed the kitchen area, mathematicians sometimes wandered by to toast a bagel or grab a muffin, eliciting excited nudging from the group, and some alarm from staffers unaccustomed to seeing outsiders staring at them.

Next, Dwyer took his visitors downstairs to see Renaissance's data group, where over thirty PhDs and others—including Chinese nationals and a few newly hired female scientists—were usually deep in thought near whiteboards filled with intricate formulas. The job of these scientists, Dwyer explained, was to take thousands of outside data feeds pumping nonstop into the company and scrub them clean, removing errors and irregularities so the mathematicians upstairs could use the information to uncover price patterns.

Dwyer's tour usually concluded back upstairs in Renaissance's computer room, which was the size of a couple of tennis courts. There, stacks of servers, in long rows of eight-foot-tall metal cages, were linked together, blinking and quietly processing thousands of trades, even as his guests watched. The air in the room had a different feel and smell—brittle and dry, as if they could feel volts of electricity pumping. The room helped underscore Dwyer's message: Renaissance's mathematical models and scientific approach were its backbone.

"Rarely did they come and not invest," Dwyer says.

Sometimes Simons or Brown joined client presentations to say hello and field questions. These meetings sometimes veered in unexpected directions. Once, a RIEF salesman arranged a lunch at Renaissance's Long Island office for the Robert Wood Johnson Foundation, the largest foundation dedicated to funding public-health initiatives. As the foundation's investment team entered a big conference room and shook hands with RIEF sales staffers, they distributed business cards embossed with the Wood Johnson motto: "Building a Culture of Health."

The lunch went well, and the foundation appeared close to writing a big check to RIEF. To cap things off, a thick, iced vanilla cake was placed in the middle of the table. Everyone eyed the dessert, preparing for a taste. Just then, Simons walked in, setting the room ablaze.

"Jim, can we take a picture?" asked one of the health organization's investment professionals.

As the small talk got under way, Simons began making odd motions with his right hand. The foundation executives had no clue what was happening, but nervous RIEF staffers did. When Simons was desperate for a smoke, he scrabbled at his left breast pocket, where he kept his Merits. There was nothing in there, though, so Simons called his assistant on an intercom system, asking her to bring him a cigarette.

"Do you mind if I smoke?" Simons asked his guests.

Before they knew it, Simons was lighting up. Soon, fumes were choking the room. The Robert Wood Johnson representatives—still dedicated to building a culture of health—were stunned. Simons didn't seem to notice or care. After some awkward chitchat, he looked to put out his cigarette, now down to a burning butt, but he couldn't locate an ashtray. Now the RIEF staffers were sweating—Simons was known to ash pretty much anywhere he pleased in the office, even on the desks of underlings and in their coffee mugs. Simons was in Renaissance's swankiest conference room, though, and he couldn't find an appropriate receptacle.

Finally, Simons spotted the frosted cake. He stood up, reached across the table, and buried his cigarette deep in the icing. As the cake sizzled, Simons walked out, the mouths of his guests agape. The Renaissance salesmen were crestfallen, convinced their lucrative sale had been squandered. The foundation's executives recovered their poise quickly, however, eagerly signing a big check. It was going to take more than choking on cigarette smoke and a ruined vanilla cake to keep them from the new fund.

Other than making the occasional slipup, Simons was an effective salesman, a world-class mathematician with a rare ability to connect with those who couldn't do stochastic differential equations. Simons told entertaining stories, had a dry sense of humor, and held interests far afield from science and moneymaking. He also demonstrated unusual loyalty and concern for others, qualities the investors may have sensed. Once, Dennis Sullivan, returning to Stony Brook after two decades in France, drove to Renaissance's parking lot to talk with Simons. The two spent hours speaking about math formulas, but Simons sensed Sullivan was struggling with a different kind of problem. It turned out that Sullivan, who had six children from multiple marriages over forty years, was fielding financial requests from his kids and was having difficulty deciding how to treat each fairly.

Simons sat silently, considering the dilemma before offering a Solomonic answer in just two words.

"Eventually, equal," Simons said.

The answer satisfied Sullivan, who departed feeling relieved. The meeting cemented their friendship, and the two began spending more time collaborating on mathematics research papers.

Simons could be frank about his own personal life, which also endeared him to investors and friends. When asked how someone so devoted to science could smoke so much, in defiance of statistical possibilities, Simons answered that his genes had been tested, and he had the unique ability to handle a habit that proved harmful to most others.

"When you get past a certain age, you should be in the clear," he said.

Brown was almost as smooth and capable with investors, but Mercer was another story. RIEF's marketers tried to keep him away from clients, lest he laugh at an unexpected point in a conversation or do something else off-putting. One time, when neither Simons nor Brown was around to greet representatives of a West Coast endowment, Mercer joined the meeting. Asked how the firm made so much money, Mercer offered an explanation.

"So, we have a signal," Mercer began, his colleagues nodding nervously. "Sometimes it tells us to buy Chrysler, sometimes it tells us to sell."

Instant silence and raised eyebrows. Chrysler hadn't existed as a company since being acquired by German automaker Daimler back in 1998. Mercer didn't seem to know; he was a quant, so he didn't actually pay attention to the companies he traded. The endowment overlooked the flub, becoming RIEF's latest investor.

By the spring of 2007, it was getting hard to keep investors away. Thirty-five billion dollars had been plowed into RIEF, making it one of the world's largest hedge funds. Renaissance had to institute a $2 billion per month limit on new investments—yes, the fund was built to handle $100 billion, but not all at once. Simons made plans for other new funds, initiating work on the Renaissance Institutional Futures Fund, RIFF, to trade futures contracts on bonds, currencies, and other assets in a long-term style. A new batch of scientists was hired, while staffers from other parts of the company lent a hand, fulfilling Simons's goal of energizing and unifying staffers.[1]

He still had another pressing problem to address.

In late spring 2007, Simons was in his office in a midtown New York City building—a forty-one-story glass-and-steel structure steps from Grand Central Terminal—staring at Israel Englander, a graying, fifty-seven-year-old billionaire known for his distinctive tortoiseshell glasses. The men were tense, miserable, and angry at each other. It wasn't their first confrontation.

Four years earlier, researchers Pavel Volfbeyn and Alexander Belopolsky had quit Renaissance to trade stocks for Englander's hedge fund, Millennium Management. Furious, Simons stormed into Englander's office one day, demanding that he fire the traders, a request that had offended Englander.

"Show me the proof," he told Simons at the time, asking for evidence that Volfbeyn and Belopolsky had taken Renaissance's proprietary information.

Privately, Englander wondered if Simons's true fear was the possibility of additional departures from his firm, rather than any theft. Simons wouldn't share much with his rival. He and Renaissance sued Englander's firm, as well as Volfbeyn and Belopolsky, while the traders brought countersuits against Renaissance.

Amid the hostilities, Volfbeyn and Belopolsky set up their own quantitative-trading system, racking up about $100 million of profits while becoming, as Englander told a colleague, some of the most successful traders Englander had encountered. At Renaissance, Volfbeyn and Belopolsky had signed nondisclosure agreements prohibiting them from using or sharing Medallion's secrets. They had refused to sign noncompete agreements, though, viewing the firm as underhanded for slipping them in a pile of other papers to be signed, according to a colleague. With no signed noncompete agreement to worry about, Englander figured he had the right to hire the researchers as long as they didn't use any of Renaissance's secrets.

Sitting in a plush chair across from Simons that spring day, Englander said he hadn't been privy to the details of how his hires traded. Volfbeyn and Belopolsky had told Englander and others that they relied on open-source software and the insights of academic papers and other financial literature, not Renaissance's intellectual property. Why should Englander fire them?

Simons turned furious. He was also worried. If Volfbeyn and Belopolsky weren't stopped, their trading could eat into Medallion's profits. The defections might pave the way for others to bolt. There also was a principle involved, Simons felt.

They stole from me!

Evidence had begun to mount that Volfbeyn and Belopolsky may, in fact, have taken Medallion's intellectual property. One independent expert concluded that the researchers used much of the same source code as Medallion. They also relied on a similar mathematical model to measure the market impact of their trades. At least one expert witness became so skeptical of Volfbeyn and Belopolsky's explanations that he refused to testify on their behalf. One of the strategies Volfbeyn and Belopolsky employed was even called "Henry's signal." It seemed more than a coincidence that Renaissance used a similar strategy with the exact same name developed by Henry Laufer, Simons's longtime partner.

Simons and Englander didn't make much headway that day, but a few months later, they cut a deal. Englander's firm agreed to terminate Volfbeyn and Belopolsky and pay Renaissance $20 million. Some within Renaissance were incensed—the renegade researchers had made much more than $20 million trading for Englander, and, after taking a break of several years, they'd be free to resume their activities. But Simons was relieved to put the dispute behind him and to send a message of warning to those at the firm who might think of following in the footsteps of the wayward researchers.

It seemed nothing could stop Simons and Renaissance.

=

RIEF was off to a great start and Medallion was still printing money. Peter Brown was so cocksure that he placed a bet with a colleague: If Medallion scored a 100 percent return in 2007, Brown would get his colleague's new, Mercedes E-Class car. Brown's competitive streak extended to other parts of his life. Lean and six feet tall, Brown challenged colleagues to squash matches and tests of strength in the company's gym. When Simons brought employees and their families to a resort in Bermuda for a vacation, many lounged around a swimming pool wearing knee-high black socks and sandals, watching a water volleyball game. Suddenly, a commotion disrupted the peace. Someone in the pool was lunging for the ball, spraying water in his teammates' eyes, his elbows dangerously close to the face of a nearby child.

"Who's the maniac?" an alarmed mother asked, edging closer to the pool.

"Oh, that's just Peter," a staffer said.

Both Brown and Mercer dealt in logic, not feelings. Many of the scientists and mathematicians they hired were just as brilliant, driven, and seemingly detached from human emotion. On the way home from the Bermuda trip, as staffers lined up to board the return flight, someone suggested they clear the way for a pregnant woman. Some Renaissance scientists refused. They didn't have anything against the woman, but if she truly wanted to board early, she logically would have arrived early, they said.

"It was like being with a bunch of Sheldons," says an outsider on the trip, referring to the character on the television show *The Big Bang Theory*.

As he assumed more responsibility, Brown spent more time dealing with marketing executives and others who hadn't experienced his brusque, erratic style. Like an adolescent, Brown often was irreverent, even mischievous, especially when the fund was doing well. But he became unhinged about relatively small things. Once, during a meeting, an underling inadvertently placed his phone on vibrate mode, rather than turn it off. As Brown spoke, the phone went off, shaking and toppling a stack of books. Brown's eyes widened. He stared at the phone, and then at the employee. Then he went berserk.

"Get that fucking thing out of here!" Brown screamed at the top of his lungs.

"Take it easy, Peter," said Mark Silber, the chief financial officer. "Everything will be all right."

Mercer also had an ability to calm Brown. Just being around Mercer seemed to put Brown in better spirits. Mercer didn't interact very much with most colleagues, whistling at times during the day, but he frequently huddled with Brown to produce ideas to improve the trading models. One was emotional and outgoing, the other taciturn and circumspect, a bit like the comedy duo Penn & Teller (but much less funny).

=

In July 2007, RIEF experienced a minor loss, but the Medallion fund was up 50 percent for the year, and Brown appeared positioned to win his colleague's Mercedes. Elsewhere in the economy, troubles were brewing for so-called subprime home mortgages, the kinds written by aggressive lenders to US borrowers with scuffed or limited credit histories. Worrywarts predicted the difficulties might spread, but few thought a corner of the mortgage market was capable of crippling the broader stock or bond markets. Either way, Brown and Mercer's statistical-arbitrage stock trades were market neutral, so the jitters were unlikely to affect returns.

On Friday, August 3, the Dow Jones Industrial Average plummeted 281 points, a loss attributed to concern about the health of investment bank Bear Stearns. The drop didn't seem like a big deal, though. Most senior investors were on vacation, after all, so reading into the losses didn't seem worthwhile.

By that summer, a group of quantitative hedge funds had emerged dominant. Inspired by Simons's success, most had their own market-neutral strategies just as reliant on computer models and automated trades. In Morgan Stanley's midtown Manhattan headquarters, Peter Muller—a blue-eyed quant who played piano at a local club in his free time—led a team managing $6 billion for a division of the bank called PDT. In Greenwich, Connecticut, Clifford Asness, a University of Chicago PhD, helped lead a $39 billion quantitative hedge-fund firm called AQR Capital Management. And in Chicago, Ken Griffin—who, in the late 1980s, had installed a satellite dish on his dormitory roof at Harvard to get up-to-the-second quotes—was using high-powered computers to make statistical-arbitrage trades and other moves at his $13 billion firm, Citadel.

On the afternoon of Monday, August 6, all the quant traders were hit with sudden, serious losses. At AQR, Asness snapped shut the blinds of the glass partition of his corner office and began calling contacts to understand what was happening. Word emerged that a smaller quant fund called Tykhe Capital was in trouble, while a division of Goldman Sachs that invested in a systematic fashion also was suffering. It wasn't clear who was doing the selling, or why it was impacting so many firms that presumed their strategies unique. Later, academics and others would posit that a fire sale by at least one quant fund, along with abrupt moves by others to slash their borrowing—perhaps as their own investors raised cash to deal with struggling mortgage investments—had sparked a brutal downturn that became known as "the quant quake."

During the stock market crash of 1987, investors were failed by sophisticated models. In 1998, Long-Term Capital saw historic losses. Algorithmic traders braced for their latest fiasco.

"It's bad, Cliff," Michael Mendelson, AQR's head of global trading, told Asness. "This has the feel of a liquidation."[2]

For most of that Monday, Simons wasn't focused on stocks. He and his family were in Boston following the death and funeral of his mother, Marcia. In the afternoon, Simons and his cousin, Robert Lourie, who ran Renaissance's futures-trading business, flew back to Long Island on Simons's Gulfstream G450. Onboard, they learned Medallion and RIEF were getting crushed. Simons told Lourie not to worry.

"We always have very good days" after difficult ones, he said.

Tuesday was worse, however. Simons and his colleagues watched their computer screens flash red for no apparent reason. Brown's mood turned grim.

"I don't know what the hell is going on, but it's not good," Brown told someone.

On Wednesday, things got scary. Simons, Brown, Mercer, and about six others hustled into a central conference room, grabbing seats around a table. They immediately focused on a series of charts affixed to a wall detailing the magnitude of the firm's losses and at what point Medallion's bank lenders would make margin calls, demanding additional collateral to avoid selling the fund's equity positions. One basket of stocks had already plunged so far that Renaissance had to come up with additional collateral to forestall a sale. If its positions suffered much deeper losses, Medallion would have to provide its lenders with even more collateral to prevent massive stock sales and losses that were even more dramatic.

The conference room was close by an open atrium where groups of researchers met to work. As the meeting continued, nervous staffers studied the faces of those entering and leaving the room, gauging the level of desperation among the executives.

Inside, a battle had begun. Seven years earlier, during the 2000 technology-stock meltdown, Brown didn't know what to do. This time, he was sure. The sell-off wouldn't last long, he argued. Renaissance should stick with its trading system, Brown said. Maybe even *add* positions. Their system, programmed to buy and sell on its own, was already doing just that, seizing on the chaos and expanding some positions.

"This is an opportunity!" Brown said.

Bob Mercer seemed in agreement.

"Trust the models—let them run," Henry Laufer added.

Simons shook his head. He didn't know if his firm could survive much more pain. He was scared. If losses grew, and they couldn't come up with enough collateral, the banks would sell Medallion's positions and suffer their own huge losses. If that happened, no one would deal with Simons's fund again. It would be a likely death blow, even if Renaissance suffered smaller financial losses than its bank lenders.

Medallion needed to sell, not buy, he told his colleagues.

"Our job is to survive," Simons said. "If we're wrong, we can always add [positions] later."

Brown seemed shocked by what he was hearing. He had absolute faith in the algorithms he and his fellow scientists had developed. Simons was overruling him in a public way and taking issue with the trading system itself, it seemed.

On Thursday, Medallion began reducing equity positions to build cash. Back in the conference room, Simons, Brown, and Mercer stared at a single computer screen that was updating the firm's profits and losses. They wanted to see how their selling would influence the market. When the first batch of shares were sold, the market felt the blow, dropping further, causing still more losses. Later, it happened again. In silence, Simons stood and stared.

Problems grew for all the leading quant firms; PDT lost $600 million of Morgan Stanley's money over just two days. Now the selling was spreading to the overall market. That Thursday, the S&P 500 dropped 3 percent, and the Dow fell 387 points. Medallion already had lost more than *$1 billion* that week, a stunning 20 percent. RIEF, too, was plunging, down nearly *$3* *billion*, or about 10 percent. An eerie quiet enveloped Renaissance's lunchroom, as researchers and others sat in silence, wondering if the firm would survive. Researchers stayed up past midnight, trying to make sense of the problems.

Are our models broken?

It turned out that the firm's rivals shared about a quarter of its positions. Renaissance was plagued with the same illness infecting so many others. Some rank-and-file senior scientists were upset—not so much by the losses, but because Simons had interfered with the trading system and reduced positions. Some took the decision as a personal affront, a sign of ideological weakness and a lack of conviction in their labor.

"You're dead wrong," a senior researcher emailed Simons.

"You believe in the system, or you don't," another scientist said, with some disgust.

Simons said he did believe in the trading system, but the market's losses were unusual—more than twenty standard deviations from the average, a level of loss most had never come close to experiencing.

"How far can it go?" Simons wondered.

Renaissance's lenders were even more fearful. If Medallion kept losing money, Deutsche Bank and Barclays likely would be facing billions of dollars of losses. Few at the banks were even aware of the basket-option arrangements. Such sudden, deep losses likely would shock investors and regulators, raising questions about the banks' management and overall health. Martin Malloy, the Barclays executive who dealt most closely with Renaissance, picked up the phone to call Brown, hoping for some reassurance. Brown sounded harried but in control.

Others were beginning to panic. That Friday, Dwyer, the senior executive hired two years earlier to sell RIEF to institutions, left the office to pitch representatives of a reinsurance company. With RIEF down about 10 percent for the year, even as the overall stock market was up, customers were up in arms. More important for Dwyer: He had sold his home upon joining Renaissance and invested the proceeds in Medallion. Like others at the firm, he had also borrowed money from Deutsche Bank to invest in the fund. Now Dwyer was down nearly a million dollars. Dwyer had battled Crohn's disease in his youth. The symptoms had abated, but now he was dealing with sharp aches, fever, and terrible abdominal cramping; his stress had triggered a return of the disease.

After the meeting, Dwyer drove to Long Island Sound to board a ferry to Massachusetts to meet his family for the weekend. As Dwyer parked his car and waited to hand his keys to an attendant, he imagined an end to his agony.

Just let the brakes fail.

Dwyer was in an emotional free fall. Back in the office, though, signs were emerging that Medallion was stabilizing. When the fund again sold positions that morning, the market seemed to handle the trades without weakening. Some attributed the market's turn to a buy order that day by Asness of AQR.

"I think we'll get through this," Simons told a colleague. "Let's stop lightening up." Simons was ordering the firm to halt its selling.

By Monday morning, Medallion and RIEF were both making money again, as were most other big quant traders, as if a fever had broken. Dwyer felt deep relief. Later, some at Renaissance complained the gains would have been larger had Simons not overridden their trading system.

"We gave up a lot of extra profit," a staffer told him.

"I'd make the same decision again," Simons responded.

=

Before long, Renaissance had regained its footing. Growing turbulence in global markets aided Medallion's signals, helping the fund score gains of 86 percent in 2007, nearly enough for Brown to win the Mercedes. The newer RIEF fund lost a bit of money that year, but the loss didn't seem a huge deal.

By early 2008, problems for subprime mortgages had infected almost every corner of the US and global stock and bond markets, but Medallion was thriving from the chaos, as usual, rising over 20 percent in the year's first few months. Simons revived the idea of selling as much as 20 percent of Renaissance.

In May 2008, Simons, Brown, and a few other Renaissance executives flew to Qatar to meet representatives of the country's sovereign-wealth fund, to discuss selling a piece of Renaissance. Because they arrived on a Friday, a day of prayer for Muslims, their meetings couldn't be scheduled until the next day. The hotel's concierge recommended the group try dune bashing, a popular form of off-roading in which four-wheel-drive vehicles climb and then slide down steep sand dunes at high speeds and dangerous angles, much like a desert roller coaster. It was a brutally hot day, and Brown and others hit the hotel's swimming pool. But Simons headed out into the desert with Stephen Robert, an industry veteran and former chief executive of the investment firm Oppenheimer, whom Simons had hired to oversee Renaissance's marketing and strategic direction.

Before long, they were riding dunes that seemed as high as mountains at such breakneck speeds that their vehicle almost tipped over. Simons turned pale.

"Jim, are you okay?" Robert shouted over the vehicle's engine.

"We could get killed!" Simons yelled back, fear in his voice.

"Relax, they do this all the time," Robert told him.

"What if this tips over?" Simons responded. "People think I'm pretty smart—I'm going to die in the dumbest way possible!"

For another five minutes, Simons was gripped with terror. Then, suddenly, he relaxed, color returning to his face.

"I got it!" Simons yelled to Robert. "There's a principle in physics: We can't tip over unless the tires have traction! We're in sand, so the tires have nothing to grab on to!"

Simons flashed a smile, proud he'd figured out a most relevant scientific problem.

=

Glen Whitney wasn't nearly as relaxed.

After the dinner at Jim Simons's home where it was decided that Alexey Kononenko wouldn't be punished for his behavior, Whitney became dejected. He and Magerman had promised they would quit, but few at Renaissance believed them. Who forgoes tens of millions of dollars a year over an annoying colleague and worries about a firm's culture?

Whitney was serious, though. He saw the Kononenko decision as the last straw. Earlier, Whitney had protested Simons's decision to kick nonemployees out of Medallion. He wasn't sure a hedge fund added much to society if it just made money for employees. Once, Renaissance had seemed like a close-knit university department. Now the sharp elbows were getting to him.

In the summer of 2008, Whitney announced he was accepting a leadership role at the National Museum of Mathematics, or MoMath, the first museum in North America devoted to celebrating mathematics. Colleagues mocked him. If Whitney really wanted to improve society, some told him, he'd stay, accumulate more wealth, and then give it away later in life.

"You're leaving because you want to feel good about yourself," one colleague said.

"I have a right to personal happiness," Whitney responded.

"That's selfish," a staffer sniffed.

Whitney quit.

David Magerman also had had enough. A few years earlier, he had experienced a midlife crisis, partly due to the shocking September 11 terrorist attacks. Searching for more meaning in his life, Magerman traveled to Israel, returning more committed to Judaism. Not only was Kononenko still at the firm, but now he was co-running the entire equities business. Magerman couldn't take it anymore.

Magerman moved with his wife and three children from Long Island to Gladwyne, Pennsylvania, outside Philadelphia, searching for a calmer and more spiritual lifestyle.

=

As the global economy deteriorated throughout 2008, and financial markets tumbled, interest in a stake in Renaissance evaporated. But the Medallion fund thrived in the chaos, soaring 82 percent that year, helping Simons make over $2 billion in personal profits. The enormous gains sparked a call from a House of Representatives committee asking Simons to testify as part of its investigation into the causes of the financial collapse. Simons prepped diligently with his public-relations advisor Jonathan Gasthalter. With fellow hedge-fund managers George Soros to his right and John Paulson on his left, Simons told Congress that he would back a push to force hedge funds to share information with regulators and that he supported higher taxes for hedge-fund managers.

Simons was something of an afterthought, however, both at the hearings and in the finance industry itself. All eyes were on Paulson, Soros, and a few other investors who, unlike Simons, had successfully anticipated the financial meltdown. They did it with old-fashioned investment research, a reminder of the enduring potential and appeal of those traditional methods.

Paulson had first grown concerned about the runaway housing market in 2005, when a colleague named Paolo Pellegrini developed a price chart indicating that the housing market was 40 percent overpriced. Paulson knew opportunity was at hand.

"This is our bubble!" Paulson told Pellegrini. "This is proof."

Paulson and Pellegrini purchased protection for the riskiest mortgages in the form of credit default swaps, resulting in a $20 billion windfall over

2007 and 2008. George Soros, the veteran hedge-fund investor, placed his own CDS bets, scoring over a billion dollars in profits.[3] Baby-faced, thirty-nine-year-old David Einhorn won his own acclaim at a May 2008 industry conference when he accused investment bank Lehman Brothers of using accounting tricks to avoid billions of dollars of real-estate-related losses. Einhorn, who later attributed his success to his "critical thinking skill," was vindicated later that year when Lehman declared bankruptcy.[4]

The lesson was obvious: One *could* outsmart the market. It just took diligence, intelligence, and a whole lot of gumption. Simons's quantitative models, nerdy mathematicians, and geeky scientists, while effective, were too hard to understand, their methods too difficult to pull off, most decided.

In 2008, after RIEF dropped about 17 percent, Renaissance's researchers waved the losses off; they were within their simulations and seemed puny compared to the S&P 500's 37 percent drubbing, including dividends, that year. The scientists became concerned in 2009, however, when RIEF lost over 6 percent and the S&P 500 soared 26.5 percent. All those investors who had convinced themselves that RIEF would generate Medallion-like returns suddenly realized the firm was serious when it said it was a very different fund. Others grumbled that Medallion was still killing it while RIEF was struggling, believing something unfair was going on.

No longer in awe of Simons, RIEF investors peppered the seventy-one-year-old with tough questions in a May 2009 conference call. Simons wrote to his investors that the fund had suffered a "performance onslaught" during an "extreme market rally."

"We certainly understand our clients' discomfort," he said.[5]

Investors began to flee RIEF, which soon was down to less than $5 billion. A second fund Simons had started to trade stock futures also took on water and lost investors, while new clients dried up.

"No client on earth would touch us," says Dwyer, the senior salesman.

A year later, after some more underwhelming performance from RIEF,

Simons, who had turned seventy-two, decided it was time to pass the torch at the firm to Brown and Mercer. Medallion was still on fire. The fund, now managing $10 billion, had posted average returns of about 45 percent a year, after fees, since 1988, returns that outpaced those of Warren Buffett and every other investing star. (At that point, Buffett's Berkshire Hathaway had gained 20 percent annually since he took over in 1965.)

But Brown told a reporter the firm wasn't even sure it would keep RIEF or RIFF going, the latest sign investors had soured on the quantitative approach.

"If we assess that it's not something that's going to sell, then we'll decide it's not good to be in that business," Brown said.

As for Simons, he had devoted more than two decades to building remarkable wealth. Now he was going to spend it.

CHAPTER FOURTEEN

Jim Simons liked making money. He enjoyed spending it, too.

Stepping down from Renaissance gave Simons—who, by then, was worth about $11 billion—more time on his 220-foot yacht, *Archimedes*. Named for the Greek mathematician and inventor, the $100 million vessel featured a formal dining room that sat twenty, a wood-burning fireplace, a spacious Jacuzzi, and a grand piano. Sometimes, Simons flew friends on his Gulfstream G450 to a foreign location, where they'd join Jim and Marilyn on the super-yacht.

The ship's presence drew the attention of local media, making the aging and still-secretive mathematician unlikely international tabloid fodder.

"He was very down to earth," a taxi driver named Kenny Macrae told the *Scottish Sun* when Simons and some guests visited in Stornoway, Scotland, docking for a day trip. "He gave me a reasonable tip, too."[1]

Several years later, when Simons visited Bristol, England—the BBC speculated that Simons might be in town to purchase a British soccer team—the *Archimedes* became one of the largest ships ever to visit the city. Back home, Simons lived in a $50 million apartment in a limestone, pre-war Fifth Avenue building with stunning Central Park views. Some mornings, Simons bumped into George Soros, a neighbor in the building.

Years earlier, Marilyn had carved out space in her dressing room to launch a family foundation. Over time, she and Jim gave over $300 million to Stony Brook University, among other institutions. As Simons edged away from Renaissance, he became more personally involved in their philanthropy. More than anything, Simons relished tackling big problems. Soon, he was working with Marilyn to target two areas in dire need of solutions: autism research and mathematics education.

In 2003, Simons, who was dealing with a family member who had been diagnosed with autism, convened a roundtable of top scientists to discuss the developmental disease. He committed $100 million to fund new research, becoming the largest private donor in the field. Three years later, Simons tapped Columbia University neurobiologist Gerald Fischbach to expand his efforts. Over several years, the team established a repository of genetic samples from thousands of individuals with autism, as well as their family members, which they called the Simons Simplex Collection. The project would help scientists identify over one hundred genes related to autism and improve the understanding of the disease's biology. Research driven by the foundation would discover mutations believed to play a role in the disorder.

Separately, as technology and finance companies scooped up those with strong mathematics backgrounds, Simons became disturbed by how many math teachers in US public schools had limited education in the area themselves. Earlier in the decade, Simons had traveled to Washington, DC, to pitch the idea of providing stipends for the best mathematics teachers to reduce their temptation to join private industry. In a matter of minutes, Simons persuaded Chuck Schumer, the influential Democratic senator from New York, to support the proposal.

"That's a great idea!" Schumer boomed. "We'll get right on it."

Elated, Simons and a colleague plopped down on a couch outside Schumer's office. As a different group got off the couch to enter Schumer's office, Simons listened to their pitch and the senator's response.

"That's a great idea! We'll get right on it," Schumer said, once again.

Simons realized he couldn't count on politicians. In 2004, he helped launch Math for America, a nonprofit dedicated to promoting math education and supporting outstanding teachers. Eventually, the foundation would spend millions of dollars annually to provide annual stipends of $15,000 to one thousand top math and science teachers in New York's public middle schools and high schools, or about 10 percent of the city's teachers in the subjects. It also hosted seminars and workshops, creating a community of enthusiastic teachers.

"Instead of beating up the bad teachers, we focus on celebrating the good ones," Simons says. "We give them status and money, and they stay in the field."

Simons remained Renaissance's chairman and main shareholder, staying in regular contact with Brown, Mercer, and others. In reflective moments, Simons sometimes acknowledged having difficulty transitioning from the firm.

"I feel irrelevant," he told Marilyn one day.[2]

With time, Simons would find his philanthropic ventures as challenging as those he had encountered in mathematics and financial markets, lifting his spirits.

=

David Magerman moved with his wife and three young children to a Philadelphia suburb, searching for new meaning in his own life and perhaps a bit of peace after all those clashes at Renaissance. Magerman was eager to make a positive impact on society. Unlike Simons, who never had qualms about Renaissance's work, Magerman felt misgivings, even a bit of guilt. Magerman had devoted years of his life to helping Renaissance's wealthy employees become even richer. Now he wanted to help others.

Magerman didn't have Simons's billions, but he left Renaissance with well over $50 million, thanks to years of hefty bonuses and an enormous return on his investment in the Medallion fund. Magerman, who was beginning to adopt a Modern Orthodox lifestyle, began giving millions of dollars to needy students and Jewish day schools in the area, which had been hit hard by the 2008 economic downturn. Eventually, Magerman started his own foundation and a high school.

His new life didn't bring much serenity, however. Magerman brought his strong opinions to the world of philanthropy, insisting on so many requirements and conditions that some local leaders turned his money down, leading to hurt feelings. At one point, he was caught in a screaming match with a group of middle-school parents. Magerman joined the faculty of his alma mater, the University of Pennsylvania, lecturing in the Electrical and Systems Engineering department and giving a course on quantitative portfolio management. Disagreements arose there, too.

"The kids didn't like me; I didn't like them," he says.

Magerman helped finance a Will Ferrell movie called *Everything Must Go*, which received decent reviews but disappointed Magerman, who never saw a final cut. He agreed to watch another film he financed, *Café*, starring Jennifer Love Hewitt, hosting the actor and her boyfriend in his home theater, but Magerman wasn't a fan of that film, either.[3]

For all his faults, Magerman was the rare quant blessed with a degree of self-awareness. He began working with a therapist to eliminate, or at least tone down, his confrontational behavior, and he seemed to make progress.

By 2010, two years after leaving Renaissance, Magerman was itching to return. He missed computer programming and was a bit bored, but he also didn't want to uproot his family again. Magerman got in touch with Peter Brown and worked out an arrangement to work remotely from home, a perfect solution for someone who couldn't seem to avoid personal squabbles.

When he quit, Magerman had overseen the software responsible for executing all of Renaissance's computerized stock trades. Now Kononenko was running the effort, and it was racking up big gains. A return to that group was untenable. Instead, Magerman began doing research for Renaissance's bond, commodity, and currency-trading business. Soon, he was again participating in key meetings, his booming and insistent voice piped into speakers from the ceilings of Renaissance's conference rooms, an effect colleagues joked was like listening to "the voice of God."

"You can't win for trying, sometimes," Magerman says.

He returned to a firm on more solid ground than he had expected. Renaissance wasn't quite as collegial as it had been in the past, but the team still worked well together, perhaps even with a greater sense of urgency. By then, RIEF's returns had improved enough for Brown and Mercer to decide to keep it open for business, along with the newer fund, RIFF. The two funds managed a combined $6 billion, down from over $30 billion three years earlier, but at least investors had stopped fleeing.

Medallion, still only available to employees, remained the heart of the firm. It now managed about $10 billion and was scoring annual gains of approximately 65 percent, before the investor fees, resulting in near-record profits. Medallion's long-term record was arguably the greatest in the history of the financial markets, a reason investors and others were becoming fascinated with the secretive firm.

"There's Renaissance Technologies, and then there's everyone else," *The Economist* said in 2010.[4]

Medallion still held thousands of long and short positions at any time, and its holding period ranged from one or two days to one or two weeks. The fund did even faster trades, described by some as *high-frequency*, but many of those were for hedging purposes or to gradually build its positions. Renaissance still placed an emphasis on cleaning and collecting its data, but it had refined its risk management and other trading techniques.

"I'm not sure we're the best at all aspects of trading, but we're the best at estimating the cost of a trade," Simons told a colleague a couple years earlier.

In some ways, the Renaissance machine was more powerful than before Magerman quit. The company now employed about 250 staffers and over sixty PhDs, including experts in artificial intelligence, quantum physicists, computational linguists, statisticians, and number theorists, as well as other scientists and mathematicians.

Astronomers, who are accustomed to scrutinizing large, confusing data sets and discovering evidence of subtle phenomena, proved especially capable of identifying overlooked market patterns. Elizabeth Barton, for example, received her PhD from Harvard University and used telescopes in Hawaii and elsewhere to study the evolution of galaxies before joining Renaissance. As it slowly became a bit more diverse, the firm also hired Julia Kempe, a former student of Elwyn Berlekamp and an expert in quantum computing.

Medallion still did bond, commodity, and currency trades, and it made money from trending and reversion-predicting signals, including a particularly effective one aptly named Déjà Vu. More than ever, though, it was powered by complex equity trades featuring a mixture of complex signals, rather than simple *pairs* trades, such as buying Coke and selling Pepsi.

The gains on each trade were never huge, and the fund only got it right a bit more than half the time, but that was more than enough.

"We're right 50.75 percent of the time . . . but we're 100 percent right 50.75 percent of the time," Mercer told a friend. "You can make billions that way."

Mercer likely wasn't sharing his firm's exact trading edge—his larger point was that Renaissance enjoyed a slight advantage in its collection of thousands of simultaneous trades, one that was large and consistent enough to make an enormous fortune.

Driving these reliable gains was a key insight: Stocks and other investments are influenced by more factors and forces than even the most sophisticated investors appreciated. For example, to predict the direction of a stock like Alphabet, the parent of Google, investors generally try to forecast the company's earnings, the direction of interest rates, the health of the US economy, and the like. Others will anticipate the future of search and online advertising, the outlook for the broader technology industry, the trajectory of global companies, and metrics and ratios related to earnings, book value, and other variables.

Renaissance staffers deduced that there is even more that influences investments, including forces not readily apparent or sometimes even logical. By analyzing and estimating hundreds of financial metrics, social media feeds, barometers of online traffic, and pretty much *anything* that can be quantified and tested, they uncovered new factors, some borderline impossible for most to appreciate.

"The inefficiencies are so complex they are, in a sense, hidden in the markets in code," a staffer says. "RenTec decrypts them. We find them across time, across risk factors, across sectors and industries."

Even more important: Renaissance concluded that there are reliable mathematical relationships *between* all these forces. Applying data science, the researchers achieved a better sense of when various factors were relevant, how they interrelated, and the frequency with which they influenced shares. They also tested and teased out subtle, nuanced mathematical relationships between various shares—what staffers call *multidimensional anomalies*—that other investors were oblivious to or didn't fully understand.

"These relationships have to exist, since companies are interconnected in complex ways," says a former Renaissance executive. "This interconnectedness is hard to model and predict with accuracy, and it changes over time. RenTec has built a machine to model this interconnectedness, track its behavior over time, and bet on when prices seem out of whack according to these models."

Outsiders didn't quite get it, but the real key was the firm's engineering—how it put all those factors and forces together in an automated trading system. The firm bought a certain number of stocks with positive signals, often a combination of more granular individual signals, and shorted, or bet against, stocks with negative signals, moves determined by thousands of lines of source code.

"There is no individual bet we make that we can explain by saying we think one stock is going to go up or another down," a senior staffer says. "Every bet is a function of all the other bets, our risk profile, and what we expect to do in the near and distant future. It's a big, complex optimization based on the premise that we predict the future well enough to make money from our predictions, and that we understand risk, cost, impact, and market structure well enough to leverage the hell out of it."

How the firm wagered was at least as important as *what* it wagered on. If Medallion discovered a profitable signal, for example that the dollar rose 0.1 percent between nine a.m. and ten a.m., it wouldn't buy when the clock struck nine, potentially signaling to others that a move happened each day at that time. Instead, it spread its buying out throughout the hour in unpredictable ways, to preserve its trading signal. Medallion developed methods of trading some of its strongest signals "to capacity," as insiders called it, moving prices such that competitors couldn't find them. It was a bit like hearing of a huge markdown on a hot item at Target and buying up almost all the discounted merchandise the moment the store opens, so no one else even realizes the sale took place.

"Once we've been trading a signal for a year, it looks like something different to people who don't know our trades," an insider says.

Simons summed up the approach in a 2014 speech in South Korea: "It's a very big exercise in machine learning, if you want to look at it that way. Studying the past, understanding what happens and how it might impinge, nonrandomly, on the future."[5]

=

For a long time, Bob Mercer was a peculiar but largely benign figure within the company. Silver-haired with dark eyebrows, he favored wire-rimmed glasses and high-end shoes. Mercer whistled a lot and teased a few liberal colleagues, but, mostly, he just spoke with Peter Brown.

"He comes up with all the ideas," Brown told a colleague, likely with excess modesty. "I express them."

Mercer was truly self-contained. He once told a colleague that he preferred the company of cats to humans. At night, Mercer retreated to his Long Island estate, Owl's Nest—a nod to another creature known for wisdom, calm, and long periods of silence—where he toyed with a $2.7 million model train that ran on a track half the size of a basketball court.[6] (In 2009, Mercer sued the manufacturer, claiming he had been overcharged by $700,000. The manufacturer countered that the costs had ballooned after it was asked to finish installing the track in a rush before Mercer's daughter's wedding.)

"I'm happy going through my life without saying anything to anybody," Mercer told the *Wall Street Journal* in 2010.[7]

Those who got to know Mercer understood he was a political conservative, a National Rifle Association member who amassed a collection of machine guns as well as the gas-operated AR-18 assault rifle used by Arnold Schwarzenegger in *The Terminator*.[8] Few involved with Renaissance spent much time focusing on these views, however.

"Bob talked about the need to protect oneself from the government, and the need to have guns and gold," says an early investor in the Medallion fund. "I didn't think he was for real."

Every year or two, Mercer took a few days off to fly to Ohio State to work on computer projects with colleagues from graduate school. Mercer often treated the group to lunch at a local steakhouse, where he hummed to himself much of the meal, often with a serene smile on his face. When Mercer spoke to the academics about matters unrelated to their project, he often shared a disdain for taxes and a skepticism of climate change, recalls Tim Cooper, a physics professor. Once, Mercer rattled off an array of statistics to demonstrate that nature emits more carbon dioxide than humans. Later, when Cooper checked the data, it was accurate, but Mercer had overlooked the fact that nature absorbs as much carbon dioxide as it emits, which mankind does not.

"It sounded like someone had got to him," Cooper says. "Even a smart guy can get the details right but the big picture wrong."

Until 2008, Mercer's family foundation mostly gave money to fringe causes. Mercer helped fund work by Arthur Robinson, the biochemist in southern Oregon who was collecting thousands of vials of human urine, which Robinson believed held the key to extending human longevity. Mercer subscribed to Robinson's newsletter, which argued that low levels of nuclear radiation weren't very harmful, and could even be beneficial, and that climate science is a hoax. Mercer gave Robinson $1.4 million to buy freezers for his urine stockpile.[9]

After Barack Obama was elected president in 2008, Mercer, now worth several hundred million dollars, began to make sizable political donations. Two years later, when Robinson ran for Congress, Mercer paid $300,000 for attack ads aimed at his Democratic opponent, Representative Peter DeFazio, who had wanted to close tax loopholes and enact new taxes on certain financial trades. Mercer never told Robinson he was sponsoring the ads. (Robinson lost in a surprisingly close race.)

Mercer's emergence as a high-profile right-wing donor caused a bit of head-scratching within Republican circles. Many serious contributors want something from politicians, and it's usually reasonably clear what they're after. Mercer never asked for much in return for his cash. Political operatives concluded that Mercer was a rare breed, an ideologue driven by long-held principles. He had an intense suspicion of government and resentment of the establishment, at least in part the result of that frustrating summer writing code at the air force base in New Mexico. Like many conservatives, Mercer also had an equally intense loathing of Bill and Hillary Clinton.

By the time Mercer turned sixty-four in 2010, he was convinced government should play a minimal role in society, partly because governments empower incompetence. Mercer had worked in private industry most of his life and hadn't demonstrated much interest in public service, so it wasn't like he had a lot of experience to lean on as he formed this view. Still, policy errors gnawed at him, colleagues said, as did the alleged hypocrisy of elected officials. In conversations, Mercer emphasized the importance of personal freedoms. Some considered him an "extreme libertarian." Ayn Rand might have imagined a hero like Mercer—a tall, ruggedly handsome individualist who was a huge fan of capitalism and *always* rational and in control.

Now that he had enormous wealth, Mercer wanted to do something to alter the nation's direction. His timing was perfect. In 2010, the Supreme Court handed down a landmark decision in *Citizens United v. Federal Election Commission*, ruling that election spending by wealthy donors and others was a form of free speech protected under the First Amendment. The decision paved the way for super PACs, which could accept unlimited amounts of money to support a candidate as long as they didn't officially coordinate with the campaign.

After the decision, Simons began donating heavily to Democratic causes, while Mercer stepped up his support for Republican politicians. Mercer's penchant for privacy limited his activity, however, as did his focus on Renaissance. It was his second-oldest daughter, Rebekah, who started showing up at conservative fund-raising events and other get-togethers, becoming the family's public face, and the one driving its political strategy.

Rebekah cut a distinctive figure. "Bekah," as friends and family referred to her, was tall and auburn-haired. She favored glittery, 1950s-style cat's-eye glasses and bore a resemblance to the actor Joan Cusack. A Stanford University graduate in biology and mathematics, Rebekah spent a few years working for Magerman at Renaissance before leaving to homeschool her four children and help run a gourmet cookie store with her sisters.

Rebekah first made headlines in the spring of 2010, when she and her then-husband Sylvain Mirochnikoff spent $28 million to buy six adjoining units in the forty-one-story Heritage at Trump Place on Manhattan's Upper West Side, creating a triplex with seventeen bedrooms that was twice the size of Gracie Mansion, New York City's mayoral residence.[10]

For a while, Rebekah and her father backed traditional right-wing groups and causes, such as the Freedom Partners Action Fund, a conservative political action committee founded by billionaire industrialists Charles and David Koch and the Heritage Foundation. Sometimes, Rebekah and Bob would walk through Republican fund-raising events locked arm-in-arm. Rebekah, the more sociable of the pair, did most of the talking, while her father stood silently beside her.

The Mercers quickly lost patience with the established organizations, however, and drifted to more controversial causes, giving $1 million to a group running attack ads against a proposed mosque in the vicinity of the World Trade Center's Ground Zero in lower Manhattan.[11] Then, in 2011, the Mercers met conservative firebrand Andrew Breitbart at a conference. Almost immediately, they were intrigued with his far-right news organization, Breitbart News Network, expressing interest in funding its operations. Breitbart introduced the Mercers to his friend, Steve Bannon, a former Goldman Sachs banker, who drew up a term sheet under which the Mercer family purchased nearly 50 percent of Breitbart News for $10 million.

In March 2012, Breitbart collapsed on a Los Angeles sidewalk and died of heart failure at the age of forty-three. Bannon and the Mercers convened an emergency meeting in New York to determine the network's future, and decided that Bannon would become the site's executive chairman. Over time, the site became popular with the "alt-right," a loose conglomeration of groups, some of which embraced tenets of white supremacy and viewed immigration and multiculturalism as threats. (Bannon preferred to call himself an economic nationalist and argued that racist elements would get "washed out" of the populist movement.)

After Mitt Romney lost the 2012 presidential election, the Mercers became even more disenchanted with the establishment. That year, Rebekah stood up before a crowd of Romney supporters at the University Club of New York and delivered a scathing and detailed critique of the Republican Party, arguing that its poor data and canvassing operations held candidates back. Rebekah said it was time to "save America from becoming like socialist Europe."[12]

Bannon helped broker a deal for Mercer to invest in an analytics firm called Cambridge Analytica, the US arm of the British behavioral research company SCL Group. Cambridge Analytica specialized in the kinds of advanced data Mercer was accustomed to parsing at Renaissance, and the type of information that Rebekah said the GOP lacked. She urged organizations that benefited from her family's funds to tap Cambridge's sophisticated technological capabilities.

In 2013, Patrick Caddell, a former Democratic pollster who had turned critical of the party, shared data with Bob Mercer suggesting that voters were becoming alienated from both parties as well as most mainstream candidates. Mercer asked Caddell to do another round of polling as he collected his own data; Mercer concluded that a major shift was under way.[13]

"My God, this is a whole new world," he told Caddell.

=

In February 2014, Mercer and other conservative political donors gathered at New York's Pierre hotel to strategize about the 2016 presidential election. He told attendees he had seen data indicating that mainstream Republicans, such as Jeb Bush and Marco Rubio, would have difficulty winning. Only a true outsider with a sense of the voters' frustrations could emerge victorious, Mercer argued. Others didn't seem as convinced by his data.

He and Rebekah began searching for an outsider to shake up Washington.

"It's a philosophical thing," according to Caddell. "They think the establishment has failed and is self-serving."

For guidance, the Mercers turned to Bannon. At the time, Breitbart's online traffic was soaring, validating their faith in the political provocateur. When Mercer hosted Bannon on his 203-foot yacht, *Sea Owl*—yet another owl—Bannon wore shorts, cursed freely, belched, and held forth like a close relation, according to some people present. Bannon advised the Mercers on which political and media ventures to invest in and escorted potential beneficiaries to Rebekah's triplex at Trump Place.*

Mercer's impact extended across the Atlantic. After Breitbart started an office in London, in 2012, it began supporting politician and former commodity trader Nigel Farage's fledgling efforts to catapult the idea of the UK leaving the European Union from a fringe issue to a mainstream one. At some point, Mercer and Farage became friendly.

In 2015, Cambridge Analytica discussed ways to help the leaders of Leave.EU, the political group that supported the UK's withdrawal from the European Union. Bannon was included as part of the email traffic between the two groups, though it's not clear he read or responded to the emails. The following month, Leave.EU publicly launched a campaign to persuade British voters to support a referendum in favor of an exit from the European Union. Cambridge Analytica officials would deny doing work for Leave.EU.[14]

"Even if the firm was not paid for its services, it laid some of the early groundwork for the Leave.EU campaign," argues journalist Jane Mayer.[15]

In June 2016, the UK voted to exit the European Union. Farage was one

*When asked to comment, Bannon said there are "errors of fact" in this description of events surrounding the election and his interactions with the Mercers, though he wouldn't specify the inaccuracies. "Dude, it's not my fucking book," he said in an email.

of the leaders of that campaign, though Leave.EU wasn't selected as the effort's official organization.

"Brexit could not have happened without Breitbart," Farage says.[16]

===

As the 2016 presidential campaign got under way, the Mercers initially backed Texas Senator Ted Cruz, having been impressed by his willingness to shut the government down over debt concerns in 2013. They gave a pro-Cruz super PAC more than $13 million, but when Cruz dropped out of the race in May of that year, Rebekah accepted an invitation to meet Donald Trump's daughter Ivanka and her husband, Jared Kushner, for lunch at Trump Tower. Over sandwiches and salads, they bonded over parenting young children, among other things.[17]

Soon, the Mercers shifted their support to Trump, by then the party's effective nominee. They launched a super PAC to oppose Hillary Clinton, charging Kellyanne Conway, a veteran Republican pollster, with running the organization. Eventually, they'd become Trump's largest financial backers.

By the middle of the summer, Trump was losing ground to Clinton and victory didn't seem possible. On Saturday, August 13, the *New York Times* published a front-page story detailing the campaign's ongoing chaos. Trump wouldn't use a teleprompter during his speeches, he couldn't stay on message, and he wasn't able to tame embarrassing leaks. Republican donors were jumping ship, and a landslide victory for Clinton seemed possible, even likely.

Later that day, Bob Mercer called Bannon, asking what could be done to turn things around. Bannon outlined a series of ideas, including making Conway a more frequent presence on television to defend Trump.

"That sounds like a terrific idea," Mercer said.

Later the same day, the Mercers boarded a helicopter to the East Hampton beachfront estate of Woody Johnson, the owner of the New York Jets, where GOP backers, including Wall Street investors Carl Icahn and Steve Mnuchin, were gathering to meet Trump. Clutching the *Times* story, Rebekah made a beeline for the candidate.

"It's bad," Trump acknowledged.

"No, it's not bad—it's over," she told Trump. "Unless you make a change."

She told Trump she had a way for him to turn the election around.

"Bring in Steve Bannon and Kellyanne Conway," she said. "I've talked to them; they'll do it."[18]

The next day, Bannon took an Uber to the Trump National Golf Club in Bedminster, New Jersey. After impatiently waiting for Trump to finish a round of golf, eat some hot dogs, and then finish an ice-cream treat, Bannon made his pitch.

"No doubt you can win," Bannon told Trump. "You just have to get organized."

Before long, Bannon was running the campaign, and Conway was its manager, becoming a ubiquitous and effective television presence. Bannon helped instill order on the campaign, making sure Trump focused on two things—disparaging Clinton's character and promoting a form of nationalism that Bannon branded "America First," a slogan that seemed to echo the short-lived America First Committee, a group that had levied pressure to prevent the US from entering World War II and opposing Adolf Hitler.

Bannon made headway on Trump's current behavior, but he couldn't do anything about his past actions. On October 7, the *Washington Post* broke a story about outtake footage from the television show *Access Hollywood* in which Trump bragged, in lewd and graphic language, about kissing, groping, and trying to bed women.

"When you're a star, they let you do it," Trump said.

Mainstream Republicans condemned Trump, but the Mercers rushed out a full-throated statement of support.

"We are completely indifferent to Mr. Trump's locker-room braggadocio," they said. "We have a country to save, and there is only one person who can save it. We, and Americans across the country and around the world, stand steadfastly behind Donald J. Trump."

=

Jim Simons was torn.

Ever since he and his childhood friend, Jim Harpel, had driven across the country and witnessed some of the hardships experienced by minorities and others, Simons had leaned left politically. He sometimes supported Republican candidates, but usually backed Democrats. By the middle of 2016, Simons had emerged as the most important supporter of the Democratic Party's Priorities USA Action super PAC and a key backer of Democratic House and Senate candidates. By the end of that year, Simons would donate more than $27 million to Democratic causes. Marilyn Simons was even more liberal than her husband, and Jim's son, Nathaniel, had established a nonprofit foundation focused on climate change mitigation and clean-energy policy, issues the Trump campaign generally mocked or ignored.

As Bob Mercer's political influence grew, and his support for the Trump campaign expanded, Simons began hearing complaints from associates and others, most with the same general request: Can't you do something about him?

Simons was in a difficult position. He only recently had become aware of Mercer's alliance with Bannon and some of his other political opinions. Simons couldn't understand how a scientist could be so dismissive of the threat of global warming, and he disagreed with Mercer's views. But Simons still liked Mercer. Yes, he was a bit eccentric and frequently uncommunicative, but Mercer had always been pleasant and respectful to Simons.

"He's a nice guy," he insisted to a friend. "He's allowed to use his money as he wishes. What can I do?"

Besides, Mercer was responsible for helping Medallion achieve some of its most important breakthroughs. Simons noted to some friends that it's illegal to fire someone for their political beliefs.

"Professional performance and political views" are two separate things, Simons told someone.

Both Medallion and RIEF were enjoying strong performance, and Mercer was doing a good job leading Renaissance with Brown, who himself wasn't devoting much time on the election. Brown didn't like spending his money. He also told a friend that his wife's experience in government had helped sour him on politics. The election might even help the hedge fund by bringing a dose of volatility to financial markets, Brown told at least one person.

Mercer remained an outlier at the firm, politically, and there weren't any obvious signs that Mercer's outside activities were having a negative effect on the firm, reducing any impetus for Simons to act.

With time, that would change.

═

On Election Day, Trump's team didn't think he had a chance of winning. The Republican data team projected that Trump wouldn't win more than 204 electoral votes, and that he would get trounced in key battleground states. Staffers and others in the campaign's war room—a space in Trump Tower that once housed the set for the television show *The Apprentice*—were despondent. At 5:01 p.m., David Bossie, a close ally of Bannon and Conway who also had been installed in the campaign at the behest of Bob and Rebekah, received a phone call with early exit numbers. Trump was down in eight of eleven crucial states by 5 to 8 percentage points, he was told.

When the news was relayed to Trump, he snapped his flip phone closed and threw it across the room.

"What a waste of time and money," he said, to no one in particular.

At around nine o'clock, Bob Mercer made his way to the war room, wearing a posh three-piece gray suit. Taking a look at his outfit, Bannon joked that someone had invited Rich Uncle Pennybags, the Monopoly mascot. Melania Trump joined the room, as did Trump's children, his running mate, Indiana Governor Mike Pence, New Jersey Governor Chris Christie, and others. They ate pizza and stared at a nearby wall that was mounted with six seventy-five-inch televisions, all showing different networks.

As more disappointing numbers came in, Trump turned morose.

"Hey geniuses," he said to his team, "how's this working for us?"

At one point, Fox News's Tucker Carlson called in: "He's not going to win, will he?"

Then, the results began to turn. Around one o'clock, Trump turned to Bossie, feeling elated: "Dave, can you believe this? We just started this to have some fun."

At 2:20 a.m., Conway received a call from an Associated Press editor.

"What state are you calling?" she asked.

"We're not calling a state," he said. "We're calling the race."[19]

=

As the election approached, Simons expressed concern. Clinton led in most voter polls, but she seemed to be making strategic miscalculations. Clinton's team reached out to Simons, saying that if he was going to make additional political donations that year, he should direct them to the party's effort to win control of the Senate. The Clinton camp seemed so confident of victory that they deemed additional help for their own campaign unnecessary.

On election night, Jim and Marilyn watched the results at a friend's home. The group, all Clinton supporters, crowded around a television screen, nervous but upbeat. As the results rolled in, and it slowly became clear that Trump had a chance to win, the mood turned dark. Around 9:30 p.m., Simons had had enough.

"I'm going back to the apartment to have a drink," he told Abe Lackman, his political advisor. "Want to come?"

Simons and Lackman quietly sipped red wine as they watched Trump seal the election. Before midnight, they turned the television off. They'd seen enough.

"We were pretty depressed," Lackman says.

CHAPTER FIFTEEN

When Jim Simons looked up, there were dozens of anxious faces staring at him.

It was the morning of November 9, 2016, the day after the presidential election. Nearly fifty scientists, researchers, and other employees of the Simons Foundation had spontaneously assembled in an open space on the ninth floor of the foundation's headquarters in lower Manhattan. They were trying to come to grips with what had just happened.

The space was sun-drenched, but almost everyone at the impromptu gathering looked dour. They were concerned about the nation's future, as well as their own. It was well known that Simons had been one of the biggest supporters of Hillary Clinton's presidential campaign. Now the foundation's employees worried that the incoming Trump administration would target charitable foundations, including Simons's own. Some wondered if the foundation's tax-exempt status could be stripped as a form of retribution.

The chatter ebbed as Simons, standing near a bank of elevators in a blue blazer and tan chinos, began to speak. In measured tones, he reminded the staffers of the importance of their work. Researching autism, understanding the origins of the universe, and pursuing other worthy endeavors were long-term projects that needed to proceed, Simons said. Keep working together and try to ignore the political upheaval.

"We're all disappointed," Simons said. "The best we can do is focus on our work."

The employees slowly returned to their offices, some newly reassured.

=

Simons was somber, but Bob Mercer was celebratory.

Mercer, his daughter, Rebekah, and the rest of the family were preparing for their annual holiday party, held in early December each year at the family's Long Island estate, Owl's Nest. Mercer didn't especially enjoy speaking with colleagues or others. He was passionate about his dress-up parties, however. Since 2009, the family had welcomed hundreds of friends, business associates, and others to their mansion for an elaborate, themed costume affair.

Mercer's more-sociable wife, Diana, was usually the one at the center of the revelry. Mercer liked to sit in a quiet corner with a grandchild or play poker with one of the professional dealers hired for the evening.

This year's festivities figured to be so special even Mercer was expected to join in the fun. The chosen theme was "Villains and Heroes," and the evening's invitations featured a sword-wielding centurion crouching in an ancient ruin, facing down a serpent-haired Medusa. The Mercers directed their guests to a secret website where they received costume suggestions from film, television, comic books, and everyday life, including Superman, Captain Hook, and Mother Teresa.[1]

As the Saturday evening festivities began, investor and Trump supporter Peter Thiel, dressed as Hulk Hogan, mingled with Kellyanne Conway, who wore a Superwoman costume. Steve Bannon came as himself, a likely jab at those who deemed his insurgent political activities to be villainous—or a suggestion that he was the election's hero. As for the Mercers, Bob was dressed as Mandrake the Magician, a comic-book superhero known for hypnotizing his targets, while Rebekah came as Black Widow, covered head-to-toe in black latex.

Word spread that Donald Trump was on his way, taking a break from transition meetings and pressing cabinet decisions to join the group. A few years earlier, Mercer was just another quirky quant. To the extent he had a reputation, it was for collecting guns, backing a urine-research enthusiast among other out-there causes, and helping his enigmatic hedge fund beat the market. Now the president-elect of the United States was making the hike out to Long Island to pay homage to Mercer. Between the $26 million he had spent on Republican causes, his daughter's insistence that Trump tap Bannon and Conway to resuscitate his flailing campaign, and Breitbart News's unflinching support for the Trump campaign, Bob and Rebekah Mercer were among those most responsible for Trump's shocking victory.[2]

"The Mercers laid the groundwork for the Trump revolution," Bannon said. "Irrefutably, when you look at the donors during the past four years, they have had the single biggest impact of anybody."[3]

The president-elect and his entourage rolled up in hulking, black sport utility vehicles, and Trump stepped out wearing a black overcoat, dark suit, and a checkered tie (but no costume). He made his way through the other guests, stopping to greet Mercer, and soon was addressing the crowd. Trump joked that he'd just had his longest conversation with Mercer—"two words."[4] He lauded Mercer's support for his campaign and thanked him and his daughter for urging that he hire Bannon, Conway, and Bossie to lead the campaign, moves that gave it needed "organization," he said. Then, Trump joined the Mercers, Bannon, and Conway at the party's head table.

In the aftermath of the election, Mercer focused on running Renaissance, working as closely as ever with Peter Brown. Mercer didn't seem interested in an ambassadorship or any of the other, obvious rewards that often accrue to those backing the victors in presidential elections. Still, Bannon was slated to become the White House's chief strategist, and Conway would become a counselor to the president, ensuring that Mercer would have unparalleled access to Trump. Mercer remained one of the Republican Party's most important patrons and continued to control Breitbart News, giving him influence over the party's ascendant, antiestablishment wing.

Rebekah Mercer assumed a more active role in the new administration. For weeks, she was ensconced in Bannon's office in Trump Tower, serving as an advisor on the selection of nominees to the Trump cabinet. Mercer successfully lobbied for Senator Jeff Sessions to be chosen as attorney general, pushed hard to prevent Mitt Romney from becoming secretary of state, and played a role in the choice of lawyer Jay Clayton to lead the US Securities and Exchange Commission, even as her influence raised some eyebrows due to her father's position as co-CEO of one of the nation's largest hedge funds. Later, the president turned to one of Rebekah Mercer's longtime associates, Leonard Leo, who ran the conservative Federalist Society, for guidance on nearly all of his judicial nominees. She also made plans to lead an outside group designated to support Trump's agenda.

Rebekah Mercer was emerging as a public figure in her own right. Early that year, *GQ* magazine named Mercer the seventeenth most powerful person in Washington, DC, calling her "the First Lady of the alt-right." The family's political clout, along with its ongoing support for the president-elect, seemed assured.

=

David Magerman was miserable.

Though he was a registered Democrat, Magerman considered himself a political centrist and he sometimes voted for Republican candidates. The 2016 campaign was a different story, however. Trump had disparaged immigrants, spoken of shifting funds from public schools to charter schools, and promised to spend billions of dollars to build a security wall on the Mexican border, attitudes and policies that Magerman judged misguided or even cruel. The candidate's vow to restrict abortion rights worried Magerman and horrified his wife, Debra. After the election, Magerman unfriended almost everyone he knew on Facebook, hoping to avoid painful reminders of Trump's victory.

After the inauguration, Magerman reconsidered his position. He thought he might be able to move the administration in a more benign direction. By then, the forty-eight-year-old had spent a decade working on education-related issues. He believed that his experience might be helpful to Trump's team, or that he might be able to contribute in other areas.

In January, Magerman called Rebekah Mercer on her cell phone, but she didn't pick up. He tried her again, leaving a message that he wanted to help. Magerman got a return call, but it was from Bob Mercer. Despite his usual shyness, Mercer seemed eager to discuss the merits of Trump and various contentious political topics. They disagreed about climate change, Obamacare, and the value of a border wall, but their tone remained civil.

"He will blow things up," Mercer said about Trump.

"That's what I'm worried about," Magerman said.

"Do you really want to bring back the fear of nuclear war?" Magerman asked.

Mercer said he wasn't all that concerned about nuclear war. Before hanging up, Mercer said he had enjoyed their back-and-forth, but Magerman was left more frustrated than before.

He decided to wait to see what policies the new administration embraced. He didn't like what he saw. In late January 2017, Trump signed an executive order banning foreign nationals from seven predominantly Muslim countries from visiting the US for ninety days and suspending entry to the country for all Syrian refugees. The Senate confirmed Sessions as attorney general, and Trump continued to attack the credibility of both the US intelligence community and members of the media, actions that further irked Magerman.

Magerman wanted to do something to temper, or even counteract, the administration's policies, but he wasn't sure what to do. He made plans to donate to local Democrats, and he called Planned Parenthood, offering assistance to the nonprofit, which provides sexual health care. Magerman also tried calling Jared Kushner, Trump's influential son-in-law—to warn him about policies the administration was embracing and the influence Mercer was having—but he failed to reach him.

Magerman was beset by guilt. Mercer's foundation was invested in the Medallion fund, so Magerman felt he had personally helped provide Mercer with the resources to put Trump in office and encourage policies that Magerman found abhorrent.

"It pisses me off," he told Debra, his anger boiling over. "I've made software that makes white rich guys like Mercer even richer."

In phone calls with colleagues, Magerman complained about how Mercer made the Trump presidency possible. He shared a conversation he had had years earlier with Mercer in which, he recalled, Mercer argued that African Americans had been better off before the enactment of the Civil Rights Act of 1964, which banned discrimination in public accommodations, employment, and federally funded activities.

Word of Magerman's criticism reached Mercer. One day, as Magerman worked in his home office, his phone rang.

"I hear you're going around saying I'm a white supremacist," Mercer said. "That's ridiculous."

Magerman was caught off guard by the accusation.

"Those weren't my exact words," he told his boss, stammering.

Magerman recovered his poise.

"That's the impression I have, though," Magerman said, citing Mercer's earlier comments about the Civil Rights Act.

"I'm sure I never would have said that," Mercer responded.

Mercer then recited data that he claimed demonstrated that African

Americans enjoyed a better standard of living in the decade before the legislation, including statistics about the percentage of African Americans in various professions. He promised to send Magerman a book to prove his points.

The Civil Rights Act had "infantilized" African Americans "by making them dependent on the government," Mercer told Magerman.

Now Magerman was really upset.

"Bob—they had to use different bathrooms and water fountains!"

Magerman outlined his concerns about Trump's policy positions, rhetoric, and cabinet choices. Mercer responded that he wasn't involved in any decisions made by Trump or those close to him; he simply had wanted to prevent Clinton from being elected.

Now Magerman was really burning.

"How can you say you're not involved?" Magerman screamed, pointing to the group Rebekah Mercer had formed to boost Trump's agenda, as well as his continued close relationships with Bannon and Conway.

"You should meet Bannon. He's a sweet guy," Mercer said.

"If what you're doing is harming the country, then you have to stop!" Magerman told Mercer, before they hung up.

Mercer didn't seem especially perturbed by the conversation. He was used to having it out with more liberal members of his staff. For him, it was almost a sport. A few days later, Mercer sent Magerman a book called *Civil Rights: Rhetoric or Reality?* written in 1984 by Hoover Institution economist Thomas Sowell that the *New York Times* had called "brutally frank, perceptive, and important." The book argues that minorities began moving into higher-paying jobs in large numbers years before the passage of the Civil Rights Act, and that affirmative action had caused the most disadvantaged segments of the minority population to fall behind their white counterparts.[5]

Sowell's argument "focuses on narrow financial measures, but ignores overall human factors," Magerman says, citing one of many criticisms he and others have of the book.

Magerman was unsettled by the conversation with Mercer. He wanted to do something to stop his boss. Magerman dug through Renaissance's employee handbook to see what discipline he might face if he aired his concerns. He also spoke with Peter Brown and Mark Silber, who said they doubted Mercer had made racist comments. (Another executive joked that Mercer didn't speak enough for anyone to know if he was a racist.) Magerman understood from those conversations that he was likely on safe ground criticizing Mercer if he steered clear of saying anything about Renaissance.

In February, Magerman sent an email to a *Wall Street Journal* reporter.*

"I'm ready to take action," he wrote. "Enough is enough."

In the resulting interview, conducted at a restaurant Magerman owned in Bala Cynwyd, Pennsylvania, he held little back.

"His views show contempt for the social safety net that he doesn't need, but many Americans do," Magerman said. "Now he's using the money I helped him make to implement his worldview" by supporting Trump and proposing that "government be shrunk down to the size of a pinhead."

Magerman shared concern about his own future.

"I'd like to think I'm speaking out in a way that won't risk my job, but it's very possible they could fire me," he said. "This is my life's work—I ran a group that wrote the trading system they still use."

The morning an online version of the story appeared on the paper's website, Magerman received a phone call from Renaissance. A representative told Magerman that he was being suspended without pay and was prohibited from having any contact with the company.

=

The election was starting to cause discomfort for Mercer, as well.

He and his daughter had become so closely associated with Bannon and

*That would be yours truly.

the far-right segment of the Republican Party that they had become targets for those unhappy with the nation's lurch to the right.

At one point, the New York State Democratic Committee ran a television advertisement flashing Bob and Rebekah Mercer's faces on the screen, saying they were the "same people who bankrolled Trump's social media bot army and Steve Bannon's extremist Breitbart News."

In March 2017, about sixty demonstrators gathered outside Mercer's home, decrying his funding of far-right causes and calling for higher taxes on the wealthy. A week later, a second group held a protest, some holding signs reading: "Mercer Pay Your Taxes." Police officers closed the road in front of Owl's Nest to accommodate the protesters, who stood in the pouring rain for hours chanting criticisms of Mercer.

Mercer "played a major role in bringing about the election of Donald Trump," said Bill McNulty, an eighty-two-year-old local resident who joined the group. "We saw the corrosive and contaminating effect of dark money on politics."[6]

The Mercers received death threats, friends said, forcing the family to hire security. For a family that relished its privacy, their growing infamy was both shocking and disturbing.

=

Renaissance didn't know what to do with Magerman.

The firm rarely fires employees, even when they're unproductive, disinterested, or difficult. The risk is just too great. Even lackluster, midlevel researchers and programmers are privy to insights and understandings that may prove helpful to rivals. That was one reason Magerman felt comfortable speaking out about Mercer—he had seen others show insubordination without facing consequences. Yet, Magerman had committed a cardinal sin for any employee: He had attacked his boss in as public a fashion as possible, even suggesting he was racist. And there were few companies as publicity-shy as Renaissance—one reason many at the firm were reluctant to welcome Magerman back.

Magerman had mixed feelings of his own. He had made so much money at the firm that he didn't have to worry about the financial pain of getting fired. He loathed what Mercer was doing to the country and wanted to stop his political activity. But Magerman also remembered how kind Mercer and his wife had been to him when he first joined the firm, inviting him to dinners at Friendly's and movie nights with their family. Magerman respected Bob for his intelligence and creativity, and a big part of him still yearned to please the powerful men in his life. At that point, Magerman had spent two decades at Renaissance and he felt an appreciation for the firm. He decided that if he could go on speaking about Mercer's politics, he'd return to his old job.

As he discussed his future with Brown and others, Magerman didn't make it easy on them.

"I can't take hush money," he told them.

At one point, Magerman paid a visit to the Long Island office and was hurt that so many staffers seemed unfriendly. No one wanted to jeopardize their position at the firm by lending Magerman support, it seemed. Either that, or even left-leaning staffers thought he went about his protest the wrong way.

"People I expected to be warm and fuzzy were standoffish," he said after the encounter. "They see me as the bad guy."

Overcoming imposing obstacles, the two sides worked out a tentative agreement for Magerman to return to the fold, with conditions placed on what he could say about Mercer. The deal wasn't finalized, though. To help repair the relationship, Magerman decided to attend an April 20 poker tournament at New York's St. Regis hotel benefiting Math for America, the nonprofit that Simons had founded. The event was a highly anticipated annual showdown for quants, professional poker players, and others. Magerman knew Simons, Mercer, Brown, and other Renaissance executives would be there. Who knew, maybe Rebekah Mercer would show up?

"I wanted to reintroduce myself and be part of the culture again," Magerman says, "to show I was making an effort."

As Magerman made the three-hour drive from his home, he began feeling anxious. He was unsure how he'd be received by his colleagues or others in attendance. At the hotel, Magerman pledged $5,000 to enter the tournament. He immediately noticed he hadn't dressed appropriately. Most of the approximately two hundred players in the carpeted, second-floor ballroom wore suits or sports jackets. The security team wore tuxedos. Magerman went with jeans and an open-collared dress shirt. It was a mistake that added to his discomfort and apprehension.

Magerman entered the poker room and immediately saw Bob Mercer. This was no time to be shy, Magerman thought. He walked right up to Mercer and complimented him on the color of his suit, which was an unusual shade of blue. Mercer smiled and said one of his daughters had picked it out, an exchange that seemed to go well.

Phew, Magerman thought.

Just after seven p.m., Magerman began playing No-Limit Hold'em at a table with Simons, a member of the Poker Hall of Fame named Dan Harrington, and a few others. When Simons ducked into a side room to smoke, Magerman followed. He apologized for the negative attention thrust on the firm after his criticism of the Mercers.

"I'm sorry how things played out," Magerman told Simons. "I respect you and want you to know that."

Simons accepted the apology and said their standoff seemed to be coming to a resolution, further buoying Magerman. Back at his table, Magerman lost some early hands but remained in good spirits, pledging an additional $15,000 for buy-ins so he could continue playing.

A few tables away, Mercer was playing against some investors and others, including sport-finance executive Chris English. Mercer won several early hands, but English detected a tell: When Mercer played a great hand, he whistled patriotic songs, including "The Battle Hymn of the Republic." When he was less confident of his cards, Mercer hummed those songs. Seizing on his discovery, English quickly won a pot over Mercer.

Magerman was on his own losing streak. Around 10:30 p.m., after consuming several glasses of twelve-year-old scotch, Magerman was out of the tournament. It was too early to go home, though, and he was still on a high from the looming rapprochement with his colleagues, so Magerman decided to walk the room and watch others play.

He approached a table that included Rebekah Mercer. She was staring at him. As Magerman got a little closer, Mercer became agitated. She called to him in anger: "Karma is a bitch."

Shaken, Magerman walked around the table and stood next to Mercer. She told Magerman that his criticism of the Mercers' support for Trump had put her family in danger.

"How could you do this to my father? He was so good to you," she said.

Magerman said he felt bad, noting that her family had played a supportive role when he joined Renaissance.

"I loved your family," Magerman told Mercer.

She wouldn't hear it.

"You're *pond scum*," Mercer told him, repeatedly. "You've been pond scum for twenty-five years. I've always known it."

Get out of here, she told Magerman. A security member approached, telling Magerman to back away from the table. He refused, dodged the security detail, and approached Simons, asking for help.

"Jim, look what they're trying to do to me," Magerman called out.

It's best if you left the event, Simons told him.

Security forced Magerman outside to the curb, threatening to call the police if he didn't leave. Boaz Weinstein, another hedge-fund investor, saw how distraught Magerman was and urged him to walk off his drinks and drive home. It took some convincing, but Magerman complied, heading for his car.

"I'm not denying I was a little impacted by the alcohol. . . . It wasn't one of my finest moments. It wasn't my intent to create a scene," Magerman said several days after the event. "But that doesn't change what she said to me . . . I didn't start the fight, and I didn't resort to the petty name calling."

Back upstairs, players buzzed about the confrontation, but the tournament went on. Soon, Bob Mercer was on a tear, rebounding from his earlier setback. Simons, Peter Muller of PDT Partners, and Brown all exited play, but Mercer kept on going. In the evening's last big pot, at around one a.m., he knocked English out of the tournament.

"He might have been humming to reverse his tell," English says, trying to explain his loss. "It was so loud, I couldn't tell."[7]

As Mercer smiled and accepted congratulations from his rivals, Magerman was on his way back to Philadelphia. Along the way, he received a text from Brown: "Best to rise above all this and just live your life without getting caught up in a battle. I honestly think you will be happier."

On April 29, Renaissance fired Magerman.

═

By the early fall of 2017, Anthony Calhoun's anger had intensified. The more the executive director of the Baltimore City Fire and Police Employees' Retirement System read about Mercer's political activities, the more they bothered him.

Backing Trump wasn't the problem for Calhoun. It was Breitbart, which had become associated with white nationalists. By then, Bannon had been pushed out of his job as the chief strategist to the president. Now he was back at Breitbart, and some expected him to push the publication to further extremes.

Mercer also had backed Milo Yiannopoulos, a right-wing provocateur who had called feminism a "cancer," once appeared to endorse pedophilia, and was barred from Twitter for abusing others.[8]

It was all too much for Calhoun. The Baltimore retirement system had $25 million invested in RIEF, and Calhoun decided to share his displeasure with Renaissance.

He picked up the phone and called a RIEF representative.

"We've got real concerns," Calhoun said.

The representative said Calhoun wasn't the only one calling with complaints about Mercer. Later, when Calhoun began speaking with industry consultants, he heard other Renaissance clients were sharing their own unhappiness with the firm. Soon, Calhoun and the rest of the board of directors of the Baltimore retirement system voted to pull its money out of RIEF.

The cash was a tiny part of the Renaissance fund, and no one at the firm was worried about any kind of exodus of investors. But in October, nearly fifty protesters picketed the hedge fund itself, saying Mercer was their target, adding to the discomfort of executives, who weren't accustomed to such negative publicity.

By October 2017, Simons was worried the controversy was jeopardizing Renaissance's future. The firm's morale was deteriorating. At least one key employee was close to quitting, while another mulled a departure. Among the most important employees to convey their concerns was Wolfgang Wander,* who had earned his PhD in high-energy physics at the University of Erlangen–Nuremberg in Bavaria, Germany. Wander headed the firm's infrastructure

*On Wander's Facebook page: "If you send me a friend request, tell me how we met and clear your page of FOX talking points, thanks!"

group, effectively making him Renaissance's most senior technology officer. Simons became convinced that Renaissance would have a tougher time competing for talent.

For more than a year, Simons had ignored Mercer's growing role in politics. Now, he felt compelled to act. On a crisp October morning, Simons dropped by Mercer's office. He said he had an important matter he needed to discuss. Simons sat in a chair opposite Mercer and came quickly to the point of his visit.

"I think it's best if you stepped down," Simons told Mercer.

It wasn't a political decision but one made to ensure the firm's future. The scrutiny on the firm "isn't good for morale," Simons said.

Mercer wasn't prepared for the news. He looked sad and hurt. Nonetheless, he accepted Simons's decision without protest.

Later, Simons told a group of students and others at MIT's business school that "there was a problem of morale at Renaissance . . . morale was getting worse."

"It wasn't an easy decision," Simons later told a friend.

=

On November 2, Mercer wrote a letter to Renaissance investors saying he was resigning as Renaissance's co-CEO but would remain a researcher at the firm. He blamed "scrutiny from the press" and said the media had unfairly linked him to Bannon.

"The press has . . . intimated that my politics marches in lockstep with Steve Bannon's," he wrote. "I have great respect for Mr. Bannon, and from time to time I do discuss politics with him. However, I make my own decisions with respect to whom I support politically."

Mercer, who said he had decided to sell his stake in Breitbart News to his daughters, clarified his political views in the letter, saying he supports "conservatives who favor a smaller, less powerful government." He also said that he had supported Yiannopoulos in an effort to back free speech and open debate, but that he regretted the move and was in the process of severing ties with him.

"In my opinion, actions of and statements by Mr. Yiannopoulos have caused pain and divisiveness," Mercer wrote.

═

In early 2018, a few months after stepping down from his job, Mercer received a call from Robert Frey, the former Renaissance executive who, after leaving the company, had founded a quantitative finance program at Stony Brook University's College of Engineering and Applied Sciences. Frey invited Mercer to lunch at a nondescript restaurant within the nearby Hilton Garden Inn, the only restaurant on Stony Brook's campus with waiter service. As they sat down, a couple of students recognized Frey and said hello, but no one seemed to notice Mercer, a likely relief to him.

Mercer looked drained. Frey knew his old friend had gone through a difficult year, so he wanted to get something out of the way before the food arrived.

During the election, Frey was unhappy with both candidates, and he couldn't bring himself to vote for either Trump or Clinton. Nonetheless, he told Mercer that he was fully within his right to actively support Trump in any way he saw fit, adding that, despite the widespread criticism, he didn't believe Mercer had done anything improper.

"There's been an imbalance in how you were treated," Frey told Mercer. "Soros and other people influence politics as much as you do, but they aren't vilified like you are."

Mercer smiled, gave a nod, but, as usual, didn't say much in response.

"Thanks," Mercer replied.

Mercer's reaction gave Frey the feeling that he should change the subject.

The friends talked about math and the market, steering clear of politics for the rest of the meal.

"I felt bad for him," Frey says.

=

Rebekah Mercer was having an even harder time of it.

Mercer shared frustrations with friends about how she and her father had been portrayed and said some unfairly accused her of supporting racist causes. The criticism had sparked a backlash. According to a friend, she once received fecal matter in the mail. Another time, a stranger insulted her in public, leaving her shaking.

In January 2018, more than two hundred scientists and other academics who supported policy action to stop climate change endorsed an open letter calling on the American Museum of Natural History, New York City's most prominent science museum, to remove Mercer from its board, on which she had served for five years. They urged the museum to "end ties to the anti-science propagandists and funders of climate science misinformation." Over a dozen protesters marched outside of the museum on Manhattan's Upper West Side, carrying placards saying, "Get Rebekah Out of Our Museum," and "Climate Change Is Real."[9]

The museum never took any action, but, in February 2018, Mercer felt the need to shift public perception. She wrote an op-ed in the *Wall Street Journal* denying that she supported "toxic ideologies such as racism and anti-Semitism," adding that she believed in "a kind and generous United States."

A month later, a new controversy erupted when Cambridge Analytica was accused of acquiring the private Facebook data of millions of users, setting off a series of government inquiries. Mercer, who was on Cambridge's board of directors and helped oversee the company's operations, came in for a new round of scrutiny and negative media coverage.

By the middle of 2018, Bob and Rebekah Mercer were pulling back from politics. The Mercers had broken with Bannon soon after he was quoted making a critical comment about Trump's family, leaving the Mercers without a political consigliere. In the lead-up to the 2018 midterm elections, Mercer made just under $6 million in disclosed political contributions, down from almost $10 million in the previous midterm elections in 2014, and over $25 million in 2016.

"They've fallen off the grid," a leading member of the conservative movement said of the Mercers in late 2018. "We don't hear much from them."

Friends said the unexpected blowback they each experienced prompted a shift to a lower-key approach, with smaller political contributions and little regular communication with Trump or members of his administration.

"They were so much more successful in the political arena than they expected, it took off like a rocket," said Brent Bozell, a friend who runs the Media Research Center, a conservative nonprofit. "There's bitterness . . . people have disappointed them."[10]

Part of the reason for the disappointment, friends said, was that most of the biggest donors to the Trump campaign received something for their generosity. The Mercers never asked for anything. Yet, other financial executives—even those who hadn't supported Trump during his presidential run, such as Blackstone Group Chief Executive Stephen Schwarzman—were the ones regularly speaking with the president.

The Mercers also made strategic flubs. In June 2018, Bob Mercer gave half a million dollars to a political action committee backing Kelli Ward, who drew criticism for accusing the family of Senator John McCain for timing the announcement of the end of McCain's cancer treatment to undercut her campaign. Ward was trounced in that year's Arizona Republican Senate primary.

As the president and the Republican Party began gearing up for the 2020 election, the Mercers remained well positioned to influence the campaign. They still were close to Conway. And, while they no longer had Bannon as a conduit to communicate to Trump or others, the Mercers were big backers of a PAC that had supported US National Security Advisor John Bolton, maintaining their access to power. The Mercers told friends they were happy the Trump administration had cut taxes and chosen conservative judges, among other moves, suggesting they didn't regret becoming so involved in national politics.

Still, Rebekah Mercer seemed more focused on other issues, most far from the headlines, such as working to boost free speech on college campuses.

In October 2018, when she was honored at a Washington, DC, gala, Mercer shared concerns about the level of discourse on college campuses, saying schools "churn out a wave of ovine zombies steeped in the anti-American myths of the radical left, ignorant of basic civics, economics, and history, and completely unfit for critical thinking."[11]

Wearing a red, flowing gown and her distinctive diamond-studded glasses as she spoke to hundreds in the hall, Mercer served notice that she would continue to push to limit the role of government and make sure politicians emphasized "personal responsibility."

Calling President Trump "a force of nature," Mercer indicated that she'd continue to play an active role in the nation's politics, no matter the backlash she and her father had endured, and would remain involved in "the struggle for the soul of our country."

"I will not be silenced," she said.

conduct a comprehensive [illegible] of [illegible] among other [illegible] [illegible] [illegible] [illegible] [illegible] [illegible] [illegible] [illegible]

[illegible] [illegible] [illegible] [illegible] [illegible] [illegible] [illegible] [illegible] [illegible] In October [illegible] [illegible] [illegible] [illegible] [illegible] Wall Street [illegible] [illegible] [illegible] [illegible] [illegible] [illegible] [illegible] [illegible] [illegible] [illegible] [illegible] [illegible] [illegible] [illegible] [illegible] [illegible]

[illegible] [illegible] [illegible] [illegible] [illegible] [illegible] [illegible] [illegible] [illegible] [illegible] personal responsibility.

[illegible] [illegible] [illegible] [illegible] [illegible] [illegible] [illegible] [illegible] [illegible] [illegible] [illegible] [illegible]

[illegible] [illegible] [illegible] [illegible] [illegible]

CHAPTER SIXTEEN

Never send a human to do a machine's job.

Agent Smith in the film *The Matrix*

The stock market was collapsing and Jim Simons was worried.

It was late December 2018, and Simons and his wife, Marilyn, were at the Beverly Hills Hotel visiting family in the Los Angeles area over the Christmas holiday. Simons, dressed in chino pants and a polo shirt, was trying to relax in a hotel famous for its poolside bungalows and pink-and-green décor, but he couldn't stop watching the stock market. It was tumbling amid growing concerns about an economic downturn. That month, the S&P 500 index fell nearly 10 percent, the worst December performance since 1931.

At that point, Simons was worth about $23 billion. Somehow, though, each day's loss felt like a fresh punch to the gut. Part of it was that Simons had made substantial financial commitments to his charitable foundation, which employed hundreds of staffers, and other organizations. That wasn't really why he was so dismayed, though. Simons knew he'd be more than fine no matter what happened with the market. He just hated losing money, and he was growing anxious about when the pain would stop.

Simons reached for a phone to call Ashvin Chhabra, a Wall Street veteran hired to run Euclidean Capital, a firm managing the personal money of Simons and his family. Simons told Chhabra he was concerned about the market's outlook. It seemed like a good idea to place some negative bets against stocks, moves that would serve as protection in case the sell-off got even worse. Simons asked Chhabra's opinion about what they should do.

"Should we be selling short?" Simons asked.

Chhabra hesitated, suggesting that they avoid acting until the market had calmed, a course of action Simons agreed to follow. A day later, stocks firmed. The collapse was over.

Hanging up, neither Simons nor Chhabra focused on the rich irony of their exchange. Simons had spent more than three decades pioneering and perfecting a new way to invest. He had inspired a revolution in the financial world, legitimizing a quantitative approach to trading. By then, it seemed everyone in the finance business was trying to invest the Renaissance way: digesting data, building mathematical models to anticipate the direction of various investments, and employing automated trading systems. The establishment had thrown in the towel. Today, even banking giant JPMorgan Chase puts hundreds of its new investment bankers and investment professionals through mandatory coding lessons. Simons's success had validated the field of quantitative investing.

"Jim Simons and Renaissance showed it was possible," says Dario Villani, a PhD in theoretical physics who runs his own hedge fund.

The goal of quants like Simons was to *avoid* relying on emotions and gut instinct. Yet, that's exactly what Simons was doing after a few difficult weeks in the market. It was a bit like Oakland A's executive Billy Beane scrapping his statistics to draft a player with the clear look of a star.

Simons's phone call is a stark reminder of how difficult it can be to turn decision-making over to computers, algorithms, and models—even, at times, for the inventors of these very approaches. His conversation with Chhabra helps explain the faith investors have long placed in stock-and-bond pickers dependent on judgment, experience, and old-fashioned research.

By 2019, however, confidence in the traditional approach had waned. Years of poor performance had investors fleeing actively managed stock-mutual funds, or those professing an ability to beat the market's returns. At that point, these funds, most of which embrace traditional approaches to investing, controlled just half of the money entrusted by clients in stock-mutual funds, down from 75 percent a decade earlier. The other half of the money was in index funds and other so-called passive vehicles, which simply aim to match the market's returns, acknowledging how challenging it is to top the market.[1]

Increasingly, it seemed, once-dependable investing tactics, such as grilling corporate managers, scrutinizing balance sheets, and using instinct and intuition to bet on major global economic shifts, amounted to too little. Sometimes, those methods helped cripple the reputations of some of Wall Street's brightest stars. In the years leading up to 2019, John Paulson, who made billions predicting the 2007 subprime-credit crisis, suffered deep losses and shocking client defections.[2] David Einhorn, a poker-playing hedge-fund manager once known as "King David" for anticipating Lehman Brothers' 2008 collapse, saw his own clients bolt amid poor performance.[3]

In Newport Beach, California, Bill Gross, an investor known to chafe when employees at bond powerhouse PIMCO spoke or even made eye contact with him, saw his returns slip ahead of his shocking departure from the firm.[4] Even Warren Buffett's performance waned. His Berkshire Hathaway trailed the S&P 500 over the previous five, ten, and fifteen years leading up to May 2019.

Part of the problem was that traditional, actively managed funds no longer wielded an information advantage over their rivals. Once, sophisticated hedge funds, mutual funds, and others had the luxury of poring over annual reports and other financial releases to uncover useful nuggets of overlooked information. Today, almost any type of corporate financial figure is a keystroke or news feed away, and can be captured instantly by machines. It's almost impossible to identify facts or figures not fully appreciated by rival investors.

At the same time, a crackdown on insider trading, as well as a series of regulatory changes aimed at ensuring that certain investors couldn't obtain better access to corporate information, resulted in a more even playing field, reducing the advantages wielded by even the most sophisticated *fundamental* investors. No longer could big hedge funds receive calls from brokers advising them of the imminent announcement of a piece of news, or even a shift in the bank's own view on a stock.

Today, the fastest-moving firms often hold an edge. In late August 2018, shares of a small cancer-drug company called Geron Corporation soared 25 percent after its partner, Johnson & Johnson, posted a job listing. The opening suggested that a key regulatory decision for a drug the two companies were developing might be imminent, a piece of news that escaped all but those with the technology to instantly and automatically scour for job listings and similar real-time information.[5]

Quant investors had emerged as the dominant players in the finance business. As of early 2019, they represented close to a third of all stock-market trades, a share that had more than doubled since 2013.[6]

Spoils have accrued from that dominance. In 2018, Simons made an estimated $1.5 billion, while the founders of rival quant firm Two Sigma Investments earned $700 million each. Ray Dalio of Bridgewater Associates—which is a systematic, rules-based investment firm, but not quantitative—made $1 billion, as well. Israel Englander, Simons's combatant in the fight over the two renegade Russian traders, pulled in $500 million.[7]

In early 2019, Ken Griffin, who focuses on quant and other strategies at his Chicago-based firm, Citadel, dropped jaws after he spent $238 million for a New York penthouse, the most expensive home ever sold in the country. (Griffin already had purchased several floors of a Chicago condominium for nearly $60 million, as well as a Miami penthouse for the same amount, not to mention $500 million for a pair of paintings by Jackson Pollock and Willem de Kooning.)

There are reasons to think the advantages that firms like Renaissance enjoy will only expand amid an explosion of new kinds of data that their computer-trading models can digest and parse. IBM has estimated that 90 percent of the world's data sets have been created in the last two years alone, and that forty zettabytes—or forty-four trillion gigabytes—of data will be created by 2020, a three-hundred-fold increase from 2005.[8]

Today, almost every kind of information is digitized and made available as part of huge data sets, the kinds that investors once only dreamed of tapping. The rage among investors is for *alternative data*, which includes just about everything imaginable, including instant information from sensors and satellite images around the world. Creative investors test for money-making correlations and patterns by scrutinizing the tones of executives on conference calls, traffic in the parking lots of retail stores, records of auto-insurance applications, and recommendations by social media influencers.

Rather than wait for figures on agricultural production, quants examine sales of farm equipment or satellite images of crop yields. Bills of lading for cargo containers can give a sense of global shifts. Systematic traders can even get cell phone–generated data on which aisles, and even which shelves, consumers are pausing to browse within stores. If you seek a sense of the popularity of a new product, Amazon reviews can be scraped. Algorithms are being developed to analyze the backgrounds of commissioners and others at the Food and Drug Administration to predict the likelihood of a new drug's approval.

To explore these new possibilities, hedge funds have begun to hire a new type of employee, what they call *data analysts* or *data hunters*, who focus on digging up new data sources, much like what Sandor Straus did for Renaissance in the mid-1980s. All the information is crunched to get a better sense of the current state and trajectory of the economy, as well as the prospects of various companies. More adventurous investors may even use it to prepare for a potential crisis if, say, they see a series of unusual pizza deliveries at the Pentagon in the midst of an international incident.

Exponential growth in computer processing power and storage capabilities has given systematic traders new capabilities to sift through all that data. According to Singularity Hub, by around 2025, $1,000 will likely buy a computer with the same processing power as the human brain. Already, hedge-fund firm Two Sigma has built a computing system with more than one hundred teraflops of power—meaning it can process one hundred trillion calculations a second—and more than eleven petabytes of memory, the equivalent of five times the data stored in all US academic libraries.[9]

All that power allows quants to find and test many more predictive signals than ever before.

"Instead of the hit-and-miss strategy of trying to find signals using creativity and thought," a Renaissance computer specialist says, "now you can just throw a class of formulas at a machine-learning engine and test out millions of different possibilities."

Years after Simons's team at Renaissance adopted machine-learning techniques, other quants have begun to embrace these methods. Renaissance anticipated a transformation in decision-making that's sweeping almost every business and walk of life. More companies and individuals are accepting and embracing models that continuously learn from their successes and failures. As investor Matthew Granade has noted, Amazon, Tencent, Netflix, and others that rely on dynamic, ever-changing models are emerging dominant. The more data that's fed to the machines, the smarter they're supposed to become.

A quip by novelist Gary Shteyngart sums up the future path of the finance industry, and the direction of broader society: "When the shrinks for their kids are replaced by algorithms, that'll be the end; there'll be nothing left."

═

For all the enthusiasm building around the quantitative approach, its limitations also are clear. It's not easy to process the information and discover accurate signals in all that noisy data. Some quants have argued that picking stocks is harder for a machine than choosing an appropriate song, recognizing a face, or even driving a car. It remains hard to teach machines to distinguish between a blueberry muffin and a Chihuahua.

Some big firms, including London's Man AHL, mostly use machine-learning algorithms to determine how and when to make their trades, or to map connections between companies and do other kinds of research, rather than to develop automated investment decisions.

For all the advantages quant firms have, the investment returns of most of these trading firms haven't been that much better than those of traditional firms doing old-fashioned research, with Renaissance and a few others the obvious exceptions. In the five years leading up to spring of 2019, quant-focused hedge funds gained about 4.2 percent a year on average, compared with a gain of 3.3 percent for the average hedge fund in the same period. (These figures don't include results from secretive funds that don't share their results, like Medallion.) Quantitative investors face daunting challenges because the information they sift is always changing—unlike data in other fields, such as physics—and pricing histories for stocks and other investments are relatively limited.

"Say you're trying to predict how stocks will perform over a one-year horizon," Richard Dewey, a veteran quant, says. "Because we only have decent records back to 1900, there are only 118 nonoverlapping one-year periods to look at in the US."[10]

And it can be hard to build a trading system for some kinds of investments, such as troubled debt—which relies on judge rulings, legal maneuverings, and creditor negotiations. For those reasons, there likely will remain pockets of the market where savvy traditional investors prosper, especially those focused on longer-term investing that algorithmic, computer-driven investors tend to shy away from.

═

The rise of Renaissance and other computer-programmed traders has bred concern about their impact on the market and the potential for a sudden sell-off, perhaps sparked by computers acting autonomously. On May 6, 2010, the Dow Jones Industrial Average plummeted one thousand points in what came to be known as the "flash crash," a harrowing few minutes in which hundreds of stocks momentarily lost nearly all their value. Investors pointed the finger at computer-programmed trading firms and said the collapse highlighted the destabilizing role computerized trading can play, but the market quickly rebounded. Prosecutors later charged a trader operating out of his West London home for manipulating a stock-market-index futures contract, laying the groundwork for the decline.[11]

To some, the sudden downturn, which was accompanied by little news to explain the move, suggested the rise of the machine had ushered in a new era of risk and volatility. Automated trading by computers is a scary concept for many, much as airplanes flown by autopilot and self-driving cars can frighten, despite evidence that those machines improve safety. There's reason to believe computer traders can amplify or accelerate existing trends.

Author and former risk manager Richard Bookstaber has argued that risks today are significant because the embrace of quant models is "system-wide across the investment world," suggesting that future troubles for these investors would have more impact than in the past.[12] As more embrace quantitative trading, the very nature of financial markets could change. New types of errors could be introduced, some of which have yet to be experienced, making them harder to anticipate. Until now, markets have been driven by human behavior, reflecting the dominant roles played by traders and investors. If machine learning and other computer models become the most influential factors in markets, they may become less predictable and maybe even less stable, since human nature is roughly constant while the nature of this kind of computerized trading can change rapidly.

The dangers of computerized trading are generally overstated, however. There are so many varieties of quant investing that it is impossible to generalize about the subject. Some quants employ momentum strategies, so they intensify the selling by other investors in a downtown. But other approaches—including *smart beta*, factor investing, and *style investing*—are the largest and fastest-growing investment categories in the quant world. Some of these practitioners have programmed their computers to buy when stocks get cheap, helping to stabilize the market.

It's important to remember that market participants have always tended to pull back and do less trading during market crises, suggesting that any reluctance by quants to trade isn't so very different from past approaches. If anything, markets have become more placid as quant investors have assumed dominant positions. Humans are prone to fear, greed, and outright panic, all of which tend to sow volatility in financial markets. Machines could make markets *more* stable, if they elbow out individuals governed by biases and emotions. And computer-driven decision-making in other fields, such as the airline industry, has generally led to fewer mistakes.

=

By the summer of 2019, Renaissance's Medallion fund had racked up average annual gains, before investor fees, of about 66 percent since 1988, and a return after fees of approximately 39 percent. Despite RIEF's early stumbles, the firm's three hedge funds open for outside investors have also outperformed rivals and market indexes. In June 2019, Renaissance managed a combined $65 billion, making it one of the largest hedge-fund firms in the world, and sometimes represented as much as 5 percent of daily stock-market trading volume, not including high-frequency traders.

The firm's success is a useful reminder of the predictability of human behavior. Renaissance studies the past because it is reasonably confident investors will make similar decisions in the future. At the same time, staffers embrace the scientific method to combat cognitive and emotional biases, suggesting there's value to this philosophical approach when tackling challenging problems of all kinds. They propose hypotheses and then test, measure, and adjust their theories, trying to let data, not intuition and instinct, guide them.

"The approach is scientific," Simons says. "We use very rigorous statistical approaches to determine what we think is underlying."[13]

Another lesson of the Renaissance experience is that there are more factors and variables influencing financial markets and individual investments than most realize or can deduce. Investors tend to focus on the most basic forces, but there are dozens of factors, perhaps whole dimensions of them, that are missed. Renaissance is aware of more of the forces that matter, along with the overlooked mathematical relationships that affect stock prices and other investments, than most anyone else.

It's a bit like how bees see a broad spectrum of colors in flowers, a rainbow that humans are oblivious to when staring at the same flora. Renaissance doesn't see all the market's hues, but they see enough of them to make a lot of money, thanks in part to the firm's reliance on ample amounts of leverage. Renaissance has endured challenging periods in the past, however, and it stands to reason that the firm will find it difficult to match its past success as markets evolve and staffers try to keep up. In moments of honest reflection, current and former employees marvel at their gains and acknowledge the hurdles ahead.

The gains Simons and his colleagues have achieved might suggest there are more inefficiencies in the market than most assume. In truth, there likely are fewer inefficiencies and opportunities for investors than generally presumed. For all the unique data, computer firepower, special talent, and trading and risk-management expertise Renaissance has gathered, the firm only profits on barely more than 50 percent of its trades, a sign of how challenging it is to try to beat the market—and how foolish it is for most investors to try.

Simons and his colleagues generally avoid predicting pure stock moves. It's not clear any expert or system can reliably predict individual stocks, at least over the long term, or even the direction of financial markets. What Renaissance does is try to anticipate stock moves relative to other stocks, to an index, to a factor model, and to an industry.

During his time helping to run the Medallion fund, Elwyn Berlekamp came to view the narratives that most investors latch on to to explain price moves as quaint, even dangerous, because they breed misplaced confidence that an investment can be adequately understood and its futures divined. If it was up to Berlekamp, stocks would have numbers attached to them, not names.

"I don't deny that earnings reports and other business news surely move markets," Berlekamp says. "The problem is that so many investors focus so much on these types of news that nearly all of their results cluster very near their average."

=

Days after Rebekah Mercer had David Magerman tossed from the poker-night festivities at New York's St. Regis hotel, Renaissance fired the computer scientist, ending any chance of a rapprochement between the warring sides.

Magerman filed two lawsuits—a federal civil rights claim against Robert Mercer and a wrongful termination suit against Renaissance and Mercer. In both cases he alleged that Mercer had him terminated from Renaissance for "engaging in protected activity."

"Mercer's conduct is an outrageous attempt to deny Magerman his constitutional and federal statutory rights," stated the ten-page complaint filed in federal court in Philadelphia.

Magerman acknowledged that Renaissance's employee handbook prohibited him from publicly disparaging the firm or its employees, but he said he had obtained approval from at least one Renaissance executive before sharing his concerns with the *Wall Street Journal* earlier that year.

Magerman nursed hurt feelings. It still bothered him that his old workmates had given him the cold shoulder.

Slowly, both he and his former firm began moving past their dispute, though. As unhappy as Magerman had been about Mercer's political activity, and as adamant as he was about his right to speak out, he never had wanted to anger Simons, Brown, or his other colleagues. Some days, Magerman even missed being close to Mercer.

"I worked for Renaissance for over twenty years, they're the one place I ever worked in my professional life," he told a reporter. "I had an obligation to inform the public. . . . And that was the end of it, as far as I'm concerned, except that I got suspended and fired."[14]

In 2018, after months of negotiations, the two sides reached an amicable settlement, with Magerman exiting Renaissance with the right to invest in Medallion, like other retirees. Soon, Magerman, now fifty years old, adopted a new cause: combating powerful social media companies. He gave nearly half a million dollars to a coalition lobbying to break up Facebook and accepted a senior position at a Philadelphia venture-capital firm to work with fledgling data-related companies.

"I feel very good about where I am now, mentally and personally," he said late in 2018. "I wouldn't quite go as far to say there's no hard feelings. But, you know, I've definitely moved on."[15]

═

After Mercer stepped down as Renaissance's co–chief executive officer in November 2017, staffers were skeptical much would change at the company. Mercer was still employed at Renaissance, and he continued to be within earshot of Brown. Surely he'd go on reining in Brown's impulses, these employees said. Unlike other researchers, Mercer reported directly to Brown, a sign of his continued prominence. How much different were things really going to be?

Almost immediately after announcing he was stepping down, however, Mercer assumed a less prominent role at the firm. He didn't participate in senior meetings and seemed out of the loop. The shift sparked nervousness among employees who worried that Brown would rush into ill-advised decisions without Mercer to help guide him. Staffers feared the change would hurt Renaissance's returns at a time more investment firms were rushing into quant trading, resulting in more potential competition.

Brown seemed to sense the dangers. He responded by tweaking his management style. Brown still kept the same manic pace, sleeping in the Murphy bed in his office most weekday nights. But he began leaning on other senior staffers, asking for input from a mixed group of colleagues. The shift steadied the firm and helped Medallion end 2018 with a flourish, scoring gains of about 45 percent that year, besting the performance of almost every investment firm in a year the S&P 500 dropped over 6 percent, its worst performance since 2008. Renaissance's three funds open for investors, the Renaissance Institutional Equities Fund, the Renaissance Institutional Diversified Alpha Fund, and the Renaissance Institutional Diversified Global Equity Fund, all topped the market, as well. Money poured into the three funds, and Renaissance's overall assets surged past $60 billion, making it one of the largest hedge-fund firms in the world.

"I think everything is under control," Simons said late in 2018. "As long as you keep making money for investors, they're generally pretty happy."[16]

═

In the spring of 2018, Simons celebrated his eightieth birthday. His family's foundation marked the occasion with a series of lectures focused on Simons's contributions to the field of physics. Academics and others toasted Simons at a nearby hotel. A month later, he hosted family and friends on his ship, the *Archimedes*, for a nighttime cruise around Manhattan.

A distinct stoop in Simons's shoulders accented his advancing age, but he was razor-sharp, asking probing questions and supplying humorous quips throughout the festivities.

"I promise not to turn eighty again," he joked to the crowd.

Simons seemed to have arrived at a comfortable landing spot in his life. He had pushed Mercer out of the top job at Renaissance, relieving pressure, and the company was thriving with Brown at the helm. Even the Magerman imbroglio seemed in the rearview mirror.

Simons still felt pressures, though. Important life goals remained unmet and it didn't take a PhD in mathematics to understand he likely didn't have a huge amount of time to accomplish them. Simons maintained a daily routine that seemed aimed at improving his chances of satisfying his remaining ambitions. Most mornings, Simons woke around 6:30 a.m. and headed to Central Park to walk several miles and exercise with a trainer. On daylong hikes organized by his foundation, Simons usually led the way, leaving young staffers huffing and puffing behind him. Simons even switched to slightly healthier electronic cigarettes, at least during some meetings, his beloved Merits tucked deep into a breast pocket.

Simons continued to check in with Brown and other Renaissance executives, chairing meetings of the firm's board of directors. Once in a long while, he suggested an idea to improve the operation. Simons's focus was elsewhere, however. That year, he spent $20 million backing various Democratic political candidates, helping the party regain control of the House of Representatives.

The Simons Foundation, with an annual budget of $450 million, had emerged as the nation's second-largest private funder of research in basic science. Math for America, the organization Simons helped found, provided annual stipends of $15,000 to over one thousand top math and science teachers in New York City. It also hosted hundreds of annual seminars and workshops, creating a community of skilled and enthusiastic teachers. There were signs the initiative was helping public schools retain the kinds of teachers who previously had bolted for private industry.

One can see contradictions, even hypocrisies, in some of Simons's life decisions. Renaissance spent years legally converting short-term gains into long-term profits, saving its executives billions of dollars in taxes, even as Simons decried a lack of spending by the government on basic education in science, mathematics, and other areas. Some strident critics, including author and activist Naomi Klein, have questioned the growing influence of society's "benevolent billionaires," who sometimes single-handedly allocate resources and determine priorities in the nonprofit world at a time of stretched government budgets. Simons also can be criticized for hiring waves of top scientists and mathematicians for his hedge fund, even while lamenting about the talent that private industry siphoned from the public sphere and how many schools are unable to retain top teachers.

Simons hasn't poured his billions into vanity projects, however. He dedicated cash and creativity to efforts that may benefit millions. There are convincing signs his charitable investments could lead to real change, maybe even breakthroughs, perhaps during his lifetime. Simons could be remembered for what he did with his fortune, as well as how he made it.

EPILOGUE

Jim Simons dedicated much of his life to uncovering secrets and tackling challenges. Early in life, he focused on mathematics problems and enemy codes. Later, it was hidden patterns in financial markets. Approaching his eighty-first birthday in the spring of 2019, Simons was consumed with two new difficulties, likely the most imposing of his life: understanding and curing autism, and discovering the origins of the universe and life itself.

True breakthroughs in autism research hadn't been achieved and time was ticking by. Six years earlier, the Simons Foundation had hired Louis Reichardt, a professor of physiology and neuroscience who was the first American to climb both Mount Everest and K2. Simons handed Reichardt an even more daunting challenge: improve the lives of those with autism.

The foundation helped establish a repository of genetic samples from 2,800 families with at least one child on the autism spectrum, accelerating the development of animal models, a step toward potential human treatments. By the spring of 2019, Simons's researchers had succeeded in gaining a deeper understanding of how the autistic brain works and were closing in on drugs with the potential to help those battling the condition. A trial drew closer to test a drug that might help as many as 20 percent of those suffering from the disorder.

"It will be the first drug to have some effect on some people," Simons said. "I think we have a better than even chance of success."

Simons was just as hopeful about making headway on a set of existential challenges that have confounded humankind from its earliest moments. In 2014, Simons recruited Princeton University astrophysicist David Spergel, who is known for groundbreaking work measuring the age and composition of the universe. Simons tasked Spergel with answering the eternal question of how the universe began. Oh, and please try to do it in a few years, while I'm still around, Simons said.

Simons helped fund a $75 million effort to build an enormous observatory with an array of ultrapowerful telescopes in Chile's Atacama Desert, a plateau 17,000 feet above sea level featuring especially clear, dry skies. It's an ideal spot to measure cosmic microwave radiation and get a good look into creation's earliest moments. The project, led by a group of eight scientists including Spergel and Brian Keating—an astrophysicist who directs the Simons Observatory and happens to be the son of Simons's early partner, James Ax—is expected to be completed by 2022. Among other things, the observatory will search for distant evidence of the Big Bang, the theorized event in which the universe came into existence.[1]

Many scientists assume the universe instantaneously expanded after creation, something they call *cosmic inflation*. That event likely produced gravitational waves and twisted light, or what Keating calls "the fingerprint of the Big Bang." Scientists have spent years searching for evidence of this phenomenon, each effort meeting crushing defeat, with decades of close calls but ultimate futility. The Simons Observatory represents one of the best chances yet of discovering these faint echoes of the pangs of the universe's birth, providing potential evidence that the universe had a beginning.

"Jim is pushing to get answers soon," Spergel says.

Simons himself expresses skepticism about the Big Bang theory and whether his giant telescope will meet its goal and produce evidence of cosmic inflation. Subscribing to a view that time never had a starting point, Simons simultaneously supports work by Paul Steinhardt, the leading proponent of the noninflationary, *bouncing* model, an opposing theory to the Big Bang.

"It's always been aesthetically pleasing to me to think time has gone on forever," Simons says.

Sounding much like a hedge-fund trader, Simons figures he'll be a winner no matter what the different teams discover. If his instincts are proven accurate and inflation isn't found, Simons will feel vindicated and scientists like Steinhardt will pick up the torch. If the Spergel-Keating group finds evidence backing the Big Bang theory, "We win a Nobel and we're all dancing in the streets," Simons says.

He remains just as eager for answers to other questions that have flummoxed civilization for ages. His foundation supported scientific collaborations aimed at gaining an understanding of how life began, what early life was like, and whether there might be life elsewhere in our solar system or on planets outside our solar system.

"All religions have covered the topic and I've always been curious," he says. "I feel we're getting closer to finding out."

=

On a brisk day in mid-March 2019, Simons and his wife flew on their Gulfstream jet to an airport outside Boston. There, they were met and driven to the Cambridge, Massachusetts, campus of the Massachusetts Institute of Technology, Simons's alma mater, where he was scheduled to deliver a lecture. Wearing a tweed sports jacket, tan khakis, a crisp blue shirt, and loafers, with no socks, Simons addressed hundreds of students, academics, and local businesspeople, reflecting on his career, and the post-election turbulence at Renaissance.

Answering a question about why he didn't stop Bob Mercer's political activities, Simons said, "I think he's a little crazy," to a smattering of cheers.

"But he's extremely bright. I couldn't fire him because of his political beliefs."

Asked which professional investors students should turn to for guidance, Simons struggled for an answer, a quant still skeptical investors can forecast markets. Finally, he mentioned his neighbor in Manhattan, hedge-fund manager George Soros.

"I suppose he's worth listening to," Simons said, "though he sure talks a lot."

Simons shared a few life lessons with the school's audience: "Work with the smartest people you can, hopefully smarter than you . . . be persistent, don't give up easily.

"Be guided by beauty . . . it can be the way a company runs, or the way an experiment comes out, or the way a theorem comes out, but there's a sense of beauty when something is working well, almost an aesthetic to it."

Simons discussed his most recent passions, including his efforts to understand the universe's creation and mankind's origins.

"It's entirely possible we're alone," he said, arguing that intelligent life might solely exist on planet Earth, thanks to a confluence of favorable factors likely not found elsewhere.

For a brief moment, Simons looked at Marilyn, sitting in the audience's front row next to their grandson, a graduate student at Harvard.

"We've had a lot of luck," he said.

After an ovation from the audience, Simons extended a modest wave. Walking slowly, he made his way out of the hall, his family close behind.

ACKNOWLEDGMENTS

This book was a passion project. For over two years, I had the privilege of spending countless hours with innovative and often eccentric mathematicians, scientists, code breakers, and quant pioneers in the United States and abroad.

It was also among the most imposing challenges of my career. In high school, I never got past pre-calculus. In college, I discussed mathematical concepts, but applying them was another matter entirely. The next algorithm I create will be my first. Without the support, encouragement, and advice of practitioners in the field, groundbreaking academics, and selfless others, this book wouldn't be in your hands.

Hal Lux was my rock—a font of sage advice and valuable perspective. I also relied upon Aaron Brown, Andrew Sterge, Richard Dewey, Rasheed Sabar, and Dario Villani. I'm truly grateful for your intelligence, expertise, and guidance.

Nick Patterson, Greg Hullender, Sandor Straus, Elwyn Berlekamp, Robert Frey, Stephen Robert, David Dwyer, Howard Morgan, and many other Renaissance veterans provided important insights about various periods of the firm's history. Raimo Bakus, Richard Stern, Ernest Chan, Philip Resnik, and Paul Cohen shared their own experiences at IBM. Vickie Barone was my math tutor. Michael Pomada, Brian Keating, and Sam Enriquez were kind enough to read my manuscript and contribute helpful comments.

Lee Neuwirth, Irwin Kra, Robert Bryant, Leonard Charlap, Simon Kochen, Lloyd Welch, David Eisenbud, Jeff Cheeger, Dennis Sullivan, John Lott, Cumrun Vafa, and Phillip Griffiths answered endless questions with uncommon patience and wisdom. I also appreciate the assistance of Stefi Baum, Greg Hayt, Yuri Gabovich, John J. Smith, David Spergel, Rishi Narang, and Sharon Bertsch McGrayne.

My publisher, Adrian Zackheim, and my editor, Merry Sun, provided unwavering support, boundless enthusiasm, and savvy judgment. I consider myself lucky to have them in my corner. Jacob Urban was an indefatigable and gifted research assistant, and Anastassia Gliadkovskaya helped in many ways down the stretch, as did Nina Rodriguez-Marty.

I'm grateful for the support of friends, colleagues, and family members, including Ezra Zuckerman Sivan, Shara Shetrit, Harold Mark Simansky, Adam Brauer, Ari Moses, Joshua Marcus, Stu Schrader, Marc Tobin, Eric Landy, Kirsten Grind, and Jenny Strasburg. Enormous thanks go to Moshe and Renee Glick, who always have my back—on and off the softball field. I appreciate the support of AABJD's Sunday sluggers. Tova and Aviva shared love and support. Jerry, Alisha, Hannah, and Aiden Blugrind, David and Shari Cherna, and Douglas and Elaine Eisenberg all encouraged my efforts while feeding both my stomach and spirits. Avigaiyil Goldscheider somehow kept me going and put a smile on my face at three a.m.

Gio Urshela, DJ LeMahieu, and Aaron Judge entertained me in the early evening. Justin Vernon, Rhye, Randy Crawford, Donny Hathaway, Natalie Merchant, Miles Davis, and Franz Schubert calmed and comforted me through the night.

I'd like to thank the *Wall Street Journal*'s managing editor, Matt Murray, and Charles Forelle, the editor of the paper's Business and Finance section, for blessing this project.

ACKNOWLEDGMENTS

Growing up, I didn't particularly enjoy English class. Diagramming sentences left me miserable and a high-school teacher criticized me for writing too many papers about the Holocaust, dousing my enthusiasm for her class. Most of what I know about writing comes from *reading*—books from the Providence Public Library, clever critiques of my work from my late father, Alan Zuckerman, and thought-provoking or entertaining articles cut out and shared by my mother, Roberta Zuckerman. My parents' love and lessons still guide me.

Last but in no way least, my wife, Michelle, played a crucial role making this book a reality. As I struggled to understand hidden Markov models and explain stochastic differential equations, she soothed, cheered, and encouraged me. I appreciate you more each day. My book is dedicated to my sons, Gabriel Benjamin and Elijah Shane. Even Jim Simons couldn't have developed a model capable of predicting the happiness you've given me.

APPENDIX 1

	Net Returns	Management Fee*	Performance Fee	Returns Before Fees	Size of Fund	Medallion Trading Profits**
1988	9.0%	5%	20%	16.3%	$20 million	$3 million
1989	-4.0%	5%	20%	1.0%	$20 million	$0
1990	55.0%	5%	20%	77.8%	$30 million	$23 million
1991	39.4%	5%	20%	54.3%	$42 million	$23 million
1992	33.6%	5%	20%	47.0%	$74 million	$35 million
1993	39.1%	5%	20%	53.9%	$122 million	$66 million
1994	70.7%	5%	20%	93.4%	$276 million	$258 million
1995	38.3%	5%	20%	52.9%	$462 million	$244 million
1996	31.5%	5%	20%	44.4%	$637 million	$283 million
1997	21.2%	5%	20%	31.5%	$829 million	$261 million
1998	41.7%	5%	20%	57.1%	$1.1 billion	$628 million
1999	24.5%	5%	20%	35.6%	$1.54 billion	$549 million
2000	98.5%	5%	20%	128.1%	$1.9 billion	$2,434 million
2001	33.0%	5%	36%	56.6%	$3.8 billion	$2,149 million

* Fees are charged by the Medallion fund to its investors, which in most years represents the firm's own employees and former employees.

** Gross returns and Medallion profits are estimates—the actual number could vary slightly depending on when the annual asset fee is charged, among other things. Medallion's profits are before the fund's various expenses.

APPENDIX 1

	Net Returns	Management Fee*	Performance Fee	Returns Before Fees	Size of Fund	Medallion Trading Profits**
2002	25.8%	5%	44%	51.1%	$5.24 billion	$2.676 billion
2003	21.9%	5%	44%	44.1%	$5.09 billion	$2.245 billion
2004	24.9%	5%	44%	49.5%	$5.2 billion	$2.572 billion
2005	29.5%	5%	44%	57.7%	$5.2 billion	$2.999 billion
2006	44.3%	5%	44%	84.1%	$5.2 billion	$4.374 billion
2007	73.7%	5%	44%	136.6%	$5.2 billion	$7.104 billion
2008	82.4%	5%	44%	152.1%	$5.2 billion	$7.911 billion
2009	39.0%	5%	44%	74.6%	$5.2 billion	$3.881 billion
2010	29.4%	5%	44%	57.5%	$10 billion	$5.750 billion
2011	37.0%	5%	44%	71.1%	$10 billion	$7.107 billion
2012	29.0%	5%	44%	56.8%	$10 billion	$5.679 billion
2013	46.9%	5%	44%	88.8%	$10 billion	$8.875 billion
2014	39.2%	5%	44%	75.0%	$9.5 billion	$7.125 billion
2015	36.0%	5%	44%	69.3%	$9.5 billion	$6.582 billion
2016	35.6%	5%	44%	68.6%	$9.5 billion	$6.514 billion
2017	45.0%	5%	44%	85.4%	$10 billion	$8.536 billion
2018	40.0%	5%	44%	76.4%	$10 billion	$7.643 billion
	39.1% average net returns			66.1% average returns before fees		$104,530,000,000 total trading profits

Average Annual Returns

66.1% gross

39.1% net

The above profits of $104.5 billion represent those of the Medallion fund. Renaissance also profits from three hedge funds available to outside investors, which managed approximately $55 billion as of April 30, 2019. (*Source:* Medallion annual reports; investors)

APPENDIX 2

Returns Comparison

Investor	Key Fund/Vehicle	Period	Annualized Returns*
Jim Simons	Medallion Fund	1988–2018	39.1%
George Soros	Quantum Fund	1969–2000	32%†
Steven Cohen	SAC	1992–2003	30%
Peter Lynch	Magellan Fund	1977–1990	29%
Warren Buffett	Berkshire Hathaway	1965–2018	20.5%‡
Ray Dalio	Pure Alpha	1991–2018	12%

(*Source:* For Simons, Dalio, Cohen, Soros: reporting; for Buffett: Berkshire Hathaway annual report; for Lynch: Fidelity Investments.)

* All returns are after fees.

† Returns have fallen in recent years as Soros has stopped investing money for others.

‡ Buffett averaged 62% gains investing his personal money from 1951 to 1957, starting with less than $10,000, and saw average gains of 24.3% for a partnership managed from 1957 to 1969.

NOTES

Introduction

1. "Seed Interview: James Simons," *Seed*, September 19, 2006.
2. Gregory Zuckerman, Rachel Levy, Nick Timiraos, and Gunjan Banerji, "Behind the Market Swoon: The Herdlike Behavior of Computerized Trading," *Wall Street Journal*, December 25, 2018, https://www.wsj.com/articles/behind-the-market-swoon-the-herdlike-behavior-of-computerized-trading-11545785641.

Chapter One

1. D. T. Max, "Jim Simons, the Numbers King," *New Yorker*, December 11, 2017, https://www.newyorker.com/magazine/2017/12/18/jim-simons-the-numbers-king.
2. James Simons, "Dr. James Simons, S. Donald Sussman Fellowship Award Fireside Chat Series. Chat 2," interview by Andrew Lo, March 6, 2019, https://www.youtube.com/watch?v=srbQzrtfEvY&t=4s.

Chapter Two

1. James Simons, "Mathematics, Common Sense, and Good Luck" (lecture, American Mathematical Society Einstein Public Lecture in Mathematics, San Francisco, CA, October 30, 2014), https://www.youtube.com/watch?v=Tj1NyJHLvWA.
2. Lee Neuwirth, *Nothing Personal: The Vietnam War in Princeton 1965–1975* (Charleston, SC: BookSurge, 2009).
3. Paul Vitello, "John S. Toll Dies at 87; Led Stony Brook University," *New York*

Times, July 18, 2011, https://www.nytimes.com/2011/07/19/nyregion/john-s-toll-dies-at-87-led-stony-brook-university.html.

4. James Simons, "Simons Foundation Chair Jim Simons on His Career in Mathematics," interview by Jeff Cheeger, Simons Foundation, September 28, 2012, https://www.simonsfoundation.org/2012/09/28/simons-foundation-chair-jim-simons-on-his-career-in-mathematics.
5. Simons, "On His Career in Mathematics."

Chapter Three

1. Simons, "Mathematics, Common Sense, and Good Luck."
2. William Byers, *How Mathematicians Think: Using Ambiguity, Contradiction, and Paradox to Create Mathematics* (Princeton, NJ: Princeton University Press, 2007).
3. Private papers from Lenny Baum, provided by his family.
4. Richard Teitelbaum, "The Code Breaker," *Bloomberg Markets*, January 2008.
5. James Simons, "Jim Simons Speech on Leonard E. Baum" (speech, Leonard E. Baum Memorial, Princeton, NJ, August 15, 2017), https://www.youtube.com/watch?v=zN0ah7moPlQ.
6. Simons, "On His Career in Mathematics."
7. Simons, "Jim Simons Speech on Leonard E. Baum."

Chapter Four

1. Byers, *How Mathematicians Think*.

Chapter Five

1. James R. Hagerty and Gregory Zuckerman, "Math Wizard Elwyn Berlekamp Helped Bring Sharp Images from Outer Space," *Wall Street Journal*, May 1, 2019, https://www.wsj.com/articles/math-wizard-elwyn-berlekamp-helped-bring-sharp-images-from-outer-space-11556735303.
2. Brian Keating, *Losing the Nobel Prize: A Story of Cosmology, Ambition, and the Perils of Science's Highest Honor* (New York: W. W. Norton, 2018).

Chapter Six

1. James B. Stewart, *Den of Thieves* (New York: Simon & Schuster, 1991).

Chapter Seven

1. Geoffrey Poitras, *The Early History of Financial Economics, 1478–1776: From Commercial Arithmetic to Life Annuities and Joint Stocks* (Cheltenham, UK: Edward Elgar, 2000).

2. Mark Putrino, "Gann and Gann Analysis," *Technical Analysis of Stocks & Commodities*, September 2017.
3. Brian Stelter, "Gerald Tsai, Innovative Investor, Dies at 79," *New York Times*, July 11, 2008, https://www.nytimes.com/2008/07/11/business/11tsai.html; John Brooks, *The Go-Go Years: The Drama and Crashing Finale of Wall Street's Bullish 60s* (New York: Weybright and Talley, 1973).
4. Andrew W. Lo and Jasmina Hasanhodzic, *The Evolution of Technical Analysis: Financial Prediction from Babylonian Tablets to Bloomberg Terminals* (Hoboken, NJ: John Wiley & Sons, 2010).
5. Douglas Bauer, "Prince of the Pit," *New York Times*, April 25, 1976, https://www.nytimes.com/1976/04/25/archives/prince-of-the-pit-richard-dennis-knows-how-to-keep-his-head-at-the.html.
6. Emanuel Derman, *My Life as a Quant: Reflections on Physics and Finance* (Hoboken, NJ: John Wiley & Sons, 2004).
7. Edward O. Thorp, *A Man for All Markets: From Las Vegas to Wall Street, How I Beat the Dealer and the Market* (New York: Random House, 2017).
8. Scott Patterson, *The Quants: How a New Breed of Math Whizzes Conquered Wall Street and Nearly Destroyed It* (New York: Crown Business, 2010).
9. Patterson, *The Quants*.
10. Michelle Celarier, "How a Misfit Group of Computer Geeks and English Majors Transformed Wall Street," *New York*, January 18, 2018, http://nymag.com/intelligencer/2018/01/d-e-shaw-the-first-great-quant-hedge-fund.html.
11. Hal Lux, "Secretive D. E. Shaw & Co. Opens Doors for Customers' Business," *Investment Dealers' Digest*, November 15, 1993.
12. G. Bruce Knecht, "Wall Street Whiz Finds Niche Selling Books on the Internet," *Wall Street Journal*, May 16, 1996, https://www.wsj.com/articles/SB832204437381952500.

Chapter Eight

1. Ingfei Chen, "A Cryptologist Takes a Crack at Deciphering DNA's Deep Secrets," *New York Times*, December 12, 2006, https://www.nytimes.com/2006/12/12/science/12prof.html.
2. John F. Greer Jr., "Simons Doesn't Say," *Financial World*, October 21, 1996.

Chapter Nine

1. Peter Lynch, "Pros: Peter Lynch," interview with *Frontline*, PBS, May 1996, www.pbs.org/wgbh/pages/frontline/shows/betting/pros/lynch.html; and Peter Lynch with John Rothchild, *One Up on Wall Street* (New York: Simon & Schuster, 2000).

2. Sebastian Mallaby, *More Money Than God: Hedge Funds and the Making of a New Elite* (New York: Penguin Press, 2010).
3. Michael Coleman, "Influential Conservative Is Sandia, UNM Grad," *Albuquerque Journal,* November 5, 2017, https://www.abqjournal.com/1088165/influential-conservative-is-sandia-unm-grad-robert-mercer-trump-fundraiser-breitbart-investor-has-nm-roots.html.
4. Robert Mercer, "A Computational Life" (speech, Association for Computational Linguistics Lifetime Achievement Award, Baltimore, Maryland, June 25, 2014), http://techtalks.tv/talks/closing-session/60532.
5. Stephen Miller, "Co-Inventor of Money-Market Account Helped Serve Small Investors' Interest," *Wall Street Journal,* August 16, 2008, https://www.wsj.com/articles/SB121884007790345601.
6. Feng-Hsiung Hsu, *Behind Deep Blue: Building the Computer That Defeated the World Chess Champion* (Princeton, NJ: Princeton University Press, 2002).

Chapter Ten

1. Peter Brown and Robert Mercer, "Oh, Yes, Everything's Right on Schedule, Fred" (lecture, Twenty Years of Bitext Workshop, Empirical Methods in Natural Language Processing Conference, Seattle, Washington, October 2013), http://cs.jhu.edu/~post/bitext.

Chapter Eleven

1. Hal Lux, "The Secret World of Jim Simons," *Institutional Investor,* November 1, 2000, https://www.institutionalinvestor.com/article/b151340bp779jn/the-secret-world-of-jim-simons.
2. Robert Mercer interviewed by Sharon McGrayne for her book, *The Theory Would Not Die: How Bayes' Rule Cracked the Enigma Code, Hunted Down Russian Submarines, and Emerged Triumphant from Two Centuries of Controversy* (New Haven, CT: Yale University Press, 2011).
3. Brown and Mercer, "Oh, Yes, Everything's Right on Schedule, Fred."
4. Jason Zweig, "Data Mining Isn't a Good Bet for Stock-Market Predictions," *Wall Street Journal,* August 8, 2009, https://www.wsj.com/articles/SB124967937642715417.
5. Lux, "The Secret World of Jim Simons."
6. Robert Lipsyte, "Five Years Later, A Female Kicker's Memorable Victory," *New York Times,* October 19, 2000, https://www.nytimes.com/2000/10/19/sports/colleges-five-years-later-a-female-kicker-s-memorable-victory.html.

7. Roger Lowenstein, *When Genius Failed: The Rise and Fall of Long-Term Capital Management* (New York: Random House, 2000).
8. Suzanne Woolley, "Failed Wizards of Wall Street," *BusinessWeek*, September 21, 1998, https://www.bloomberg.com/news/articles/1998-09-20/failed-wizards-of-wall-street.
9. Timothy L. O'Brien, "Shaw, Self-Styled Cautious Operator, Reveals It Has a Big Appetite for Risk," *New York Times*, October 15, 1998, https://www.nytimes.com/1998/10/15/business/shaw-self-styled-cautious-operator-reveals-it-has-a-big-appetite-for-risk.html.
10. *Abuse of Structured Financial Products: Misusing Basket Options to Avoid Taxes and Leverage Limits: Hearings before the Permanent Subcommittee on Investigations of the Committee on Homeland Security and Governmental Affairs*, 113th Congress (2014) (statement of Peter Brown, Chief Executive Officer, Renaissance Technologies), https://www.govinfo.gov/content/pkg/CHRG-113shrg89882/pdf/CHRG-113shrg89882.pdf.

Chapter Twelve

1. McGrayne, *The Theory That Would Not Die: How Bayes' Rule Cracked the Enigma Code, Hunted Down Russian Submarines, and Emerged Triumphant from Two Centuries of Controversy.*
2. Lux, "The Secret World of Jim Simons."
3. *Abuse of Structured Financial Products* (statement of Peter Brown).
4. Katherine Burton, "Inside a Moneymaking Machine Like No Other," *Bloomberg*, November 21, 2016, https://www.bloomberg.com/news/articles/2016-11-21/how-renaissance-s-medallion-fund-became-finance-s-blackest-box.
5. George Gilder, *Life after Google: The Fall of Big Data and the Rise of the Blockchain Economy* (Washington, DC: Regnery Gateway, 2018).
6. Simon Van Zuylen-Wood, "The Controversial David Magerman," *Philadelphia Magazine*, September 13, 2013, https://www.phillymag.com/news/2013/09/13/controversial-david-magerman.
7. Scott Patterson and Jenny Strasburg, "Pioneering Fund Stages Second Act," *Wall Street Journal*, March 16, 2010, https://www.wsj.com/articles/SB10001424052748703494404575082000779302566.
8. Zachary Mider, "What Kind of Man Spends Millions to Elect Ted Cruz?" *Bloomberg*, January 20, 2016, https://www.bloomberg.com/news/features/2016-01-20/what-kind-of-man-spends-millions-to-elect-ted-cruz.
9. William J. Broad, "Seeker, Doer, Giver, Ponderer," *New York Times*, July 7, 2014,

https://www.nytimes.com/2014/07/08/science/a-billionaire-mathematicians-life-of-ferocious-curiosity.html.

Chapter Thirteen

1. Christine Williamson, "Renaissance Believes Size Does Matter," *Pensions & Investments*, November 27, 2006, https://www.pionline.com/article/20061127/PRINT/611270744/renaissance-believes-size-does-matter.
2. Patterson, *The Quants*.
3. Gregory Zuckerman, *The Greatest Trade Ever: The Behind-the-Scenes Story of How John Paulson Defied Wall Street and Made Financial History* (New York: Broadway Books, 2009).
4. Tae Kim, "Billionaire David Einhorn Says the Key to Investing Success Is 'Critical Thinking,'" CNBC, December 26, 2017, https://www.cnbc.com/2017/12/26/david-einhorn-says-the-key-to-investing-success-is-critical-thinking.html.
5. Susan Pulliam and Jenny Strasburg, "Simons Questioned by Investors," *Wall Street Journal*, May 15, 2009, https://www.wsj.com/articles/SB124235370437022507.

Chapter Fourteen

1. Alice Walker, "Billionaire Mathematician Jim Simons Parks £75 million Super Yacht during Tour of Scotland," *Scottish Sun*, July 15, 2018, https://www.thescottishsun.co.uk/fabulous/2933653/jim-simons-super-yacht-billionaire-scotland-tour.
2. Simons, "On His Career in Mathematics."
3. Van Zuylen-Wood, "The Controversial David Magerman."
4. Ryan Avent, "If It Works, Bet It," *Economist*, June 14, 2010, https://www.economist.com/free-exchange/2010/06/14/if-it-works-bet-it.
5. James Simons, "My Life in Mathematics" (lecture, International Congress of Mathematics, Seoul, South Korea, August 13, 2014), https://www.youtube.com/watch?v=RP1ltutTN_4.
6. John Marzulli, "Hedge Fund Hotshot Robert Mercer Files Lawsuit over $2M Model Train, Accusing Builder of Overcharge," *New York Daily News*, March 31, 2009, https://www.nydailynews.com/news/hedge-fund-hotshot-robert-mercer-files-lawsuit-2m-model-train-accusing-builder-overcharge-article-1.368624.
7. Patterson and Strasburg, "Pioneering Fund Stages Second Act."
8. Joshua Green, *Devil's Bargain: Steve Bannon, Donald Trump, and the Storming of the Presidency* (New York: Penguin Press, 2017).
9. Mider, "Ted Cruz?"
10. Juliet Chung, "Mega Merger: Six Apartments May Make One," *Wall Street Journal*,

April 27, 2010, https://www.wsj.com/articles/SB10001424052748704446704575207193495569502.

11. Ben Smith, "Hedge Fund Figure Financed Mosque Campaign," *Politico*, January 18, 2011, https://www.politico.com/blogs/ben-smith/2011/01/hedge-fund-figure-financed-mosque-campaign-032525.
12. Vicky Ward, "The Blow-It-All-Up Billionaires," *Highline*, March 17, 2017, https://highline.huffingtonpost.com/articles/en/mercers.
13. Gregory Zuckerman, Keach Hagey, Scott Patterson, and Rebecca Ballhaus, "Meet the Mercers: A Quiet Tycoon and His Daughter Become Power Brokers in Trump's Washington," *Wall Street Journal*, January 8, 2017, https://www.wsj.com/articles/meet-the-mercers-a-quiet-tycoon-and-his-daughter-become-power-brokers-in-trumps-washington-1483904047.
14. Carole Cadwalladr, "Revealed: How US Billionaire Helped to Back Brexit," *Guardian*, February 25, 2017, https://www.theguardian.com/politics/2017/feb/26/us-billionaire-mercer-helped-back-brexit.
15. Jane Mayer, "New Evidence Emerges of Steve Bannon and Cambridge Analytica's Role in Brexit," *New Yorker*, November 17, 2018, https://www.newyorker.com/news/news-desk/new-evidence-emerges-of-steve-bannon-and-cambridge-analyticas-role-in-brexit.
16. Nigel Farage, "Farage: 'Brexit Could Not Have Happened without Breitbart,'" interview by Alex Marlow, Turning Point USA Student Action Summit, December 20, 2018, https://www.youtube.com/watch?v=W73L6L7howg.
17. Matea Gold, "The Rise of GOP Mega-donor Rebekah Mercer," *Washington Post*, September 14, 2016, https://www.washingtonpost.com/politics/the-rise-of-gop-mega-donor-rebekah-mercer/2016/09/13/85ae3c32-79bf-11e6-beac-57a4a412e93a_story.html.
18. Green, *Devil's Bargain*.
19. Corey R. Lewandowski and David N. Bossie, *Let Trump Be Trump: The Inside Story of His Rise to the Presidency* (New York: Center Street, 2017).

Chapter Fifteen

1. Jonathan Lemire and Julie Pace, "Trump Spent Saturday Night at a Lavish 'Villains and Heroes' Costume Party Hosted by Some of His Biggest Donors," Associated Press, December 3, 2016, https://www.businessinsider.com/trump-attends-mercer-lavish-villains-and-heroes-costume-party-2016-12.
2. Matea Gold, "The Mercers and Stephen Bannon: How a Populist Power Base Was Funded and Built," *Washington Post*, March 17, 2017, https://www.washingtonpost.com/graphics/politics/mercer-bannon.

3. Jane Mayer, "The Reclusive Hedge-Fund Tycoon behind the Trump Presidency," *New Yorker*, March 17, 2017, https://www.newyorker.com/magazine/2017/03/27/the-reclusive-hedge-fund-tycoon-behind-the-trump-presidency.
4. Zuckerman et al., "Meet the Mercers."
5. William Julius Wilson, "Hurting the Disadvantaged," review of *Civil Rights: Rhetoric or Reality?* by Thomas Sowell, *New York Times*, June 24, 1984, https://www.nytimes.com/1984/06/24/books/hurting-the-disadvantaged.html.
6. David M. Schwartz, "Robert Mercer's North Shore Home Draws Tax Demonstrators," *Newsday*, March 28, 2017, https://www.newsday.com/long-island/politics/spin-cycle/protest-at-robert-mercer-s-li-home-1.13329816.
7. Gregory Zuckerman, "Renaissance Feud Spills Over to Hedge Fund Poker Night," *Wall Street Journal*, April 28, 2017, https://www.wsj.com/articles/renaissance-feud-spills-over-to-hedge-fund-poker-night-1493424763.
8. Jeremy W. Peters, "Milo Yiannopoulos Resigns from Breitbart News after Pedophilia Comments," *New York Times*, February 21, 2017, https://www.nytimes.com/2017/02/21/business/milo-yiannopoulos-resigns-from-breitbart-news-after-pedophilia-comments.html.
9. Robin Pogrebin and Somini Sengupta, "A Science Denier at the Natural History Museum? Scientists Rebel," *New York Times*, January 25, 2018, https://www.nytimes.com/2018/01/25/climate/rebekah-mercer-natural-history-museum.html.
10. Gregory Zuckerman, "Mercer Influence Wanes as Other Washington Donors Emerge," *Wall Street Journal*, November 4, 2018, https://www.wsj.com/articles/mercer-influence-wanes-as-other-washington-donors-emerge-1541350805.
11. Zuckerman, "Mercer Influence Wanes."

Chapter Sixteen

1. "Morningstar Reports US Mutual Fund and ETF Fund Flows for April 2019," *PR Newswire*, May 17, 2019, https://finance.yahoo.com/news/morningstar-reports-u-mutual-fund-130000604.html.
2. Gregory Zuckerman, "Architect of Greatest Trade Ever Hit by Losses, Redemptions Postcrisis," *Wall Street Journal*, April 27, 2018, https://www.wsj.com/articles/architect-of-greatest-trade-ever-hit-by-losses-redemptions-postcrisis-1524837987.
3. Gregory Zuckerman, "'This Is Unbelievable': A Hedge Fund Star Dims, and Investors Flee," *Wall Street Journal*, July 4, 2018, https://www.wsj.com/articles/this-is-unbelievable-a-hedge-fund-star-dims-and-investors-flee-1530728254.
4. Gregory Zuckerman and Kirsten Grind, "Inside the Showdown Atop PIMCO, the World's Biggest Bond Firm," *Wall Street Journal*, February 24, 2014, https://www

.wsj.com/articles/inside-the-showdown-atop-pimco-the-worlds-biggest-bond-firm-1393298266.

5. George Budwell, "Why Geron Corporation's Stock Is Charging Higher Today," Motley Fool, August 28, 2018, https://www.fool.com/investing/2018/08/28/why-geron-corporations-stock-is-charging-higher-to.aspx.
6. Data based on report by TABB Group.
7. Nathan Vardi, "Running the Numbers," *Forbes*, April 30, 2019.
8. "The Four Vs of Big Data," infographic, IBM Big Data & Analytics (website), https://www.ibmbigdatahub.com/sites/default/files/infographic_file/4-Vs-of-big-data.jpg?cm_mc_uid=16172304396014932905991&cm_mc_sid_50200000=1494235431&cm_mc_sid_52640000=1494235431.
9. Bradley Hope, "Five Ways Quants Are Predicting the Future," *Wall Street Journal*, April 1, 2015, https://blogs.wsj.com/briefly/2015/04/01/5-ways-quants-are-predicting-the-future.
10. Richard Dewey, "Computer Models Won't Beat the Stock Market Any Time Soon," *Bloomberg*, May 21, 2019, https://www.bloomberg.com/news/articles/2019-05-21/computer-models-won-t-beat-the-stock-market-any-time-soon.
11. Aruna Viswanatha, Bradley Hope, and Jenny Strasburg, "'Flash Crash' Charges Filed," *Wall Street Journal*, April 21, 2015, https://www.wsj.com/articles/u-k-man-arrested-on-charges-tied-to-may-2010-flash-crash-1429636758.
12. Robin Wigglesworth, "Goldman Sachs' Lessons from the 'Quant Quake,'" *Financial Times*, September 3, 2017, https://www.ft.com/content/fdfd5e78-0283-11e7-aa5b-6bb07f5c8e12.s
13. "Seed Interview: James Simons."
14. Marcus Baram, "The Millionaire Critic Who Scared Facebook Now Wants to Help 'Fix the Internet,'" *Fast Company*, December 11, 2018, https://www.fastcompany.com/90279134/the-millionaire-critic-who-scared-facebook-wants-to-help-fix-the-internet.
15. Baram, "The Millionaire Critic Who Scared Facebook."
16. Richard Henderson, "Renaissance Founder Says Hedge Fund Has Overcome Trump Tension," *Financial Times*, March 15, 2019, https://www.ft.com/content/7589277c-46d6-11e9-b168-96a37d002cd3.

Epilogue

1. Gary Robbins, "UCSD Gets $40 Million to Study Infancy of the Universe," *San Diego Union-Tribune*, May 12, 2016, https://www.sandiegouniontribune.com/news/science/sdut-ucsd-simons-telescopes-2016may12-story.html.

[illegible]

Epilogue

[illegible]

INDEX

INDEX

PENGUIN PARTNERSHIPS

Penguin Partnerships is the Creative Sales and Promotions team at Penguin Random House. We have a long history of working with clients on a wide variety of briefs, specializing in brand promotions, bespoke publishing and retail exclusives, plus corporate, entertainment and media partnerships.

We can respond quickly to briefs and specialize in repurposing books and content for sales promotions, for use as incentives and retail exclusives as well as creating content for new books in collaboration with our partners as part of branded book relationships.

Equally if you'd simply like to buy a bulk quantity of one of our existing books at a special discount, we can help with that too. Our books can make excellent corporate or employee gifts.

Special editions, including personalized covers, excerpts of existing books or books with corporate logos can be created in large quantities for special needs.

We can work within your budget to deliver whatever you want, however you want it.